Wordsworth's "Slumber"
and the
Problematics of Reading

D1610656

Wordsworth's "Slumber" and the Problematics of Reading

Brian G. Caraher

The Pennsylvania State University Press
University Park, Pennsylvania

For Susan,
lovely other, whose laughter light
is ringing in my ears

Library of Congress Cataloging-in-Publication Data

Caraher, Brian.
    Wordsworth's "Slumber" and the problematics of reading / Brian G.
Caraher.
        p.   cm.
    Includes bibliographical references (p.   ) and index.
    ISBN 0-271-00720-6
    1. Wordsworth, William, 1770–1850—Criticism and interpretation.
2. Reader-response criticism.   I. Title.
PR5888.C33   1991
821'.7—dc20   90–7478
                                                                        CIP

It is the policy of The Pennsylvania State University Press to use acid-free paper for the
first printing of all clothbound books. Publications on uncoated stock satisfy the
minimum requirements of American National Standard for Information Sciences—
Permanence of Paper for Printed Library Materials, ANSI Z39.48–1984.

Contents

Acknowledgments

This book is a compact one, but it has been some time in the making. I can now trace a tentative path of development back to one of my earliest days in graduate school, to the afternoon of November 8, 1974, when I was a member of an audience gathered to hear Max Black and M. H. Abrams speak about Wittgenstein, meaning, and the problem of the indeterminacy of literary texts. That Friday afternoon constituted a scene of reading and a moment of recognition for me: two eminent scholars and thinkers grappling with the text of William Wordsworth's "A slumber did my spirit seal" and a host of interpretive and theoretical issues it either focused or prompted. Wordsworth's text operated primarily as an exemplary sample of how to interpret or how not to interpret, given various conventions and conditions. The discussion of the problematical issues involved in reading such a text as "A slumber," though, drew my attention toward reading a text that had seemed to me for several years to be very difficult to comprehend. I remember recognizing that afternoon something strange about not only the problems of interpreting it but something strange about the very process of reading Wordsworth's poem. As readers of this book will recognize, I have made something of that now-distant scene of reading and of recognition— though I do not privilege the moment of it in any way. The moment, though, at least in some of its locality and particularity, should be acknowledged and thanked.

I also wish to acknowledge and thank a number of friends and colleagues who have assisted, encouraged, and supported me through a number of drafts and versions of this book. Art Efron, Irving Massey, and Mary Childers read and critiqued a very early version of a good deal of this material; I hope the book can live up to their welcome words of guidance.

David Bleich, David Downing, Elizabeth A. Flynn, John Kilgore, and Barry Kroll have read various drafts of sections of the book or essays incorporated within it and have offered helpful criticism and encouragement. Many graduate and undergraduate students at Indiana University have also helped me to sound out, refine, and corroborate many of the patterns of reading, particular interpretations, and theoretical constructions that I describe and advance here. Classroom teaching has both strongly enhanced and tryingly deferred the completion of the project. Don Bialostosky and Ken Johnston have read late drafts of the entire book and have kindly given very sound advice, welcome suggestions for revision, and timely encouragement. I also wish to thank Philip Winsor of Penn State Press; he has been a wonderfully supportive and understanding editor from the beginning.

Earlier versions of some of the material presented in the first six chapters of Part Two have appeared in *Reader, The Journal of Mind and Behavior,* and *Works and Days.* I thank the editors of these journals for kindly letting me adapt and augment my earlier arguments and formulations here. I also acknowledge and thank the editors of *The Wordsworth Circle* for allowing me to reprint (and revise as an appendix) an article that originally appeared in their pages.

I dedicate this book most particularly and most fondly to my wife, Susan, who has kept a great sense of humor through a demanding time and the vagaries of an odd profession. I plan to follow up many of the critical and theoretical issues explored in this book in a companion book or sequel, tentatively entitled *The Joyce of Reading: The Problematics of Reading Joyce's "Ulysses."*

Prologue: An Introduction to Induction and Literary Pragmatics

This book develops a pragmatist model of literary understanding—it engages in detail the nature and the implications
of what can be called "literary pragmatics." It pursues a closely
reasoned investigation of what is involved in generating and securing
warrantable interpretations of specific literary works, and it does so
through fully developed instances of literary reading and interpretation
and a carefully argued theoretical model of literary experience and
inquiry. Accordingly, this book strives to come to terms with the ways
in which real readers reading and interpreting literary works can, and
quite often do, handle the evidence of their activity of reading. What
follows, then, possesses a clearly theoretical orientation and focus.
However, from the first page, the pragmatic is never slighted or lost
sight of in a cloud of speculation. Indeed, this book begins with a
particular case in practical criticism and proceeds inductively both to
clarify the case and to draw out the theoretical issues that demand to
be clarified and conceptually elaborated. This conceptual elaboration
is deferred until Part Two, but the deferral is justified by the exigencies
of an inductive way of proceeding.

Moreover, throughout the book, I emphasize the close reading and
interpreting of the writings of literary critics. Such attention to the
rhetoric, assumptions, and insights of other informed readers must form
the basis of any useful and sustained exploration of the pragmatics of
literary reading and literary inquiry. Critical writing is the repository, as it
were, of the evidence of keen and powerful reading. The recovery of such

evidence, and all the critical strategies brought to bear upon it, would seem essential to the conduct and justification of an inductive method. Theory should not authorize, ordain, predetermine, or prefigure fact, actuality, and practice. In the best sense of its operation, theory moves in tandem with practice, once summoned to help probe an indeterminate or problematic situation; and it moves tentatively, with concepts never too distant from answerable percepts.

The choice of inductive method, furthermore, is intimately related not only to my attempt to realign the relationship of critical practice and theoretical conceptualization but also to my desire to handle critical conflict, divergence, and disagreement. Critical practice and theoretical construction in literary studies have notoriously been rife with conflict. Though such interpretive and conceptual disagreement will and should continue to yield often strongly marked divergences and stances, there is much to be gained in seeking strategies for coping with such conflict. The choice of inductive method offers one clear, though frequently neglected, strategy for handling disagreement. Its conceptual merits can best be appreciated by characterizing it in terms that delineate its methodological differences with deduction or the hypothetico-deductive method of thought and inquiry.

Very generally considered, deduction constitutes a mode of inquiry as well as argumentation that places a premium upon the analytic consistency and coherence of statements that appear to support a thesis, theory, or hypothesis. Deductive thinking, inquiry, and argumentation thus strive to advance a theory that stands or falls on the formal and analytic merit of its supporting statements. If the support fails to cohere or is found to be analytically inconsistent—that is, if the theory's support is self-contradictory—then the theory itself fails. The value and the validity of a deductive theory rides completely upon the nature of the support that can be deduced and analyzed in its favor. This close linkage of support to theoretical hypothesis, of course, seems highly desirable, logically speaking. However, there is a great price to pay for such strong logical linkage. Deductive inquiry and argumentation ultimately tend to be a matter of semantics and also tend to simplify, if not trivialize, conceptual conflict and disagreement.

One generally imagines, perhaps following the arguments of Karl R. Popper, that the logic of inquiry and cognitive discovery involves advancing a hypothesis that must be tested and either validated or invalidated by its logically deductive support.[1] Questions of logical validity or formal justification are foremost, indeed all-consuming, here. However, there is a crucial and seemingly unavoidable logical and semantic circularity in this basic structure of deductive reasoning and argumentation. Concern for the validity or justification of the deductive inferences, implications, and conclusions of a theory mandates the testing of the theory by seeking either to corroborate or to falsify its logically deductive conclusions.[2] Though facts and consequences purportedly assist in this process of corroboration or refutation, the real weight of proof falls upon the formal coherence and consistency of the theoretical conjecture or hypothesis with its deductive premises and conclusions. Of course, troublesome and highly problematical "facts" and unforeseen "consequences" can always be brought against a deductive theory. However, the logical and semantic connectedness of a thesis with its deductive support and conclusions constitutes the real measure of proof or disproof. Troublesome or conflictually irremediable facts and consequences can stand outside the issue of formal coherence and consistency and the question of deductive validity or justification. Accordingly, a deductive theory tends to be logically and semantically circular. Its support, premises, inferences, and conclusions must already be contained within it, and the supporting statements and conclusions must already be implicit within the thesis. Semantic articulation (restatement and recharacterization) brings out and affirms the full semantic load of a deductive thesis or theoretical conjecture. Perhaps the most telling instances of this logical and semantic circularity in deduction are arithmetical and algebraic formulas. For instance, the algebraic notation "$3y - 1 = 2$" contains the premise or inference that "$3y = 3$" as well as the conclusion that "$y = 1$." The very nature of algebraic axioms, rules,

1. See Karl R. Popper, *The Logic of Scientific Discovery* [translation and revision of *Logik der Forschung*, 1934] (New York: Harper & Row, 1965), pp. 27–33.

2. Ibid., pp. 32–33. See also Karl R. Popper, *Conjectures and Refutations: The Growth of Scientific Knowledge* (New York: Basic Books, 1962), especially pp. 33–65, 215–50. Perhaps the best adaptation of Popper's work to the purposes of literary theory can be found in Ralph W. Rader, "Fact, Theory, and Literary Explanation," *Critical Inquiry* 1 (December 1974): 245–72. Rader's essay is especially good at making the point that "problematical facts" should be used as "critical tests" for hypotheses (pp. 246–47). However, he discriminates between "objective problematic facts" and "the facts of the literary text [that] do not speak for themselves" (p. 272). This pivotal, indeed saving distinction for his hypothetico-deductive model of theory construction in literary studies poses a trying epistemological dilemma.

and notation is calibrated to perform such deductive inquiries and arguments time and again without reference beyond the internal coherence and consistency of algebraic statements. Moreover, classic logical syllogisms—such as "All human beings are mortal. Socrates was a human being. Therefore, Socrates was mortal."—actually already contain their premises and conclusions within the terms that constitute their theses. The very definition of a human being contains the logical connection with human mortality and the semantic connection with such individuals as Socrates or even John and Jane Doe.[3] Indeed deductive thinking, inquiry, and argumentation work well once cognitively secure and relatively well-tested theses or theories have been developed and accepted *by other means*. The corroboration or the refutation of a theoretical conjecture along deductive lines, then, is generally a matter already well determined by the way in which the thesis has been articulated and by the operations already implicit in the analytic and semantic ramifications of that thesis. Deductive or hypothetico-deductive arguments offer succinct, often simple, and logically nonproblematical or nonconflictual (that is to say, circular) ways to extend the logical and semantic implications of theories over broader domains of cases.

Very generally considered, induction constitutes a major source of those *other means* by which cognitively secure and relatively well-tested hypotheses or theories come to be developed and accepted by humanists and scientists engaged in inquiry and the extension of the limits of human knowledge. Inductive method comes under severe attack by Karl Popper, primarily because its proponents leave the results of this method of inquiry and cognitive discovery open to relative degrees of probability or reliability.[4] However, the probabilistic character of induction should not be regarded so much as a weakness in the degree of logical linkage of thesis and support as a manifest strength in dealing with the weight of facts and the competition among rival theories or hypotheses. Inductive method

3. Notice that the troublesome or problematical cases of Jesus of Nazareth (Christ) or Siddhartha Gautama (Buddha), or even Elijah or Lazarus, seem never to arise in typical discussions of this classical logical syllogism concerning human mortality. Such cases would prompt skeptical reservation or disbelief or might occasion the consideration of the social, cultural, and ideological beliefs and attitudes that impinge upon all modes of inquiry and argumentation—deduction included.

4. Popper, *The Logic of Scientific Discovery*, pp. 27–30, 251–65, and *Conjectures and Refutations*, pp. 280–92.

generally works from particular and often provocative cases toward increasingly more capacious and conceptually interesting levels of generalization. Along the way, additional, often numerous, and even problematical examples are studied as test cases for the generalizations that have been generated by the inquiry or through the pathways of the argument. Unlike deductive inquiries or arguments, in which the logical and semantic circularity of theory and support predominates, induction relies upon the ability to recognize and evaluate the distinctive evidence afforded by particular cases in terms of a range of conflicting or rival theories that strive to account for such evidence. The exigencies and the contingencies of fact—that is to say, the often troublesome and problematic evidence of specific cases—tend to achieve a degree of perceptual clarity and conceptual power that they structurally lack in deductive thinking, with its general concern for analytic coherence and consistency. The notoriously stunning inductive methods of Edgar Allan Poe's amateur detective C. Auguste Dupin and Arthur Conan Doyle's private investigator Sherlock Holmes offer clear cases in point about how inductive inquiry can operate in dealing with particular, often problematic cases.[5] Both fictional detectives must synthesize explanatory hypotheses on the basis of their appraisal of the manifold facts and contingencies of cases and test these hypotheses against rival theories competing for explanatory scope and adequacy. Inductive inquiry and argument presuppose a contest and a conflict among contending hypotheses. The test or proof of an inductive hypothesis is not *strictly* the presence (corroboration) or lack (refutation) of analytic coherence and consistency in the formal structure of the inquiry. Much more important, the overall constitution of an inductive inquiry reveals a thinker (or group of thinkers) engaging a range of rival hypotheses and attempting to pose and weigh evidence that eventually tends to support one of the hypotheses as the most plausible, probable, and cognitively adequate to the known facts and declared contingencies of the

5. Of course, Conan Doyle is well known for characterizing the method of Holmes as "deductive," but this label does not square at all with the practices of his fictional character. Moreover, Umberto Eco and Thomas A. Sebeok have collected and edited a group of ten essays that examine the methods of inquiry of not only Dupin and Holmes but also other inductive thinkers such as Charles S. Peirce and Sigmund Freud. Eco and Sebeok as well as the majority of their contributors prefer to use Peirce's term "abduction" in order to characterize a preliminary step of inductive method concerned with causal or genetic explanation. For my purposes, this Peircean distinction within the domain of inductive method will not be promoted. See Eco and Sebeok, eds., *The Sign of Three: Dupin, Holmes, Peirce* (Bloomington: Indiana University Press, 1983), especially pp. vii–ix, 11–55, 119–34, 154–69, 181–83, 198–220.

case. Well-established, socioculturally accepted, and cognitively secure hypotheses can eventually serve as the primary premises of deductions or deductive theories. However, inductive inquiry often constitutes the pathway and the procedures by which such hypotheses come to be constructed as relatively secure premises available for the activity of deductive inquiry and argumentation.

Inductive inquiry and argumentation, then, can handle critical conflict and disagreement at a level at which they are the most telling and consequential. The issue of critical conflict is not and should not be regarded merely as a matter of preference or the accidental consequence of a local community of interpreters. Indeed, critical conflict involves critical method, the recognition and evaluation of evidence, the selection and articulation of rival hypotheses, and the manner in which various bodies of evidence are regarded as confirming one contending hypothesis while failing to sanction adequately the explanatory scope and adequacy of other conjectural possibilities.[6] The very manner in which thinkers handle conflict and regard evidence as applicable and confirmable in a given case has a lot to do with the way they will handle conflict and evidence in new cases. Human beings in and through various acts of inquiry and argument build up a workable repertoire of cases and skills in practical reasoning and judgment. The very ways in which particular persons construe and cope with evidence and critical conflict at the level of critical inquiry has everything to do with the possibilities for recognizing and adjudicating critical disagreement at the level of conclusions or evaluative judgments. There would seem to be no other fully constructive manner in which to engage productively the issue of critical divergence other than to look closely at the complicated, often implicit pathways of an inquiry or an argument and to reconstruct them carefully along the lines of a fully reasoned inductive approach.

I have tried to do precisely this kind of close, reasoned examination of the exfoliating pathways of an inductive inquiry. In Part One, "Dreaming the Death of the Lovely Other: A Case of Murder and the Romantic Imagination," I concern myself with the adjudication of three possible readings of William Wordsworth's poem "A slumber did my spirit seal." I address various problems encountered in the experience of reading the

---

6. See Israel Scheffler, *The Anatomy of Inquiry* (New York: Borzoi Books, 1963), pp. 299–302, and Nelson Goodman, *Fact, Fiction, and Forecast* (Cambridge, Mass.: Harvard University Press, 1955).

poem, as well as the choice and development of literary, social, and historical contexts for following out and enriching its implications. The poem links up not only with numerous other works and issues in Wordsworth's own rich canon of texts but also with various preoccupations of some later Romantic authors. Moreover, the fate of the speaker or the narrator of Wordsworth's lyric can be recognized as fully representative of the fate of numerous critical readers of the work—namely, the slumbrous failure to interact. This approach to reading Wordsworth and the critical writings of his own readers deliberately departs from a recent tendency in theoretically informed studies of the poet's work that claim that Wordsworth's "poetry maintains the priority of the poem's production over its understanding or reception."[7] This tendency, largely influenced by the theory and practice of the late Paul de Man, generally promotes an incommensurability between imaginative figurality and retrospective or temporal understanding. I will maintain, instead, that the activity of reading Wordsworth's poetry can lead critical readers into a recognition of the poetry's cognitive and performative fusion of imaginative construction and temporal unfolding.[8]

In order to extend the possible ramifications of this way of attending to a poem, readings of two other so-called "Lucy" poems—"Strange fits of passion have I known" and "She dwelt among the untrodden ways"—will be offered. The interpretation of all three of these poems, moreover, bears out the subtle, surprising, and deftly modulated workings of a death fantasy. These diverse lyric expressions of such a fantasy significantly pivot

7. Cynthia Chase and Andrzej Warminski, Introduction to "Wordsworth and the Production of Poetry," a special issue of *Diacritics* 17 (Winter 1987): 2. See especially the essays by de Man, Warminski, Chase, Reeve Parker, and Cathy Caruth in this issue of *Diacritics*. A special issue of the *Centennial Review* 33 (Fall 1989): 301–510, edited by A. C. Goodson, seems to counter the ethos of Chase and Warminski's approach to the figural anteriority of Wordsworth's productions by exhibiting a fine set of essays that highlights ways in which the construction of intelligible experience in Wordsworth depends upon critical understanding of the poet's complex engagements with a wide set of philosophical, scientific, and poetic issues and interlocutors. See especially the essays by Goodson, Fred Wilson, Gerald Bruns, Don Bialostosky, Julie Ellison, and Laura Haigwood.

8. There has been some recent work on examining Wordsworth's poetry, especially some of *Lyrical Ballads*, in relation to theories of reading. For instance, see Susan Edwards Meisenhelder, *Wordsworth's Informed Reader: Structures of Experience in His Poetry* (Nashville, Tenn.: Vanderbilt University Press, 1988), and Regina Hewitt, "Towards a Wordsworthian Phenomenology of Reading: 'The Childless Father' and 'Poor Susan' as Paradigms," *Essays in Literature* 16 (1989): 188–202. Both Meisenhelder and Hewitt draw heavily from the work of Wolfgang Iser in order to underscore the structured experience of reading Wordsworth's poems as that which elicits moral and social effects in the implied reader.

upon the markedly self-involved or solipsistic powers of the lyrics' narrators and their failure to interact with the reality of otherness. I will argue, furthermore, that this curious situation has direct significance for insistent critical patterns of reading these poems and of characterizing lyric figurations of the nature of poetic imagination.

The brief interchapter presents interpretations of three letters from 1799, letters that were written by one of Wordsworth's most celebrated readers and interpreters, Samuel Taylor Coleridge. I attempt to demonstrate that the language, action, and intriguing preoccupations of Wordsworth's three "Lucy" lyrics infiltrate and help articulate the language and revealing fantasies of Coleridge's attempts to deal with the loss of his own son Berkeley. Coleridge's emotionally trying scenes of grief and fantasy seem eerily emblematic of so much subsequent critical failure to interact carefully, fully, and self-reflexively.

In Part Two, "Realigning Literary Reading and Critical Inquiry: Interaction and the Problematics of Reading," I pursue a fully theoretical exposition of an interactional model of reading that treats the interaction of reader and poem as a critical inquiry into the boundaries and interdependencies of self and others. The general framework here derives from major writings by the American pragmatist philosopher John Dewey. His work in logic, epistemology, and social psychology provides a solid and capacious foundation for literary theorists interested in understanding the connections between literary reading and inquiry and the ordinary patterns of purposive activity in human experience. Various gleanings from and critiques of passages and concepts in Dewey and a number of other theoretically inclined writers are coordinated in order to produce a critical analysis of Dewey's phenomenology of experience that is amenable to literary studies. The goal is to seek out a thorough treatment of Dewey and the work of related thinkers in order to articulate a cogent and compelling model of the procedures and local practices of literary inquiry. In particular, Dewey's notion of cognitive inquiry into experience yields the concept of the "problematic"—Dewey's name for a form of critical inquiry that attends to artistic events as being characteristically problem generating and that helps to describe and elaborate conceptually the felt qualities of such events. A given "problematic"—developed in the course of reading and rereading a specific poetic text, for example—centers and guides the particular ways in which a real reader actively engages the text and the ways in which the text acts upon and guides that reader. This interactional model of reading also draws upon Stephen C. Pepper's work in aesthetics and the theory of evidence as well as Ludwig Wittgenstein's writings on understanding and being guided by a scriptoral notation. I develop this interactional model of reading, of course, in relation to various contemporary and competing models of the act of literary reading and response.

This model, however, stands in critical contrast with some fairly recent appropriations of Dewey and pragmatism in the interests of confronting major issues in literary theory. Richard Rorty most specifically and Stanley Fish, Walter Benn Michaels, and Steven Knapp more generally have striven to show the pertinence of "pragmatism" to questions of interpretation, meaning, conventions, and intentions in literary theory.[9] Rorty's image of Dewey and conception of Deweyan pragmatism have much to recommend them. Nevertheless, as his projection of a literary and cultural pragmatism slides toward a Fishean, unprincipled, purportedly antiessentialist and antifoundationalist epistemological position, Rorty departs significantly from the principled experiential basis of Dewey's work in the theory of logic, epistemology, and social psychology. As David B. Downing has remarked:

> What Rorty's reading of Dewey misses is the extent to which, following the deconstruction of Aristotelian metaphysics, *Dewey's reconstruction of the pragmatic patterns of inquiry resisted the foundational grounds of certainty which Aristotle claimed for his logic.* Instead, Dewey did not seek to assay the transcendental rules of knowledge; rather *he sought systematically to reconstruct the relative and contingent patterns of inquiry which have been deployed in social history, critical theory, and scientific practice,* and secondly, he hoped further to clarify those patterns so they might be more useful in the tasks of social amelioration and cultural transformation. In other words, while Rorty champions Dewey's edifying, conversational, and antifoundationalist modes, he resists *Dewey's pragmatic efforts to outline the logical patterns to those conversations.*[10] (italics mine)

9. See especially Richard Rorty, "Texts and Lumps," *New Literary History* 17 (Autumn 1985): 1–16, and "Philosophy without Principles," *Critical Inquiry* 11 (March 1985): 459–65. See also the contributions by Knapp and Michaels and by Fish in *Against Theory: Literary Studies and the New Pragmatism,* ed. W. J. T. Mitchell (Chicago: University of Chicago Press, 1985).

10. David B. Downing, "Deconstruction's Scruples: The Politics of Enlightened Critique," *Diacritics* 17, 3 (Fall 1987): 75.

Downing's eloquent evocation of Dewey's reconstructive pragmatism yields a succinct image of the Dewey that I will be in critical dialogue with in this book. My own account of Dewey and the possibilities of Deweyan pragmatism for fundamental questions in literary theory will strive to reconstruct a more philosophically principled pragmatist—indeed, one who is deeply engaged in thinking through the pragmatic, contingent, yet logical patterns that structure the intensive conversation of critical inquiry into literary reading.

This turn to a more philosophically principled reconstruction of Dewey's pragmatism answers well to the terms of the postmodern crisis in the legitimation of knowledge that Jean-François Lyotard graphs so starkly in his well-known monograph *The Postmodern Condition*.[11] For Lyotard the condition of postmodern possibilities of knowledge is strongly marked by the failure of the grand, modern metanarratives of the systematic legitimation of knowledge (pp. xxiv–xxv, 37, 41). Neither the metanarrative of the liberatory, empowering potential of knowledge in the service of the people nor the metanarrative of the speculative, systematic organization of all fields of knowledge in the encyclopedic expansion of rational disinterestedness and spiritual growth can legitimate the practices of knowledge in a world where technology, efficiency, and performance determine the status of what will count as knowledge (pp. 31–53). It would appear that the condition of postmodern knowledge goes without foundations because the former, legitimating, and grand stories of the epistemological foundations of knowledge have been deconstructed by the spiritless hegemony of new discursive practices that remake the field of the knower and the known into a technologically mediated economy and circulation of discrete information. However, nostalgia for the lost organicism of the old metanarratives of legitimation should not lead one to the thoughtless postmodern leap of despair into "the dissolution of the social bond and the disintegration of social aggregates into a mass of individual atoms thrown into the absurdity of Brownian motion"—the very ethos of Jean Baudrillard's odd simulation of the postmodern condition (p. 15). Instead, Lyotard recognizes that the postmodern condition most fully encountered leads one to engage in a turn toward pragmatics or toward close analysis of moves and effects in various

---

11. Jean-François Lyotard, *The Postmodern Condition: A Report on Knowledge*, trans. Geoff Bennington and Brian Massumi (Minneapolis: University of Minnesota Press, 1984). Quotations will be from this translation and will be cited parenthetically throughout the ensuing paragraph.

"language games" of local knowledge and performative expertise (pp. 9–11, 43). Postmodern legitimation of knowledge must reside, then, in local inquiries into the pragmatics of specific fields of cognitive practice. Grand, overarching metanarratives will not suffice. They tend to offer major premises or hegemonic hypotheses from which all fields of knowledge and cognitive procedures must be logically and systematically deduced. The postmodern condition of knowledge forces thinkers and would-be theorists of disciplinary activity to realize that the field of knowledge yields a complex, heterogeneous assortment of knowledge games with a varying mix of rules, procedures, conventions, purposes, and modes of practical effectivity. Particular disciplines and disciplinary theorists need to recognize this situation and to inquire into the pragmatics of their own local "language game," what Lyotard also calls "the game of inquiry" (p. 15). For Lyotard the foundational or legitimating move in the playing of such a cognitively significant game involves the situation of the self or subject "in a fabric of relations" that constitutes an inescapable "social bond" for any given human being (p. 15). Real agents, actual human selves or subjects, center the play of local knowledges; their own practices and self-governing prescriptions become legitimated, not by some "universal metalanguage," but within socially shared "linguistic practice and communicational interaction" (pp. 40–41, 35–36). This situation echoes Dewey's emphasis upon locating and conceptualizing those local, contingent, and pragmatic patterns of the practice of knowledge. For Dewey and for Lyotard the interactive and inquiring human individuals both center and help legitimate local knowledges by seeking to explore and to articulate the pragmatics that comprise the real moves and experienced effects of language games that ineluctably bind them socially, even agonistically, to other selves adept at playing the same games.

Lyotard prefers the term "language game"; Rorty promotes the term "conversation"; Dewey elects to use the notion of "inquiry" into "cognitive situations" whose local logics or practical patterns of knowledge need to be articulated and clarified by the agent (or agents) most directly involved. Through a critical inquiry into the procedures and practices of literary understanding that I conduct in the second part of this book, I have striven to articulate what I take to be the pragmatics of the "language game" or "conversation" of literary reading and critical inquiry. In many respects, Part Two offers the core of a Deweyan "literary pragmatics." However, the first half of the book remains central to any inductive inquiry into the pragmatics of literary experience. Indeed, the second part returns allusively and even insistently to comment upon the literary-theoretical relevance of the interpretive, critical, and scholarly moves rehearsed in Part One. My explicit intention in setting the architecture of the book in this way rests upon the belief that the second part would supply a much fuller theoretical description and conceptual defense of the model of literary reading and critical inquiry that the first half enacts as a matter of local practice. I have deliberately chosen this structure because of my already avowed conviction in the aptness and relevance of inductive method and procedures for the field of literary studies. Nevertheless, the second part cannot be used to deduce, educe, or otherwise produce the sort of thick descriptive particulars of the first part. In ways that will become clear as the whole book unfolds, the latter half forms a *conceptual report* on what the first half *enables* the critical reader to *undergo qualitatively.* In Part One then, I ask my reader to play the role of a critical sleuth—a Dupin or a Holmes—examining the curious evidences and cover-ups of a case of the Romantic imagination, both lyrical and critical, at deadly play. In Part Two I ask that same reader to examine carefully the structure of critical assumptions and procedures that can be judged as warranted and legitimated by and through the detective spadework of Part One.

In general, any worthwhile theory of literary reading must be able to test itself through and against well-known, representative, and paradigmatic texts. To have chosen relatively unknown or unconsidered pieces as my case studies would have called attention to new, even noncanonical texts. However, a freshly integrated model of literary reading needs to be demonstrated through how effectively and persuasively it can handle the problems that have been generated in reading and in theorizing the reading of well-known works. Wordsworth's "A slumber did my spirit seal," as well as "Strange fits of passion" and "She dwelt among the untrodden ways," provide ideal and highly productive examples. This small gathering of powerfully suggestive texts permits the sort of intensive textual, literary-historical, and interpretive scholarship that can be attuned to the recurrent critical issues and theoretical problems that a model of reading must delve into and with which it must come to conceptually precise terms. This book, then, is offered as simultaneously an exacting study in practical criticism and historical scholarship and a careful elaboration of a theory of literary reading. My belief and my contention would be that such practice and such theory necessarily demand such intimate connection.

PART ONE

DREAMING THE DEATH
OF THE LOVELY OTHER:
A Case of Murder
and the
Romantic Imagination

My basic procedure has been to locate a text that has caused a fair amount of dissension; to locate within the text the main points of divergence among the critics; and, at each point, to map out a pattern of variation. The next task was to ascertain the cause of variation, and, from each cause, to draw out a point of critical theory.

—*Philip Hobsbaum,* Theory of Criticism

A slumber ought not to seal the reader's spirit as he reads this poem, or any other poem.

—*Cleanth Brooks, "Irony as a Principle of Structure"*

The necessary immanence of the reading in relation to the text is a burden from which there can be no escape. It is bound to stand out as the irreducible philosophical problem raised by all forms of literary criticism.

—*Paul de Man,* Blindness and Insight

It is when these [professors of literature] overextend their art, when they become a little *murderous, that they also become interesting.*

—*Geoffrey Hartman, "Centaur: Remarks on the Psychology of the Critic"*

Thus almost everywhere there can be found striking omissions, disturbing repetitions, palpable contradictions, signs of things the communication of which was never intended. The distortion of a text is not unlike a murder. The difficulty lies not in the execution of the deed but in doing away with the traces.

—*Sigmund Freud,* Moses and Monotheism

It is a monstrous thing to see in the same heart and at the same time this sensibility to trifles and this strange insensibility to the greatest objects. It is an incomprehensible enchantment, and a supernatural slumber, which indicates as its cause an all-powerful force.

—*Blaise Pascal,* Pensées, #194

I say "her," but the pronoun is one of the most terrifying masks man has invented; what came to Charles was not a pronoun, but eyes, looks, the line of the hair over a temple, a nimble step, a sleeping face.

—John Fowles, The French Lieutenant's Woman

. . . to speak a little metaphysically, words are not a mere vehicle, *but they are* powers *either to kill or to animate.*

—Wm. Wordsworth, letter to Wm. R. Hamilton, Dec. 23, 1829

On "Strange fits," "She dwelt" and "I travelled" he said: "These poems were written in Germany, 1799." On "Three years": "1799. Composed in the Hartz Forest." Of "A slumber" he said nothing at all.

—Hugh Sykes Davies, "Another New Poem by Wordsworth"

1

A Familiar Confusion
and
Shared Features of Experience

Perhaps even before you began reading this sentence your attention was drawn to the lyric presented below. If so, more than likely, you immediately recognized it in its familiarity: one of the "Lucy" poems by William Wordsworth. It is probably one of the most recognizable, read, and discussed lyrics in the canon of English literature. And it is to be written about yet again as I ask you to read it once more.

> A slumber did my spirit seal;
>   I had no human fears:
> She seemed a thing that could not feel
>   The touch of earthly years.
>
> No motion has she now, no force;
>   She neither hears nor sees;
> Rolled round in earth's diurnal course,
>   With rocks, and stones, and trees.

Perhaps a familiar confusion has returned. The reference of the pronoun "she," so often taken to mean "Lucy," is not so clear upon first reading the poem after some time away from it. Perhaps this lack of clarity, this confusion, in reference occurred most sharply in one's very first reading of the poem, before one had learned that it was a "Lucy" poem and that "she" was in actuality the Lucy who is referred to by name in the other four poems of the group.[1] Yet all too often we can fictionalize an original and pristine reading. This fictionalizing of a first reading may happen because we desire the authority of a pure and unqualified beginning or because we wish to avoid the fact that repetition or recurrence of some situation through time may be our only and all-too-human way of learning to see and understand it.[2]

Perhaps, instead, some form of controlled experiment could yield original and seemingly unqualified responses by numerous readers of the poem. These responses, either uniformly or predominantly, would reveal the confusion in the reference of "she" in Wordsworth's poem. However, the primary result of a controlled experiment may not be authentic responses at all but evidence of the motivation and extent of the experimenter's control and desires in what is an ineradicably contrived situation. Frequently, the principles that an experimenter seeks to establish or verify are already present within the operational procedures he or she has chosen.[3]

Nevertheless, the experience of a confusion in the reference of "she" is very real, I contend, even though seemingly difficult to locate or verify in some unqualified or scientific fashion. I propose that this experience of a confusion is a basic and necessary piece of literary evidence in any

1. See *The Poetical Works of William Wordsworth*, ed. Ernest de Selincourt and Helen Darbishire, rev. ed., 5 vols. (Oxford: Clarendon Press, 1952–59). (The volumes of this edition will hereinafter be cited parenthetically as *PW*, I, *PW*, II, *PW*, III, *PW*, IV, and *PW*, V.) The four other poems of the so-called "Lucy" group are "Strange fits of passion have I known," "She dwelt among the untrodden ways," "I travelled among unknown men," and "Three years she grew in sun and shower." The first three lyrics are grouped together as poems VII, VIII, and IX in the section "Poems Founded on the Affections" in *PW*, II, pp. 29–31. "Three years she grew" and "A slumber" are placed together as poems X and XI in the section "Poems of the Imagination" on pp. 214–16 of the same volume.

At least two critics have chosen to add two additional lyrics to the "Lucy" group. George Maclean Harper, in *William Wordsworth: His Life, Works and Influence*, rev. ed. (London, 1929), assigns "I met Louisa in the shade" and "Dear Child of Nature, let them rail" to the "Lucy" group (p. 292). John Jones, in *The Egotistical Sublime: A History of Wordsworth's Imagination* (London: Chatto & Windus, 1954), includes "The Danish Boy" and "Lucy Gray" in his group of seven "Lucy" poems, all of which share "the highly stylized Lucy setting" (pp. 71–72). For a general survey of the problem of the "Lucy" poems as a distinct and integral group, see Herbert Hartman, "Wordsworth's 'Lucy' Poems: Notes and Marginalia," *PMLA* 49 (1934): 134–42.

2. I will discuss some consequences of fictionalizing beginnings in the general context of literary studies at the beginning of Chapter 8; see pp. 133–35.

3. For an extended commentary on the methodology of controlled experiments and some reader-response theories, see Chapter 8, pp. 135–58.

comprehensive description and explanation—that is to say, interpretation—of "A slumber did my spirit seal."

Before I offer an interpretation, it is best to start with a ground-level accounting of how and why a referential confusion is not only possible but plausible in reading or in rereading this poem after some time away from it. The first two lines introduce a slumbrous and insensitive speaker, though with a very curious grammatical turn of phrase in the first line. Perhaps we may be slightly piqued at the assuredness of tone or bravado that the speaker manages in asserting so directly his insensitivity while in his slumber: "I had no human fears." Yet we accept or just go along with the opening, or perhaps even identify provisionally with the speaker because of the easy transference conventionally permitted us when we read or recite the pronoun "I" in written passages.[4] But regardless of the terms we swiftly make in agreeing to go on reading, the pronoun "she" in line three demands an antecedent, which we can and may acknowledge to be "my spirit." This demand is not an unusual or excessive one; it is natural to the situation. When the pronouns "my" and "I" occur in the first and second lines, their demands for an antecedent, a reference, are met by the assumption of a speaker; we are aware that the speaker of a poem, if not the poet himself, appears in it through the use of the pronoun "I." However, uses of the pronouns "he," "she," and "it" presuppose a reference in order to be meaningful in a situation; we either know the antecedent for the pronoun being used or we look about for it.[5] It appears

4. Hearing the poem read aloud by someone else would probably diminish, if not incapacitate, the ease of this identification or transference. In the oral-aural situation, the reciter of the poem can readily assume the role of the "I" both personally and for the auditors.

5. A critical assumption at work here is that a strict dichotomy cannot be drawn between ordinary and literary discourse. With respect to ordinary and to literary uses of language, pronouns must presuppose a reference in order to be meaningful. Differences will and do occur, but they occur as *different uses* of the same basic linguistic process or strategy. A poem beginning with the pronoun "he" or "she," for instance, can insist on suspending clarification of the referent being presupposed. A reader, then, may ascribe the reference to a persona of the author, a generalized human type, or someone who becomes associated with the figure being drawn; that is, a writer can deliberately manipulate the linguistic operation of a pronoun's presupposing a reference because it is understood that a basic linguistic process will insist upon fulfilling itself. It is unreasonable to posit a pronoun in either ordinary or literary discourse of any kind and not expect an auditor or reader to try to look about for an antecedent or reference. Notice how the pronouns in Thomas Hardy's four-poem cycle "She, to Him," initially so abstract and unattached, provoke the curiosity of the reader. The poems themselves elaborate concrete antecedents for the initial unspecified relation of female speaker to male auditor. See *Collected Poems of Thomas Hardy* (New York: Macmillan, 1925), pp. 11–13.

that the only possible antecedent for "she" in the first stanza is "my spirit," and while we are reading through that stanza the presupposition of "my spirit" as the reference of "she" can be naturally enough made. The lines "She seemed a thing that could not feel / The touch of earthly years" strike us as further amplification of the nature of the slumber that has sealed the speaker's spirit. We are directed toward making this connection by the colon at the end of line two. It directs us forward, indicating that what follows is an amplification or a case in point of how the speaker "had no human fears."[6] If a reader, either by cultural conditioning or gender or by

---

6. The punctuation at the end of line two has always been a colon, from the first publication of "A slumber" in 1800 through all subsequent printings of the poem authorized by Wordsworth during his lifetime. I have checked with two separate copies of volume two of the 1800 edition of *Lyrical Ballads* (London, 1800), p. 53: one deposited in the Wordsworth Room of the Lilly Library at Indiana University [described as Item 7 in Russell Noyes, *The Indiana Wordsworth Collection* (Boston: Hall, 1978), p. 5] and the other deposited in the SUNY at Buffalo Library's Poetry/Rare Books Collection. This invariance in punctuation becomes truly remarkable when the punctuation of the other lines of the lyric in its 1800 appearance is compared with various later editions. The punctuation for line one and all of stanza two is altered by Wordsworth through the various republications of the poem, beginning with the 1802 edition of *Lyrical Ballads* and continuing through the 1805 edition until the 1850 edition of *Poetical Works*. The 1800 version of "A slumber" is minimally punctuated, but the original choice of a colon at the end of the second line would appear to be a deliberately important one in the light of subsequent major punctuating and repunctuating of many other lines. A colon also appears at the end of line two in Coleridge's transcription of "A slumber" for Thomas Poole in a letter dated April 6, 1799. This transcription is the earliest extant version of the poem and is based on a copy, now lost, that Wordsworth had sent to Coleridge soon after composing the poem. See S. T. Coleridge, *Collected Letters*, Vol. I, ed. E. L. Griggs (Oxford: Clarendon Press, 1956), p. 480 (hereinafter cited parenthetically as Griggs, I). I stress the facts of Wordsworth's punctuation because his use of the colon, as will be seen, should be included in a full interpretation of "A slumber."
The 1800 version of "A slumber" reads as follows:

> A slumber did my spirit seal,
>   I had no human fears:
> She seem'd a thing that could not feel
>   The touch of earthly years.
>
> No motion has she now, no force
>   She neither hears nor sees
> Roll'd round in earth's diurnal course
>   With rocks and stones and trees!

The general effects of Wordsworth's subsequent punctuation of the poem are to: (1) slow down the movement—here perhaps too quick—of the reader through the lines; (2) lend the lines a greater somberness or muted quality; and (3) clarify the logical and grammatical relations among clauses and phrases.
Perhaps it could be objected that Wordsworth himself says that he is "no adept" at punctuation.

familiarity with lyric tropology, has no hesitation in referring a feminine personal pronoun back to the noun "spirit," then the presupposition is made and the first stanza is read. Some misgivings are possible, and this dissonance will resound all the more in the confusion awaiting a reading of the first two lines of the second stanza.

However, it is possible to avoid acknowledging "my spirit" as the antecedent of "she" by assuming that "she" will be clarified later on in the poem. In this event, a full stop in attention is made at the end of line two, as if a period were placed there instead of a colon. The "she" is still confusing, because there is no antecedent for it, no preparation for its appearance. However, the third line is begun as if a new sentence and a whole new thought were commencing. This construing of grammar and the attention given it permits one to assume that clarification of who "she" is will arrive later on, and so we proceed. However, stanza two offers no such clarity, and we are surprised and even shocked to find already lifeless someone whose identity baffles us.

Strictly speaking, the ascription of "Lucy" as the reference or antecedent of "she" in line three is completely unwarranted.[7] Such an ascription transfers the knowledge of other "Lucy" poems, as well as the various arrangements of and commentaries upon them, prematurely and prejudicially upon "A slumber did my spirit seal." Comparisons are to be made, but a pronoun in one poem should not be forced to presuppose an antecedent found only in another poem.

In a letter to Humphry Davy of July 29, 1800, in which he encloses the poems "Hart-leap Well," "There was a Boy," "Ellen Irwin," and the first thirty-six lines of "The Brothers" (the four poems that immediately precede the first three "Lucy" poems in *Lyrical Ballads*), Wordsworth says: "You would greatly oblige me by looking over the enclosed poems and correcting any thing you find amiss in the punctuation a business at which I am ashamed to say I am no adept." However, the two letters (#133, 134) that precede this one to Davy (#135) in the collected *Letters* contain numerous typographical corrections prepared by Wordsworth for the printers Messrs. Biggs and Cottle and transcribed in Coleridge's and Dorothy Wordsworth's hands. Included are many alterations in punctuation for poems being set for the 1800 edition. Such attention implies some measure of care on Wordsworth's part for the fine distinctions in rhythm, feeling, and meaning that accurate punctuation can achieve. See *The Letters of William and Dorothy Wordsworth*, Vol. I, *The Early Years, 1787–1805*, ed. Ernest de Selincourt; rev., 2d ed., C. L. Shaver (Oxford: Clarendon Press, 1967), pp. 289, 285–88 (hereinafter this volume will be cited parenthetically as EY).

7. There is an important semantic difference between the words "presupposition" and "ascription." The presupposition of a reference involves the capacity to assume beforehand or to take for granted that the particular act of referring will and does work successfully—or "felicitously," to use J. L. Austin's term. The ascription of a reference involves conscious imputing or attributing, usually after the fact, of a reference that may have been unclear or confusing.

The second stanza, though, yields a confusion. We are surprised or
even shocked to discover that "she" has become insensate, has ceased to
exist by truly becoming a thing. But our confusion lies in the fact that the
pronoun "she" in the lines "No motion has she now, no force; / She
neither hears nor sees" now definitely seems to indicate another person,
rather than the "spirit" of the narrator. Who has become insensate? Who
has become a thing? Is the speaker presenting his own slumbrous lapsing
into death or describing a woman dead to all feeling? Such is the confusion we experience when the lines are fleshed out in complete sentences
and interrogatives. The surprise or shock of death (or a deathlike state) that
is communicated so resoundingly in the final two lines of the second
stanza does not resolve our confusion, but heightens it. We want to know
who "she" really is; we need to know whose death it is that surprises or
shocks us so abruptly. Thus we have the motive to reread the lyric and
clarify the antecedent of "she."[8] However, because there is no internal

8. Perhaps here can be located an origin for the surprisingly insistent impulse to discover the
"true identity" of the "Lucy" figure. Herbert Hartman, pp. 137–38, briefly notes eight different
proposals for "the original of Lucy."
    The most plausible of them is perhaps best formulated by Catherine Macdonald Maclean in
Dorothy and William Wordsworth (London: Cambridge University Press, 1927), pp. 49–58.
Maclean claims that the five so-called "Lucy" poems plus "Among all lovely things my Love had
been," "Louisa," and "Child of Nature" "are all based on moods, emotions and states of feeling
which were part of the poet's life with his sister, and which could not have been part of his life
with any other woman. . . . In these poems he expresses the most romantic relationship and
deepest devotion of his life" (p. 56). H. W. Garrod ["Wordsworth's Lucy," *The Profession of Poetry*
(Oxford: Clarendon Press, 1929), pp. 80–81, 86–87] and F. W. Bateson [*Wordsworth: A
Re-interpretation*, 2d ed. (London: Longmans, Green, 1956), p. 67] concur, on the whole, with
Maclean's selection.
    H. M. Margoliouth, however, makes yet another proposal for Lucy's original: Margaret (Peggy)
Hutchinson, the younger sister of Wordsworth's wife. Peggy died unexpectedly of consumption
in 1796; Margoliouth claims that "A slumber" is written as her epitaph and that in "Strange fits,"
"She dwelt," and "I travelled among unknown men" Wordsworth continues his thoughts about
the surprising early death of his acquaintance. See Margoliouth, *Wordsworth and Coleridge,
1795–1834* (London: Oxford University Press, 1953), pp. 52–58.
    Both of these proposals seem reasonable and are well argued, and it is probably the case that
Dorothy and Peggy both lend biographical elements that Wordsworth fuses in various ways in his
"she" and his "Lucy." However, "Lucy" is not all biographical, for as Garrod and Herbert
Hartman both point out there are significant *literary* sources for "Lucy." Garrod proposes a
possible connection between the line "And Lucy, at her wheel, shall sing" from Samuel Rogers's
"Mine be a cot beside the hill" and the English setting of Wordsworth's "I travelled among
unknown men" (p. 90). Earlier Lucys also appear in lyrics by Tickell ("Colin and Lucy"),
Lyttelton, Edward Moore, and Chatterton ("The Happy Pair") (p. 91). Lucy, then would take on
"the life of a purely ideal creation" (p. 91); she would be, in essence, a literary fiction. Herbert
Hartman notes yet another literary Lucy: William Collins's "Song: the Sentiments Borrowed from

clarification of the referential confusion, it is here that we find ourselves appealing outside the poem and our reading of it to the "Lucy" of "Strange fits of passion have I known" and "She dwelt among the untrodden ways" for clarification. This appeal seems inevitable, unless we are to dismiss the poem as poorly or confusingly contrived.[9]

My point here is that we do experience a confusion about who "she" is *while we are reading the poem*. This confusion is a basic fact involved in reading this particular lyric, and the desire to clarify or resolve this confusion is a basic fact in immediately rereading it and searching out its connections to the other "Lucy" poems. We must learn how to read "Lucy," or image her forth, in place of the three uses of "she" in the poem. This knowledge is not offered us at first reading, or even when we return to "A slumber" after some absence.

I have used "we," "us," and "our" in accounting for the referential confusion concerning "she" because this confusion is something we all *can* experience. However, a number of recent critics of the neo-Kantian assumptions of subjective universality and aesthetic distance contend that critical uses of the pronouns "we," "us," and "our" serve, in practice, to mask the "I" who is actually lurking behind them. Generally, these critics believe that some form of subjectivity should be the basic paradigm for literary studies.[10] Now, it would be unreasonable to claim that every

---

Shakespeare," a poem published in February 1788, a year before Wordsworth wrote his "Remembrance of Collins" (p. 141). "The name itself, it would seem, had become a neo-Arcadian commonplace, an eighteenth century elegiac fixture" (Hartman, p. 141). Quite rightly, Herbert Hartman does not argue solely for this conclusion. Neither a psychobiographical analysis nor a study of literary derivation and convention addresses all that is at play in "A slumber" and the other "Lucy" poems.

Mary Moorman's discussion of the identity of "Lucy" is compatible with this assessment. For Moorman, Wordsworth's "poetic creation of Lucy" involves many elements—Margaret's early death, Dorothy's and Mary Hutchinson's sorrow over this death, Dorothy herself, and Samuel Rogers's poem—and is not reducible to any one of them. See Mary Moorman, *William Wordsworth: A Biography; The Early Years, 1770–1803* (Oxford: Clarendon Press, 1957), pp. 423–25 (hereinafter cited parenthetically as Moorman, I).

As I will argue, Wordsworth's art carries us beyond the limits of these forms of analysis. Wordsworth reworks and fuses events from his acquaintances with Dorothy and Margaret (and perhaps others) as well as his readings of ballads and elegies in order to achieve his own work.

9. See the second paragraph of Chapter 3, pp. 40–42.

10. See Norman Holland, *Poems in Persons: An Introduction to the Psychoanalysis of Literature* (New York: Norton, 1973), pp. 3–4; and David Bleich, *Readings and Feelings: An Introduction to Subjective Criticism* (Urbana, Ill.: NCTE, 1975), pp. 7, 20, 49. In passing, Holland and Bleich discuss the question of subjectivity in literary studies and its bearing on their critical paradigms in an issue of *New Literary History*. See Bleich, "The Subjective Paradigm in

reader does or must experience a referential confusion in reading "A slumber." However, the "we" must and does begin with an "I." It is myself, one reader, who experiences the confusion over the reference of "she"; it is *my* experience, and I know it to be so. However, in this instance, what makes *my* experience *possible for me*? A number of things do, but what is important about them is that I share them with a great many other readers. Specifically, my knowledge of how pronouns are used in English is routinely called into play here. It is a form of shared knowledge so fundamental that it runs the risk of being minimized or sidelined as trifling. When I hear someone using a third-person-singular pronoun, I either know its antecedent already or understand that it will soon be clarified. If neither happens, then I am left puzzled or I ask for clarification.[11] I also know that listeners or readers of my uses of such pronouns also follow these same habits; they do not understand what I am saying if they claim not to exercise these fundamental linguistic habits. Now this is a shared and comprehensive form of knowledge for speakers of English. A more refined but still shared and shareable form of knowledge is an awareness of the literary uses of the pronoun "she." In this instance, knowledge of previous uses of the feminine personal pronouns in designating human and divine spirits is relevant.[12] This knowledge gets

---

Science, Psychology and Criticism," *NLH* 7 (Winter 1976): 313–34; and Holland, "The New Paradigm: Subjective or Transactive?," pp. 335–46.

11. See the discussion of pronouns and the presupposition of antecedents or references in footnote 5, p. 17. Again, the risk here lies in overlooking the fact that even our linguistic play with the pronouns "he," "she," or "it" in conversation and in poems assumes and playfully manipulates our search and need for an antecedent or referent. The pleasure and instruction found in such play stems from manipulating, altering, sidetracking, or even frustrating the conventional linguistic act of presupposition. Notice what happens in reading the following "pieces" by Robert Creeley:

> It's strange. It's   ———it
> all fallen   it———
> to grey.

See Creeley, *Pieces* (New York: Scribner's, 1969), pp. 78 and 17.

12. Familiarity with lyrics by Wyatt, Surrey, Sidney, Jonson, Herbert, and Crashaw would be very much to the point here. The work of the latter two poets also intersects with medieval and Renaissance religious writings in which the human spirit or soul is frequently imaged as female, usually as either a humble supplicant or a beloved of the Lord. See, for example, the second sentence of the first chapter of Book 3, "Internal Consolation," of Thomas à Kempis, *The Imitation of Christ*, trans. Aloysius Croft and Harold Bolton (Milwaukee, Wis.: Bruce, 1940), p. 83: "Blessed is the soul who hears the Lord speaking within her, who receives the word of consolation from His lips." Wordsworth had a copy of *De imitatione Christi* in his library at Rydal

called into play in making plausible for many readers the initial and immediate presupposing of "my spirit" as the antecedent of "she." These two specific forms of shared knowledge are integral parts of a reader's general linguistic and literary competence, and these general competencies are necessary to any individual reading of "A slumber did my spirit seal."

And last, but perhaps most fundamentally, I can share with others an awareness of what having an experience involves. As John Dewey phrases this awareness,

> we have *an* experience when the material experienced runs its course to fulfillment. Then and then only is it integrated within and demarcated in the general stream of experience from other experiences. A piece of work is finished in a way that is satisfactory; a problem receives its solution; a game is played through; a situation, whether that of eating a meal, playing a game of chess, carrying on a conversation, writing a book, or taking part in a political campaign, is so rounded out that its close is a consummation and not a cessation. Such an experience is a whole and carries with it its own individualizing quality and self-sufficiency. It is *an* experience.[13]

Thus we assume that reading a short lyric will offer us *an* experience; we will experience a certain body of linguistic and literary material running its course to fulfillment through our agency as its reader, and we will witness a closure to our experience when it achieves a distinct and self-sufficient character. The closure is not of necessity always the end or result that one desires, nor is the course of an experience always pleasing. Yet an experience always entails an engagement of a person with some material, some thing or work or event, so that an ending, a finality, a consummation, is achieved. A beginning is implied, but only because the experience achieves closure; we can only infer or reasonably reconstruct beginnings of experience, because an experience does not stand out or become "demarcated in the general stream of experience" until it achieves

Mount; it is listed in the "Rydal Mount Loan Book" kept by Wordsworth as well as in a catalogue of Wordsworth's library made by his clerk John Carter. See C. L. Shaver and A. C. Shaver, *Wordsworth's Library: A Catalogue* (New York: Garland, 1979), p. 144.

13. John Dewey, *Art as Experience* (New York: Capricorn Books, 1958; orig. pub. 1934), p. 35.

or is on the way to achieving a consummation.[14] Only at this point can
we recognize an experience of ours as "a whole" and recognize "its own
individuating quality and self-sufficiency." Otherwise, what could have
been an experience lies undeveloped and indistinct in the general stream
of experience.[15]

Generally, we have a sense of the definitive features an experience
characteristically possesses and can recognize them emerging again and
again in our experiences. For now, it is sufficient to summarize these
features as being: (1) a body of material found within the general stream
of human experience, (2) an agent who by nature experiences and is
capable of having distinct and individualized experiences, (3) an experience that emerges from the general stream of experience by standing out
or becoming demarcated temporally and specifically through running its
course to fulfillment or consummation, and (4) the achieved or consum-
mated experience that "carries" along with it and yields "its own
individualizing quality and self-sufficiency," its own distinct and developed character. These definitive features of an experience I share with
anyone who is capable of having an experience. It is by no means
necessary, however, that I or anyone else be clearly aware of all these
features in order to have an experience. It is the case that a great many
people, even students and researchers of experience among them, value
only one or two of these features, sometimes to the disregard or exclusion
of the others. These features are manifestly general. However, they
distinguish four essentials that any extended discussion of the nature of
experience will hover about and perhaps light upon.[16]

In specifically literary terms, these four definitive features of having an
experience would be: (1) a literary work, (2) a reader, (3) the activity of
reading, the temporal interaction of work and reader, and (4) the quality

14. In *Beginnings: Intention and Method* (New York: Basic Books, 1975), Edward W. Said
would appear to support this conclusion at one juncture in his text: "To identify a point as a
beginning is to classify it after the fact" (p. 29). *Beginnings*, as well as Said's book, will be
discussed in the first part of Chapter 8.

15. Because such an inconclusive "experience" lies undeveloped and indistinct it may
contribute to a sense of recognition or déjà vu in the future when a similar or perhaps identical
experience is developed and made distinct, individual, and self-sufficient.

16. To introduce basic notions into the development of this first chapter and to mark out the
ground of my discussion, I have presented rather general expositions of the notions of shared
forms of linguistic and literary knowledge and of awareness of what having an experience
involves. I will develop these notions at greater length and with attention to opposing viewpoints
and counterarguments in the second part of this book.

or character developed and made distinct within and through the temporal interaction of work and reader. These terms transfer easily enough to a consideration of the basic features of the experience of referential confusion upon first reading "A slumber" or rereading it after some time. There is a work (the poem), a reader (me), the process of reading, and the quality of a confusion that is developed and made distinct in the course of the literary interaction. These definitive features of having an experience of Wordsworth's brief lyric, like the features of an experience in general, are neither exhaustive nor rigorous and are not intended to be. They merely sketch out provisionally the pragmatic grounds for a shared awareness of what having a literary experience can involve. Particular responses to and readings of literary works scarcely ever remain completely idiosyncratic. Indeed, grammatically and rhetorically structured effects tend to induce recognitions that can surface in one's own reading of a literary work yet can also be witnessed structuring the terms and features of readings by other readers. Specific grammatical and literary competencies are at issue here, as well as broadly definitive features of what having a literary experience is often taken to mean by readers. These factors only begin to dramatize pragmatically the social, shareable status of literary response and interpretive procedures.

2

One Line of Interpretation: "She" as "Spirit"

There is an extended argument for an autonomous reading of "A slumber did my spirit seal" that "turns on the antecedent of the pronoun 'she' in the third line and in the second stanza." Hugh Sykes Davies has conducted a painstaking job of critical sleuthing into philological, bibliographical, and manuscript evidence to demonstrate the plausibility of an interpretation based on the observation that "she" can refer to "my spirit." His article was discussed but not disproved by three respondents in the pages of *Essays in Criticism* and has since been frequently footnoted but not discussed in a number of more recent attempts to read the "Lucy" poems as a narrative sequence.[1] Davies's exposition is not grounded in an experience of referential confusion encountered while reading the poem but instead pivots upon the purported "autonomy" of the poem. As Davies maintains,

> if a upholder of the traditional interpretation is ungallantly pressed about it, he will be found to maintain that the word "Lucy," though admittedly not to be found in this poem, is conspicuous in four other poems so inseparably and intimately linked with this one that there is no difficulty whatever in transferring it from one or all of them into this poem, thus "supplying" (as the old grammarians were fond of saying) what was wanting in it, and bringing it into line with the proper and received views. This

---

1. H. S. Davies, "Another New Poem by Wordsworth," *Essays in Criticism* 15 (April 1965): 135. The respondents to Davies's article will be discussed later on in this chapter, and some of the attempts to read the "Lucy" poems as a narrative sequence will be examined in Chapter 7.

rather remarkable procedure rests, in fact, on the no less remarkable assumption that the poem is not autonomous, and that it
must be read as one of a "group" of poems. The new interpretation, on the other hand, assumes that the poem *is* autonomous,
and that the antecedent for "she" must therefore be the one noun
within the text fitted by meaning and number to fill this function,
the word "spirit" in the first line.[2]

All the evidence that Davies goes on to assemble is aimed at supporting
this claim for the poem's autonomy and, consequently, for the ascription
of "my spirit" as the only reference for "she."

Davies begins his argument by showing examples from throughout
Wordsworth's writings that represent the latter's characteristic uses of "the
three traditional components of the human personality, 'soul,' 'mind' and
'spirit.'" Wordsworth, Davies notices,

> was consistent only in the gender of the pronoun for "soul"; in his
> verse, at any rate, this was always feminine. For "mind" on
> the other hand, he wavered between the feminine and the
> neuter. . . . With "spirit" he was even more variable. The word
> is antecedent to a pronoun twenty-five times in his verse; six of
> these pronouns are masculine, ten neuter and nine feminine. But
> the variation is not entirely random, for the masculine was always
> used when "spirit" stood for some supernatural being . . .[3]

Wordsworth also used feminine pronouns for such antecedents as "hope,"
"city," "town," and "earth"; and Davies concludes "that Wordsworth's
choice of gender in pronouns was both variable and personal, and that to
represent 'spirit' by the feminine pronoun was well within the usual usage
of his verse."[4] Thus, within the limits of Wordsworth's own poetic practice
alone, there are numerous pretexts for the noun "spirit," as well as for
other nouns, to occur as an antecedent of feminine pronouns.

Coleridge, however, some time after Wordsworth had sent him a copy
of "A slumber" in a letter, speculates that Dorothy Wordsworth was the
intended referent of the pronoun "she." In a letter written on April 6,

2. Ibid., pp. 135–36.
3. Ibid., p. 136.
4. Ibid., p. 138.

1799, to Thomas Poole, a mutual friend of the two poets, Coleridge prefaces his own transcription of the lyric with these words: "Some months ago Wordsworth transmitted to me a most sublime Epitaph. Whether it has any reality, I cannot say. —Most probably in some gloomier moment he had fancied the moment in which his Sister might die."[5] Quite rightly, Davies understands that if Coleridge had any " 'inside' information" concerning the troublesome pronoun "there would be an end of the matter."[6] However, the available evidence points toward the conclusion that Coleridge had no special information and was merely speculating on who "she" might be. Coleridge and Wordsworth had been residing separately in relatively distant towns in Germany since October 1798, corresponding infrequently. They did not meet again until April 20, approximately two weeks after Coleridge's letter to Poole.[7] Wordsworth's original letter to Coleridge containing "A slumber" has never been located, and none of the other extant letters—including the one containing two other "Lucy" poems[8]—mentions anything about the eight-line lyric. Davies narrates these facts and also uses them to refute a "flimsy scrap of gossip" concerning a secret meeting and "metaphysical excursions" between Wordsworth and Coleridge in Göttingen in mid-January 1799.[9] Thus, there does not appear to be any evidence to show that

5. Griggs, I, p. 497; quoted by Davies, p. 138.
6. Davies, p. 138.
7. Moorman, I, p. 434, and Ch. 13, pp. 408–33, in passing.
8. A letter written by Dorothy and William to Coleridge from Goslar on the 14th or 21st of December 1798 contains drafts of two "little Rhyme poems" that later became "She dwelt among the untrodden ways" and "Strange fits of passion have I known." The same letter contains drafts of three descriptions of childhood pleasures that later became "Nutting" and two sections of Book I of *The Prelude*. See EY, pp. 235–43. The letter containing "A slumber" may have been sent anytime between November 1798 and February 1799. F. W. Bateson, pp. 213–14, dates the lyric's composition as "Late 1798 or Early 1799."
9. Davies, pp. 139–41. In his "ineffably tedious and ill-written memoirs," *Early Years and Late Reflections*, Clement Carlyon, a slender acquaintance of Coleridge, delivers a good deal of misinformation about Coleridge's and the Wordsworths' sojourn in Germany, including a ramble of a day or two with homoerotic undertones and where "Miss Wordsworth" is left behind. Coleridge's own information at the time flatly contradicts Carlyon. See Griggs, I, p. 490, and Moorman, I, p. 434.
A more recent essay on the "Lucy" poems attempts to found a reading of the lyrics on Wordsworth's supposed desire to be with Coleridge during their months in Germany. Dorothy, however, is a financial burden for Wordsworth and thus keeps the two men separated from one another—Wordsworth isolated and depressed in Goslar. In his desire to be with Coleridge, Wordsworth supposedly fantasizes the death of Dorothy in the figure of Lucy. The victimizing of "Miss Wordsworth" here is reminiscent of Carlyon's bias in favor of unhindered male

Coleridge had " 'inside' information" about "A slumber" by the time he wrote about the poem to Thomas Poole. Moreover, the very phrasing of his comment on the lyric makes it clear that Coleridge's "information" seems intended by him to be taken as mere speculation.

In connection with Coleridge's supposition that Dorothy is the "she" of "A slumber," Davies points out that Coleridge's "own linguistic habits would have prevented him from taking 'she' as referring to [the] word ['spirit'] . . . and would as surely have driven him to suppose that it must refer to some woman."[10] In contrast with Wordsworth's pronominal habits, Coleridge's use of pronouns is "much more tied down to the rule that the neuter should be used for antecedents without obvious sex." Indeed, Coleridge almost always used neuter pronouns for "soul" and invariably used masculine pronouns for "Mind" and for "spirit" whenever the latter was regarded as a supernatural being. However, where "spirit" stood for some part of the human personality, Coleridge almost always used neuter pronouns and never feminine ones, as Wordsworth was so inclined to do.[11] Thus, it is reasonable to assume that, given his characteristic uses of pronouns, Coleridge would look about for a woman as the antecedent for "she" rather than ascribe the pronoun's antecedent to the noun "spirit." Lacking the whole subsequent tradition of reading "A slumber" as merely one of a group of interconnected poems all about a mysterious "Lucy," yet knowing firsthand the closeness and affection of the Wordsworths for one another, Coleridge made a reasonable, though not really very germane, conjecture.

The next step in Davies's argument presents his clearest and strongest evidence in support of the autonomy of "A slumber" vis-à-vis the other poems in the so-called "Lucy" group. By considering the arrangements and rearrangements of the "Lucy" poems in the 1800 and 1802 editions of *Lyrical Ballads* and in the 1807 and 1815 editions of *Poems*, Davies concludes that Wordsworth's own isolating of the poems of this supposed

---

camaraderie. See Richard Matlack, "Wordsworth's Lucy Poems in Psychobiographical Context," *PMLA* 93 (1978): 46–65.

Matlack quotes a part of Carlyon's memoirs that describes Wordsworth's and Coleridge's Dorothyless rambles and says: "Although neither the Wordsworths nor Coleridge mentions such an excursion, it does seem plausible in the light of the theory of Dorothy's unwanted presence offered in this article" (p. 64). The plausibility of spurious evidence in the light of a theory, in most instances, should lead to a more careful examination of the grounds and claims of that particular theory or hypothesis. I will discuss this essay further in Chapter 5.

10. Davies, p. 139.
11. Davies, p. 139.

group in varying places and configurations in the four texts shows convincingly that "A slumber" "was clearly separable from the 'Lucy' poems, for Wordsworth himself separated it from them."[12] Instead, the whole impetus toward considering the various "Lucy" poems as a distinct group stems from their "fate at the hands of the Victorian Wordsworthians."[13] Commencing with an article by Thomas De Quincey in *Tait's Edinburgh Magazine* in 1839, in which he notes parenthetically that Wordsworth has "always preserved a mysterious silence on the subject of that 'Lucy' repeatedly alluded to or apostrophied in his poems" and that he has "heard, from gossiping people about Hawkshead, some snatches of tragical story, which, after all, might be an idle semi-fable, improved out of slight materials," a period of suppressed reference to Wordsworth's early love life arose. After the Laureate's death, these suppressed references helped suggest "insidiously powerful" rearrangements of Wordsworth's lyrics in the anthologies and selections of Victorian editors.[14] Palgrave in

---

12. Davies, p. 145. See also pp. 142–45 for all the particulars of the argument. Davies goes on to say that "A slumber" was printed after "Strange fits" and "She dwelt" in *Lyrical Ballads*, 1800, "because it had been written at very nearly the same time. And in the rearrangement of 1815, 'A slumber' was placed with 'Three years' because these two were the only 'little Rhyme poems' among *Poems of the Imagination* which had been written in Germany" (p. 146). I think Davies severely strains his argument for autonomy at this point. Later on I will discuss what these two smaller arrangements mean and, consequently, why an argument for a completely autonomous reading of "A slumber" ("Another New Poem") is unnecessary and, indeed, vitiatingly limited.

13. Ibid., p. 152.

14. De Quincey is quoted by Davies, p. 147. The context of De Quincey's remark is his discussion of Wordsworth's marriage, especially De Quincey's own "perplexity" in imagining "Wordsworth as submitting his faculties to the humilities of courtship." But then, in a curiously structured sentence—as if to whisper and then conceal a secret all in one breath, perhaps like one gossiper to another—De Quincey confides what "some of us have sometimes thought": Wordsworth was "a lover disappointed at some earlier period by the death of her he loved, or by some other fatal event." De Quincey fills in his hint at tragedy or some such "fatal event" with the parenthetical gossip quoted above and then breaks off abruptly with the remark "let this matter have been as it might, at all events he made, what for him turns out, a happy marriage."

Mary Moorman has described the circumstances of Wordsworth's and De Quincey's relationship, one that eventually culminated in several bitter attacks by the latter on Wordsworth in *Tait's* during the winter of 1839. De Quincey had been an intimate of the Wordsworths from 1803 to 1813. However, a series of disagreements over De Quincey's addiction to opium, his taking of a mistress, and other improprieties began a prolonged estrangement and period of ill-feeling among the former intimates. De Quincey expressed his resentment toward the Wordsworths' change of heart by accusing Mary Wordsworth of intellectual weakness and Wordsworth himself of ingratitude and excessive pride. See Moorman, *William Wordsworth: A Biography; The Later Years: 1803–1850* (Oxford: Clarendon Press, 1965; rpt., with corrections, 1966), pp. 234–37 (hereinafter cited as Moorman, II).

1861, Matthew Arnold in 1879, Aubrey de Vere in 1880, and A. J. Symington in 1881 grouped the so-called "Lucy poems" together as one unit but in four markedly different sequences, as if to suit their personal whims. De Vere and Symington provided commentary on Wordsworth's alleged long-lost love and the significance of the sequence each was putting forward for the reader; Palgrave even renamed two of the lyrics in order to promote their biographical interest.[15] In the 1880s the " 'Lucy' legend" passed into "the main stream of academic orthodoxy" by being accepted and repeated in scholarly works. Thus, "there was no chance" for "A slumber" to have "any independent life of its own"; "for the first time, 'A slumber' was linked, conspicuously and apparently inseparably, with the poems containing the name 'Lucy.' " This situation, moreover, "now acquired that status of a fact which needed no proof, but which would be perverse to question."[16]

Perversity or no, Davies questioned the facts of the case and found the legend and the orthodoxy wanting. He has cleared the ground for an interpretation of "A slumber" based on the observation that "my spirit" appears in the text of the poem as the only possible antecedent for "she." Unfortunately, at this point the argument begins to lose its firmness and sense of direction and becomes merely suggestive and tentative. Essentially Davies has striven to establish the textual autonomy of a poem but then has the problem of getting it to mean something in a reasonably determinate fashion. His interpretive procedure involves locating various passages of prose and poetry in the Wordsworth canon that can lend some credibility to the consequences of reading "she" as meaning the narrator's own "spirit." It is only through the similarities and affinities thus suggested that one can get a sense of what Davies's own interpretation of the poem may be; he never actually states or summarizes it clearly.

Davies points out that in almost all passages in which "the condition of being 'sealed in a slumber' " occurs in Wordsworth "the imaginative power most fully exerts itself"; the body and the senses are laid to sleep and

---

For greater detail on the relationship of Wordsworth and De Quincey, see also John E. Jordan, *De Quincey to Wordsworth: A Biography of a Relationship,* With the Letters of Thomas De Quincey to the Wordsworth Family (Berkeley and Los Angeles: University of California Press, 1962), and Hugh Sykes Davies, *Thomas De Quincey (1785–1859)* (London: Longmans, Green, 1964).

15. Palgrave renamed "She dwelt" as "The Lost Love" and "Three years" as "The Education of Nature." See Davies, "Another New Poem," p. 148.

16. Davies, "Another New Poem," pp. 148, 150–51. In general, I am following Davies's compact presentation of a great range of evidence.

the spirit falls into a powerful dream or trancelike state.[17] Moreover, the "central image" of "A slumber" is to be located in another passage written at nearly the same time while Wordsworth was in Germany:

> yet still the solitary cliffs
> Wheeled by me—even as if the earth had rolled
> With visible motion her diurnal round!

These lines occur in an "extract" from Book I of *The Prelude* (lines 458–60) that was published separately in Coleridge's *Friend* in 1809 and later in the 1815 edition of *Poems* as a poem called "Influence of Natural Objects," but it is contemporaneous in composition with "A slumber." Davies claims that

> this leaves no doubt that the central image of "A slumber" long antedated any "Lucy," real or imaginary, and that it was one of those boyhood experiences which Wordsworth had begun to record and explore at Goslar. The poem is, in fact, a sort of transformation of the experience which had been re-awakened in meditating the blank verse description—whether it was actually written down before or after it, we have no means of knowing.[18]

This final remark or admission is critical to and perhaps troublesome for Davies's interpretive procedure. It is possible that "A slumber" provided an image that became central in recalling and composing the boyhood experience and not necessarily ("this leaves no doubt") vice versa. However, chronological considerations work in Davies's favor here even though methodological difficulties appear in his relying so exclusively on the external evidence of passages similar to "A slumber" to promote an interpretation. After having argued so convincingly for the textual autonomy of "A slumber" with respect to the other so-called "Lucy" poems, Davies basically surrenders this newly won autonomy to perhaps an even more specious kind of textual heteronomy.

In Davies's view, however, the action of "A slumber" is comparable to that in "Influence of Natural Objects." Wordsworth's "own sensations remain the central theme, but instead of stopping suddenly and watching

17. Ibid., p. 153, and pp. 153–60 in passing.
18. Ibid., p. 155.

the earth visibly roll past him, he imagines himself joined with it, and in a trance-like state identified with its diurnal motion."[19] Wordsworth's imaginative power has so exerted itself that his slumbering "spirit" carries him into an entranced communion with the things of nature. His spirit has been laid asleep, and she does "not feel / The touch of earthly years": "we are laid asleep / In body, and become a living soul" ("Tintern Abbey," lines 46–47). Again, seeking external evidence to support his reading, Davies appeals to a passage in the *Diary* of Joseph Farington and to a draft for Book XIII of *The Prelude* to establish a predilection on Wordsworth's part for such trancelike states.[20]

Davies, though, fails to take into account the surprise or shock that occurs in the second stanza of "A slumber" when the present-tense verbs alert a reader to a significant temporal displacement. Regardless of the passages appealed to for evidential support, this critical shift in tense indicates an immediate and particular rupturing of a trancelike state. A slumber or a trance has occurred at some time in the past, but "now" something else is undergone or recognized as happening in the present and after an abrupt and unexpected shift forward in time. Davies's interpretation would be plausible only if lines five and six were written something like the following:

> No motion had she then, no force;
> She neither heard nor saw;

With the entire poem in the past tense, we would have a unified and unruptured sense of time and occasion. In other words, we would have a plausible context for the speaker's spirit slumbrously to join with the "earth's diurnal course"; it would all be one event, one action. Yet, as the

19. Ibid.
20. Ibid., pp. 157–59. In preference to the note on the "Immortality Ode" that Wordsworth dictated to Isabella Fenwick in 1843, in which he takes a point of view contrary to a trancelike-state interpretation, Davies enlarges upon a passage written by Joseph Farington in his *Diary* that records a meeting between Constable and Wordsworth in 1806: "He told Constable that while he was a boy going to Hawkshead school, his mind was often so possessed with images, so lost in extraordinary conceptions, that he held by a wall not knowing but he was part of it." Davies takes this as an instance for the type of slumber or trance that the "spirit" undergoes in "A slumber." Davies also notes a draft for *The Prelude*, XIII, that de Selincourt provides in which a horse, a "slumbering horse," in Davies's words, with "all his functions seal'd up" and "motion gone," "can very reasonably be taken as" an "objective correlative," "as an outward image for the inward experience which Wordsworth had so often described" (p. 159).

poem stands, a reading that takes "she" to refer to "my spirit" and does not admit a confusion concerning the antecedent of the poem's feminine pronouns should end with the death (or the imagined or vicarious death) of the speaker. A slumber sealed the speaker's spirit some time in the past such that "she seemed a thing that could not feel" the very circumstances of earthly life and human temporality. Now, abruptly transposed to the present, that spirit is recognized as stilled, is without the life and abilities she once had, and is "rolled round" with nonhuman things in an unending cycle of motion. The "spirit" has either accidentally or unwittingly extinguished herself or has vicariously, or even proleptically, undergone her own death.[21] Davies will not extend his interpretation this far, but he does concede that "the trance-like condition of the slumbering spirit in many ways resembles death, is indeed on the borders of life and death, so that confusion between the two is both possible and likely."[22]

The three critical responses published in *Essays in Criticism* do nothing ultimately to unsettle the mass of evidence that Davies has presented in favor of the feminine "spirit" of "A slumber," but they do help to recenter this evidence with regard to the confusion in the reference of "she" experienced while reading the poem. The first respondent, R. F. Storch,

21. See a remark by Paul de Man, whose full interpretation of "A slumber" I will discuss later: "Wordsworth is one of the few poets who can write proleptically about their own death and speak, as it were, from beyond their own graves. The 'she' in the poem is in fact large enough to encompass Wordsworth as well." De Man, "The Rhetoric of Temporality," *Interpretation*, ed. Charles S. Singleton (Baltimore, Md.: Johns Hopkins University Press, 1969), p. 206. In this connection also, see a passage from Dorothy Wordsworth's "Grasmere Journal" (April 29, 1802): "We then went to John's grove, sate a while at first. Afterwards William lay, and I lay, in the trench under the fence—he with his eyes shut, and listening to the waterfalls and the birds. . . . [W]e both lay still, and unseen by one another; he thought that it would be as sweet thus to lie so in the grave, to hear the *peaceful* sounds of the earth, and just to know that our dear friends were near." Dorothy's account beautifully illustrates de Man's insight. See *Journals of Dorothy Wordsworth*, Vol. 1, ed. Ernest de Selincourt (London: Macmillan, 1959), pp. 139–40 (hereinafter cited as *Journals*, I).

There is at least one critic of Wordsworth, Richard J. Onorato, who indicates, though briefly, that "A slumber" is to be read as the speaker's vicarious experience of death. The speaker's "spirit" ("she") seems dead to him ("Rolled round in earth's diurnal course / With rocks, and stones, and trees."); "the poet is not half-mourning, half-envying someone who was very like himself and who may have Life-in-Death, but rather writing numbly about himself as one experiencing Death-in-Life." It is noteworthy that Onorato takes "spirit" as the antecedent of "she." See R. J. Onorato, *The Character of the Poet: Wordsworth in "The Prelude"* (Princeton, N.J.: Princeton University Press, 1971), p. 198.

22. Davies, "Another New Poem," p. 160. Davies also suggests that this "possible and likely" "confusion" could be a reason that "A slumber" has been "so readily interpreted as an epitaph, by so many devoted and skilful readers of Wordsworth," Coleridge among them.

objects to what he sees as Davies's single-minded and laborious case against a "historical person" being regarded as the "she" of the poem:

> Mr. Davies argues that if the "she" is not Lucy, then she must be the poet's own spirit. This either/or approach seems altogether inappropriate here. The "she" can be both, as well as Dorothy, and none of these.[23]

Storch does not say *how* he *knows* that "she" can stand for more than one person or persona, only that there are several possibilities—none of which can be ruled out by biographical and external evidence. However, the second respondent, Jonathan Wordsworth, admits two possible readings and claims most-favored status for only one of them: "though Wordsworth certainly could have attributed feeling, motion, force, hearing, sight to his own spirit, it must be allowed that they are better suited to Lucy."[24] However, *how* are these two facts *known*, and why does a good critic and reader persist in claiming that Lucy is "better suited" as the referent of the poem when the grounds for such an interpretation have been undercut? Finally, the third respondent, Gene W. Ruoff, contributes by far the most probing of the three responses by presenting some additional evidence that indicates Wordsworth had planned at one time (sometime between 1807 and 1815) to place "A slumber" with two other "Lucy" poems among the category "Epitaphs and Elegiac Pieces" for his collected *Poems*.[25] This factor would and should necessitate a more complicated reading of the poem, either one that imaginatively projects the vicarious death of the narrator or one that involves a doubled or confused reference for "she." Ruoff, though, like Jonathan Wordsworth, demands a simplified reading:

> It seems hardly likely that the poet forgot for a moment what his poem was about, and I think we may safely assume that "A slumber" is, with all due deference to Mr. Storch's demand for ambiguity, a poem about the death of a girl.[26]

23. R. F. Storch, "Another New Poem by Wordsworth," *Essays in Criticism* 15 (1965): 474.
24. J. Wordsworth, "A New Poem by Wordsworth?" *Essays in Criticism* 16 (1966): 123.
25. G. W. Ruoff, "Another New Poem by Wordsworth," *Essays in Criticism* 16 (1966): 359–60.
26. Ibid., p. 360.

Ruoff opts to look only at his newfound piece of evidence and overlooks that "A slumber" was actually published among "Poems of the Imagination." It also exhibits at least one very strange ambiguity—"she" can refer to the noun "spirit" but could also refer to someone else besides. In other words, the experience of a referential confusion while reading "A slumber" could well be intentional, and an interpretation of the lyric would have to take this felt experience and this interpretive judgment into account.

3

Another Line
of
Interpretation and Stark Clarity

N ow, I take as a cue and a pretext for my own interpretation of "A
slumber did my spirit seal" a note appended to the poem by a late
Victorian editor and anthologist who, apparently, was an attentive reader:

> This poem may, and one may suppose is, often read by itself,
> when the pronoun "she" can only refer to "spirit" in the line
> before. So read, it has a high and beautiful spiritual significance,
> but, as the poem would seem to come in the cycle of Lucy poems,
> it seems certain that "she" must refer to the dead girl, and if that
> be so, the lines have a very beautiful and still more pathetic
> meaning.[1]

Here, this anthologist, Oswald Crawfurd, near the turn of the century,
and of course some years following the earlier Victorian editors of

---

1. Oswald Crawfurd, "Notes," *Lyrical Verse from Elizabeth to Victoria*, ed. O. Crawfurd
(London: Chapman and Hall, 1896), p. 434. "A slumber" is set by itself apart from any of the
other "Lucy" poems on page 291 of this anthology.

Robin Skelton also notices that "she" can have two references: "'She' refers not only to Lucy,
the incarnation of the unfallen spirit, of nature, of all that is pure, instinctive, unadulterated, but
also to 'spirit.' In this poem Lucy is clearly identified with the poet's spirit, or faculty of vision,
of extra-mundane perception." Skelton's Blakean interpretation of the poem, however, diffuses
the power and implications of this recognition. See Skelton, *The Poetic Pattern* (London:
Routledge & Kegan Paul, 1956), p. 182, and pp. 182–85 in passing.

Wordsworth, is sensitive enough to recognize two ways in which "A slumber" can be read. The first way, namely, "read by itself," follows the pattern of reading already dwelt upon in the foregoing discussion of Hugh Sykes Davies's article. In this case, the feminine pronoun "can only refer to 'spirit.'" Of course, what that "high and beautiful spiritual significance" may be remains open to speculation. A reasoned guess, however, would be that Crawfurd values rather highly the imagined or vicarious death that the slumbering spirit undergoes, at least according to the terms advanced for this interpretation so far. The second way of reading "A slumber" makes use of the consideration that the lyric "would seem to come in the cycle of Lucy poems" and would, therefore, seem to make "certain that 'she' must refer to the dead girl." In this event, we have a different meaning but an even more affecting one—the death of another seems to jar, albeit belatedly, the slumbering spirit back into the world of emotions and feelings, the world of pathos.[2] It is this second way of reading that Crawfurd apparently prefers, but he does not rule out that the first way of reading does indeed occur and with considerable merit. In effect, he admits that there are two distinct, plausible, and meaningful interpretations of the poem. The difference between them does not lie in opposing philosophical, aesthetic, or critical camps; it lies in the two possible contexts that Wordsworth offers for reading his poem. "A slumber" can be read by itself or with some attention to its place among the "Lucy" poems. It is to his credit that Crawfurd noticed that these two ways of reading can and do occur and that the context and reference of "she" is the pivotal term.

The experience of a confusion in the reference of "she" while reading

2. This is a frequent and well-respected way of reading "A slumber." F. R. Leavis, for example, discusses "the emotional power" of the lyric. The diction of the poem in its "full force" or its "potent evocative force"—localized specifically in the words "human," "thing," and "diurnal"—evokes "a certain *hubris* in the security of forgetful bliss." See F. R. Leavis, "'Thought' and Emotional Quality," *Scrutiny* 13 (1945): 54. John Speirs, in *Poetry Towards Novel* (London: Faber & Faber, 1971), pp. 141–42, states that the greatness of the emotion in "A slumber" is "the naked recognition nakedly presented of the fact that she who was alive is dead"; the final image of the poem "is one of the very few unmitigatedly tragic moments of recognition in Wordsworth's poetry." Even quite recently, Jerome J. McGann, in his call for historical studies of the ideology of Romantic poetry and criticism, echoes this conventional approach to "A slumber": "The poem offers a pathetic message for an experience of the loss of someone beloved, a comfort which yet troubles our own inevitable 'human fears,' a solace which cannot—which would not—remove the sense of pity and loss." See *The Romantic Ideology: A Critical Investigation* (Chicago: University of Chicago Press, 1983), p. 68.

"A slumber" would now seem to have a reason for being. This initial character or quality encountered in reading the lyric can alert us to two distinct lines of interpretation, depending upon which context we choose or just happen to place the poem within. Davies's article and the foregoing discussion of it still underwrite the plausibility of the interpretation that pivots on the ascription of "my spirit" as the antecedent of "she"; but there is still the evidence that Davies fails to contend with, the evidence yielded in the activity of reading the poem through. This evidence indicates that our initial presupposition of who "she" refers to does not go off cleanly. Also, the history of writings on the poem shows that there is a compulsion on the part of readers to resolve whatever confusions they have experienced by taking "she" as another, as "Lucy," or as some woman or feminine persona other than the speaker's "spirit." This interpretive tendency is lent plausibility by the two arrangements in which Wordsworth himself caused "A slumber" to be published. This remark does not run counter to the argument in favor of the textual autonomy of "A slumber" presented by Davies. His argument was primarily directed against the notion that "A slumber" occupied an integral position in a group or sequence of lyrics all about the single figure of "Lucy." The fact is that Wordsworth did not actually discourage an association of "A slumber" with at least some of the poems of the "Lucy" group. In the three editions of *Lyrical Ballads* in which "A slumber" appeared during Wordsworth's lifetime, it was the last poem in a group of three short lyrics—the first two being "Strange fits" and "She dwelt"—that were set in the midst of longer pastorals and ballads.[3] In the 1815 edition of *Poems,*

3. See *Lyrical Ballads*, Vol. II (London, 1800), pp. 50–53. The three lyrics occur as the fifth, sixth, and seventh poems; this same order was preserved in the 1802 and 1805 editions. "Lucy Gray" and "Three years she grew in sun and shower" were also published in the second volumes of these three editions but in separate and varying locations. See also Wordsworth and Coleridge, *Lyrical Ballads 1805*, ed. Derek Roper (London: Collins, 1968), pp. 168–69, 265–68, 366–70.
James Scoggins observes that Wordsworth might at one time have had a plan to publish all the so-called "Lucy" poems as one unit. In a letter to Coleridge written in May 1809, Wordsworth tentatively proposes an arrangement of his poems for an eventual collected works. Scoggins places "Strange fits," "She dwelt," "I travelled," "Three years," and "A slumber" as poems five through nine in the second part of this tentative arrangement, a part that bears the rubric of "Affections of Youth and Early Maturity." Wordsworth's only reference to such a group, however, is as "those about Lucy"; he does not specify which poems these are or in what order they are to be placed. Scoggins's arrangement, however appealing, remains only speculative. See James Scoggins, *Imagination and Fancy: Complementary Modes in the Poetry of Wordsworth* (Lincoln: University of Nebraska Press, 1966), pp. 39–40. Wordsworth's letter to Coleridge is cited and amply discussed by Scoggins.

these latter two poems were published in a threesome with "I travelled among unknown men" in the place of "A slumber." In another location and under a different heading, "A slumber" was printed immediately following "Three years she grew in sun and shower."[4] These associations are not in any way conclusive or definitive of an identification of "she" with "Lucy," but they do suggest a certain willfulness on Wordsworth's part not to hinder or discourage such an identification. That is to say, such an identification provides the impulse for a reader to take the "she" of "A slumber" as "Lucy" or some kindred "dead girl." Moreover, the other three so-called "Lucy" poems with which "A slumber" has been variously published all contain real or imagined dead girls and speakers or narrators who are affected by their deaths. The context of the publication of "A slumber" arranged and permitted by Wordsworth himself, then, certainly does not prevent certain pieces of very proximate external evidence from impinging on rereadings of and attempts to interpret the lyric. Thus, the experience of a referential confusion actually presents us with our first odd but surely reliable indication that the interpretation of the poem can proceed along two lines and certainly must do so in order to be fair to all the evidence assembled.

If the plausibility of either line of interpretation is denied or dismissed, then the charge of poor, misleading, or confusing construction on Wordsworth's part could arise. Of course, such a charge has been brought against other poems that Wordsworth wrote but almost never against "A slumber"—"the lyric which is at the powerful center of this poet's art," according to David Ferry.[5] The charge in this case would be that Wordsworth has allowed the grammar and punctuation in his first stanza to become too slack and therefore capable of misleading or confusing the reader, of leading him or her into an unfortunate and fruitless ambiguity. The poet should have placed a full stop after "I had no human fears," or, better yet, should have worked the name "Lucy" into the meter of the third line.[6] However, these suggestions are misplaced. It is best to try and

4. The ordering of these poems in the 1815 edition of *Poems* is preserved in *PW*, II, pp. 29–31, 214–16. See footnote 1, p. 16. "I travelled" was first published in *Poems in Two Volumes*, Vol. I (London, 1807), pp. 68–69. Its publication in 1815 is its first textual identification with any of the other so-called "Lucy" poems.

5. David Ferry, *The Limits of Mortality* (Middletown, Conn.: Wesleyan University Press, 1959), p. 76.

6. In a talk entitled "Wittgenstein's Views about Meaning and the Indeterminacy of Literary Texts" given on November 8, 1974, at SUNY at Buffalo, Max Black recounted Robert Graves's

understand what Wordsworth may be doing by confusing and setting the reader off on two seemingly unconnected lines of interpretation. In other words, Wordsworth's use of "she" might well be a brilliant stroke of imaginative contrivance.

The situation, then, is that two ways of reading "A slumber" are possible and defensible; yet neither one can be ruled out in favor of the other. Oswald Crawfurd's comment shows that the two ways of reading are indeed even possible for one and the same reader. Depending upon which context of the poem one consciously attends to, one or the other line of interpretation achieves relative prominence. However, in the initial activity of reading the poem, a particular reader's experience of a confusion in the reference of "she" can indicate that these two lines of interpretation have yet to be separated.

It is from this initial, felt experience of confusion that the two divergent lines of interpretation can be seen to originate, bifurcate, and proceed on their separate ways, depending for their direction upon the context a reader has chosen to develop his or her interpretation. Perhaps it is because neither the line of interpretation derived from Davies nor the conventional line of interpretation fully attends to the significance of a referential confusion experienced while reading the lyric that this initial confluence of two interpretations has not previously been noticed. However, it is now possible to see that these two divergent lines of interpretation follow the separating paths of two solutions to a single, initial experience of referential confusion. A reader traces "she" to either the speaker's "spirit" or to a dead girl, perhaps even "Lucy," and then carries out a fuller interpretation on the basis of this initial choice.

Even though we may now see how two divergent lines of interpreting "A slumber" actually arise from one experiential confusion, the problem of why Wordsworth would contrive a lyric moment first to confuse and then to dispatch readers on separate paths still remains. Is there something about this poem that would benefit from this poetic strategy? I believe there is, and it is something that draws attention away from the cold and final image of deathly passivity back toward the beginning of the lyric.

In order to determine who is really "rolled round" with such stark finality, a reader turns his or her attention back to the beginning anyway

---

attempt to remedy what he saw as confusing or misleading grammatical constructions in "A slumber" by rewriting the lyric. To date I have not been able to locate a documented reference for this attempt at reauthoring the poem.

and examines closely the grammar of the first stanza. While one pays close attention to the grammar of the first few lines of the poem, a grammatical oddity is almost certain to appear. The first line of the poem yields a syntactical and grammatical solipsism. The standard way of phrasing (and thus paraphrasing, in this case) the first line would be "A slumber sealed my spirit"; the line is still metrical, though the stress for the fourth and final iamb is lost and thereby leaves the meter of the line with a "feminine" rather than "masculine" ending.[7] The syntax of this altered line is now as straightforward as that of the other three unaltered lines of the first stanza. Wordsworth, though, employs the modal verb "do" and forms the more emphatic construction of the past tense of the verb "seal," namely "did seal." What is more, he inserts the predicate noun "my spirit" into the middle of his emphatic predicate (or verb) rather than after it. The obvious rationale for this construction is that it fits the requirements of the meter that Wordsworth employs. However, a reader cannot escape attending to how noticeably different the contrived syntax of the first line is in comparison with the standard syntax of the other lines of the first stanza. Then, all of a sudden, as a reader pores over that one initial line, a reversal in grammar can reveal the secret or hidden rationale for Wordsworth's contrivance. If a reader lets a strong stress fall on the word "did," the words "my spirit" unexpectedly appear as the subject of another sentence buried in the phrasing of the first sentence. The standard form of this unexpected sentence is "my spirit did seal a slumber" or "my spirit sealed a slumber." This sentence emerges when the thematic rather than the metrical use of the emphatic verb construction "did seal" is recognized.[8]

7. A time marker, such as "then," could be used at the end of the line to fill out the measure. The use of "then" would also clarify or make distinct on the surface structure of the poem the temporal difference between the first and second stanzas. Obviously, the rhyming word "feel" at the end of line three would also have to be replaced—perhaps by the verb "ken." Clearly this rewriting results in a noticeably different texture and, truly, a different poem. However, this experiment in clarifying and making unambiguous the grammatical and temporal structures of the lyric can also at the same time make "A slumber" more suitable to the conventional line of interpretation. By making transparent from the beginning a distinct temporal disjunction between the events of the two stanzas, the poem would have to be interpreted as the stark juxtaposition of the narrator's former imperceptivity and his present sharp awakening to fatal loss. Changing the colon to a semicolon or a period at the end of line two would be the only other alteration needed to secure textual conformity to the conventional line of interpretation.

8. Perhaps the only study of syntactical inversions as they apply to poetic processes is an article by William P. Bivens III, "Parameters of Poetic Inversion in English," *Language and Style* 13 (1979): 13–25. All three parameters for syntactic inversion that Bivens formulates apply exactly

The thematic use of this construction can pull the reader into a third way of reading "A slumber," one that lurks within the confluence of two lines of interpretation already discussed. When a reader understands that the first line can be read taking "a slumber" as a predicate noun and "my spirit" as the subject of a second, syntactically nonstandard sentence, a completely different interpretation can suddenly loom. Instead of an experience of confusion, an unnerving yet stark clarity may very well characterize one's introduction to this third way of reading. If "my spirit" "did . . . seal" "a slumber," then the speaker seems by no means slumbrous, insensitive, and imperceptive. He marks, closes, impresses, or enforces a slumber, though the passive recipient of this action is yet undeclared. The speaker now appears to be an active agent, an executor of deeds, rather than a passive undergoer of his own vicarious death fantasy or an insensitive and belated mourner of lost love. "My spirit" sealed "a slumber"; "I had no human fears:" The agent appears cold-blooded, as if inhuman. The colon then directs us into the reason why the speaker had no such fears: She, a woman, appeared to him to be a thing untouchable by age or mortality or perhaps even by blemish or change. We can possibly take "she" to be a love object or loved one of the speaker because we have been looking for the referent of "she" and a Lucy-like creature here seems quite likely. Now, in the present and separated by some undisclosed amount of time from the past moment of the first stanza, the woman has no motion or force, no life or mortality. She is left ruthlessly and shockingly a corpse among the things of a landscape denuded of their own relations to human life and livelihood. The speaker

---

to the first line of "A slumber." These parameters account for the possibility of poetic inversion and ambivalence. Bivens uses four examples of poetic inversion taken from Wordsworth, more than from any of the numerous other authors he examines. One of these is especially informative in connection with "A slumber": "A gentle answer did the old Man make" ("Resolution and Independence," line 85). Syntactically considered, this line is identical with the first line of "A slumber." It shows that the subject or noun phrase of a line can be set between auxiliary and verb, while the object or the predicate noun is situated at the beginning of the line.

At least two other critical readers of "A slumber" have noticed the syntactical inversion in the first line, but neither one fully develops its context or rationale. In "Action in Wordsworth's 'Lucy' Poems: A Reading," *Illinois Quarterly* 34 (1971): 25, Terry Otten remarks: "In point of fact, the poem is highly ambiguous, even from the first line (did slumber seal the spirit or did spirit seal the slumber?)." In "Floating Authorship," *Diacritics* 16 (1987): 12, Peggy Kamuf recognizes that "[t]he emphatic verb 'did . . . seal' allows for a grammatical interchangeability of subject and object, slumber and spirit: either a slumber sealed my spirit or my spirit sealed a slumber." She goes on to remark that such a grammatical doubling permits two readings and a corresponding ambiguity, circularity, and undecidability (pp. 12–13).

chillingly confesses a murder; the slumber that his spirit has sealed is the murder of a woman.[9] He straightforwardly admits the cold-bloodedness of the deed and offers his motive: She appeared unearthly, disembodied, immortal.

A number of finer points can lend support to this third way of reading "A slumber." The first line of the second stanza has a syntactically nonstandard sentence structure, and its subject is embedded in the middle of the sentence. This curiously mirrors the nonstandard structure of the first line of the first stanza.[10] In this first line of the second stanza—"No

9. Wordsworth's use of the word "slumber" in several other poems can support its link to a sudden, unexpected, and often violent death. In the poem "To the Daisy"—the one that is sometimes called "Sweet Flower" and that appears in *Poetical Works* between "Elegiac Stanzas" ("Peele Castle") and "Elegiac Verses" and together with them forms a threesome of elegiac pieces for the drowned John Wordsworth—Wordsworth calls his brother's watery entombment a "slumber": "Six weeks beneath the moving sea / He lay in slumber quietly" (lines 50–51). A lover of daisies and rural bowers and "the tender peace of rural thought," Wordsworth's brother is "a gentle Soul and sweet," whose violent death at sea is nonetheless a "slumber," the untimely death of an innocent (lines 23, 61; *PW*, IV, pp. 260–62). In *The Excursion*, Book VI, another innocent dies young and unexpectedly. The Pastor relates the story of Ellen, who is forsaken by her lover and left with child. Ellen, though, is bound over to nurse someone else's child because of her own "scruples" and "severe restraints and laws unjust" (lines 940, 955). The issue of the unfortunate situation is the sudden death of her "deserted child" and her struggle to go and look "Upon the last sweet slumber of her Child" before its burial (lines 969, 981; *PW*, V, p. 218). Then again, in "The Oak and the Broom" the oak warns the broom that "The little witless shepherd-boy / [may] come and slumber in [its] bower"; and if he does, both "Will perish in one hour" (lines 46–47, 50; *PW*, II, p. 132). In this instance a careless slumber can suddenly turn fatal for another young innocent. This pastoral narrative, moreover, was first published in *Lyrical Ballads* as the second poem after "A slumber."

10. The mirroring effect carries through the other three lines of each stanza. Lines two and six both use a standard subject-predicate sentence structure, and both lines contain negatives. The last two lines of both stanzas each comprise an amplification or an illustration of the first two lines of their respective stanzas. The first two lines in each stanza are built up from two independent clauses connected by a semicolon; but then the concluding lines of the two stanzas are subordinated as dependent clauses to those initial, syntactically and grammatically equipoised sentences. The subordination occurs in the first stanza through the use of the colon at the end of line two; in the second stanza, the syntactical and grammatical dependency is accomplished through the suppression of "she is" in the surface structure at the beginning of line seven. The overall effect of this syntactical and grammatical mirroring is a sense of poised balance, a deliberate pairing or doubling of linguistic elements. Here again there is evidence of a careful and deliberate imaginative contrivance on Wordsworth's part. The careful linguistic construction calls attention back to the lines that initiate the mirroring effect—the first lines of each stanza.

John E. Jordan discusses Wordsworth's "syntactic trick of repeating the subject of a sentence or an objective complement in noun and pronoun form" in a number of poems from *Lyrical Ballads*. The implication is that the poems of *Lyrical Ballads* are "experiments" employing a variety of "syntactic tricks" and showing "the mind's luxuriating in words as a form of art." See Jordan, *Why the "Lyrical Ballads"?* (Berkeley and Los Angeles: University of California Press, 1976), pp. 180–81.

motion has she now, no force;"—we clearly take the initial noun "motion" as the predicate noun of the sentence and the pronoun "she" as the subject. In contrast, as has been shown already, two ways of construing the syntax *and grammar* of the lyric's very first line are possible. However, by examining closely these two first lines, numerous similarities encourage a construing of "my spirit" as the subject of the line "A slumber did my spirit seal." Syntactically, they are both nonstandard; and, thematically, they both evoke a tone and image of immobility and sealed enclosure.[11] The syntax of the second first line comprises a syntactical solipsism: The predicate noun of the sentence both begins and ends it structurally. "No motion" is the predicate noun of "she" "has," but "no force" is the final phrase set in apposition to "no motion." It is another way of phrasing the object of the sentence, but structurally it functions to return the sentence and its thought to its point of origin—the predicate noun, "no motion." The line syntactically and thematically is self-enclosing, self-sealing, solipsistic. Once this clear and univocal solipsism is recognized in the fifth line of the lyric, the syntactical and grammatical solipsism already described for the initial line gains some internal support.[12] The two syntactically nonstandard lines of the poem call attention to themselves, and both of them yield critically important syntactical and thematic solipsisms. The first line, however, remains grammatically doubled and thereby more complex and deceptive in its solipsism than the clearer grammar of the fifth line.

11. Compare Elizabeth Drew's remark, in her chapter "Imagery" in *Discovering Poetry* (New York: Norton, 1933), p. 154, on the power and resonance of the first line of the lyric throughout the rest of the poem:

> Such a completely simple figure, for example, as 'a slumber did my spirit seal' in the Lucy poem we have already quoted, is so essential a part of the whole poem that the emotions and sensations and even the visual suggestions aroused by it vibrate through the eight lines and provide the unifying idea of the whole. Not only does the image completely sum up the emotional sense of the poet's blind confidence and sense of security in his happiness, in the first verse, but the actual vision it evokes of immobility and closed eyelids and sealed ears becomes identified at once in the second verse with Lucy's eternal sleep of death.

12. "She" is the subject in the fifth line. "My spirit" as the hidden subject of the first line is set in a structural parallelism with the pronoun it initially gets confused with in the third line of the lyric. Syntactically speaking, then, Wordsworth is engaged in a very complex play between the speaker's "spirit" and the feminine pronouns of the poem. The linguistic form of his lyric images forth or incarnates the very play between "spirit" and "she" that occurs thematically, and initially so confusingly, for the reader.

The lyric is also heavily laden with sibilants. The sounds of "c," "s," "sh," and "z" fill the atmosphere of the poem and help evoke a sense of soporific stillness and tightly sealed immobility. Every line of the poem is implicated in this evocation, but most especially lines one, five, six, and eight. The sibilants either dominate such complete lines as "A slumber did my spirit seal" and "No motion has she now, no force; / She neither hears nor sees;" or take up emphatic initial or terminal positions in such lines as "She seemed . . . / . . . years." This soporific, sealed atmosphere suddenly turns sinister and threatening when one realizes that "my spirit" can be the subject noun of the first line. As a consequence, Wordsworth's poem effectively summons up a more terrifying context in which a profusion of sibilants serves to instill a strange, even unsettling sense of the sinister. Also in this third way of reading "A slumber," the sudden recognition of the depths of the speaker's inhumanity is echoed in the technical term "diurnal."[13] Its analytic precision makes a sinister blend with the words "die," "urn," and "all" and with the grim pun that can be heard lurking within their sequence of syllables: "die yearn all."

13. Walter S. Minot, in "Wordsworth's Use of *diurnal* in 'A Slumber Did My Spirit Seal,'" *Papers on Language and Literature* 9 (1973): 319–21, collects and discusses numerous critical remarks on Wordsworth's choice of the word "diurnal." He concludes: "The poet is forcing metrical, alliterative, and conceptual emphasis on the middle syllable of the word (-*urn*-) and thus suggests by a play on sounds and words (a device Wordsworth used elsewhere) that the earth is an *urn*, a tomb or burial place" (p. 321). The other two syllables of "diurnal" also have their own playful possibilities: "die" and "all." The pronunciation of the word "diurnal" allows the word "yearn" to sound playfully within it. Minot notes that Wordsworth frequently used "the serious pun" (p. 321n).

4

The Romantic Death Fantasy
and the
Ambivalence of Solipsism

A fantasy of death looms at the core of the third way of reading "A slumber did my spirit seal." This fantasy exhibits a yearning for the death of the other who stands outside the speaker's will to power and his apparent desire to traduce and incorporate. J. M. Hawthorn, in a scarcely noticed but, I believe, seminal study of the Romantic death fantasy, explores "the strange deaths of Sally, Ann, Lucy and others" and directs critical attention to a basic process and obsession of "the Romantic mind."[1] Hawthorn asserts generally that in fiction "we use death imaginatively to gain control," and he seeks particularly

> . . . to try and isolate a specifically Romantic use of an imagined death as a means of gaining a fantasy control over a person or situation associated with sexual love. Such control . . . is sought

1. J. M. Hawthorn, "The strange deaths of Sally, Ann, Lucy, and others," *Trivium* 6 (1971): 70–80. In *Criticism in the Wilderness: The Study of Literature Today* (New Haven, Conn.: Yale University Press, 1980), pp. 63–85, Geoffrey Hartman discusses Walter Benjamin's reading of Baudelaire's sonnet "A une passante" and notes that the poet's drive toward intimacy with a woman seems to push him just as much toward a death wish, the shock of a lost and irrecoverable love object. See Walter Benjamin, "On Some Motifs in Baudelaire," *Illuminations*, ed. H. Arendt, trans. H. Zohn (New York: Harcourt, Brace and World, 1968), pp. 157–202, especially pp. 168–72. The same translation is also published in Walter Benjamin, *Charles Baudelaire: A Lyric Poet in the Era of High Capitalism*, trans. H. Zohn (London: New Left Books, 1973), pp. 107–54.

within the fantasy, and not outside; death, in fact, often becomes the dividing line between reality and fantasy.[2]

Hawthorn examines the prosaic accounts of frustrated love affairs given by William Hazlitt in his *Liber Amoris* and Thomas De Quincey in *The Confessions of an English Opium-Eater* and draws attention to the escapist, fantasy solutions that these two authors arrive at for their violent infatuations with young girls. The social class of the servant girl Sally Walker inspires and then impedes the married Hazlitt's infatuation, and De Quincey's desire for the quiescence and solitude of the opium trance and withdrawn domesticity quickly breaks off any real pursuit of his infatuation with the young prostitute Ann. Like Keats, Shelley, and Byron with their nightingales and skylarks, Hazlitt and De Quincey equivocate "when faced with pain or hardship in the real world." Instead of playing out their infatuations in the travails of loving another over the course of time, they seize upon "the imagined death of a loved one . . . as a door through which the individual concerned can escape into a larger fantasy where control over and communion with a loved one can be achieved."[3]

Only in fantasy are Hazlitt and De Quincey able to attain power and control over a feminine other in these select instances. Both of them project their young girls into "that cold bed" of "the grave" and transform any relation of dependency into one of solipsistic, imaginative incorporation. Hazlitt transforms the servant girl Sally into a feverish, diseased

2. Hawthorn, pp. 70–71.
3. Ibid., pp. 71, 73. In its literary manifestations, the Romantic death fantasy would appear to constitute the undeveloped other side of Leslie Fiedler's discussion of the Sentimental Love Religion in *Love and Death in the American Novel*, rev. ed. (New York: Dell, 1966). In general, for Fiedler, the novel is "a prose narrative in which the Seducer and the Pure Maiden [are] brought face to face in a ritual combat destined to end in marriage or death" (p. 62). The novel, the "seduction story," however, tends to sentimentalize the desire for control and incorporation of the loved one; marriage rather than murder is the name given to the end result of the "ritual combat" of seduction. Fiedler recognizes, though, that "the American *eros*" has continued much the same over the course of its history and its literature: "We continue to dream the female dead. . . ." (p. 29n). I believe Fiedler best explores the mythology of this insistent death fantasy in his chapter on the *non–love stories* of Hawthorne, Melville, Twain, and Faulkner: "The Power of Blackness: Faustian Man and the Cult of Violence" (pp. 430–505). The terror, violence, and depravity of the American Fausts are all-consuming: Otherness, in any possible manifestation, is assaulted, abased, and absorbed. There is only a single terrifying prospect: ". . . the impossibility of reciprocal love, the sadness of a world in which growing up means only learning that isolation is the lot of everyone" (pp. 478–79).

"little witch" whose grave he "trod[s]" while vicariously and violently enjoying the worms' delight in the virginity he "had never tasted." De Quincey fancies for himself "a supernatural power," "the curse of a father," which will "pursue its object with a fatal necessity of self-fulfillment" until the object—namely, Ann—is finally and totally his, whether in brothel or grave. De Quincey is also resignedly content to think of his whore "as one long since laid in the grave," while his once "fiery passion," like his memorable headmaster's unrequited love before him, "still survive[s] as an abstraction," an idealized love. These Romantic lovers wishfully and freely "fuse past and present" and declare "the powers of fantasy or dream over time"; once Sally or Ann "becomes a fantasy girl rather than a real one, her characteristics can be made to stay the same, or can be altered at will."[4] The lovely, infatuating other can fall totally under the control of her "lover" by being transformed and incorporated within his imagination. All the Romantic lover need do to conjure up such dehumanizing power is to dream the death of the lovely other and insist on living in this solitary, withdrawn, and solipsistic fantasy state.

Stanley Diamond, in the central essay of his immensely important book in philosophical anthropology, *In Search of the Primitive*, examines succinctly the "pathological loneliness" and "schizoid character" that inform "individualism" and its cult of "romantic love"—"the underlying theme in contemporary American popular culture," according to Diamond.[5] He notes that romantic love "is grounded in the sense of personal

<hr/>

4. Hawthorn, pp. 72–75. Thomas De Quincey, who for a number of years was an avid disciple and friend of Wordsworth, had an intense and various absorption in the deaths of young girls. In his discussion of De Quincey's "need for uncritical love," John E. Jordan in *De Quincey to Wordsworth* describes the disciple's fascination with the child Catharine Wordsworth (p. 211). After her death at the age of three in June 1812, De Quincey, stricken with grief, nightly stretched himself upon her grave. Many years later, in the essay "The Affliction of Childhood," published in 1845, De Quincey describes fully for the first time his intense love for his sister Elizabeth, who died at the age of seven. He confesses in great detail a clandestine visit to the room where her body lay and where he kissed her. De Quincey further dissects the large network of associations he has built upon this moment, including the death of Catharine Wordsworth and the loss of Ann in London. What emerges is a dream network or fabric in which the power of his own fantasy allegorizes, idealizes, and fuses various dead girls to suit his own morbid affliction. These fantasy girls have long since ceased to be or to resemble real ones and survive only in De Quincey's endlessly grieving imagination. See also H. S. Davies, *Thomas De Quincey*, pp. 30–31.

5. Stanley Diamond, "The Search for the Primitive," *In Search of the Primitive* (New Brunswick, N.J.: Transaction Books, 1974), p. 160. The context is the discussion of Diamond's tenth and final basic characteristic of primitive societies—"transcendence and individuation."

isolation" because of the attenuation of kinship ties under the pressure of civilized modes of socialization. Family and kinship groups become so fragmented and estranged in civilized societies that they fail to "satisfy the dependency needs of their members." The result is an intensified frustration of affective needs and the production of "a high level of infantile expectation."[6] The romantic lover craves love in perverse and solipsistic fashion. He or she desires to fulfill his or her affective and dependency needs but yearns to do so in an infantile, all-consuming way. Indeed, the romantic lover has all along been deprived of adequate and constant stimulation and resolution of dependency needs and does not know how to reciprocate adequately and humanely in the experience of love. Hence, romantic love is thoroughly idealized and completely self-centered. As Diamond characterizes this affective situation:

> It is love as an abstraction, rather than the actual loving of a person as a being in the world, that dominates the romantic consciousness and transforms the whole notion of the romantic, which implies empathy with the inwardness of the other, into its opposite—a sentimental longing, a desire to incorporate the other.[7]

This desire for incorporating the other obviously leads to further frustration, and it becomes

> . . . no more than an acting out of the bitterness of estrangement in the most intimate phases of socialization in the family of origin. Romantic love, culturally defined, is not an expression of feeling, but of frustration at feeling's absence.[8]

The standard, civilized reification of this sense of frustration at the lack of feeling, even in the very form of civilized love itself, is the desire for revenge. The romantic lover will summon violence to aid him in exacting revenge for the very absence of adequate human feeling in himself and to assist him in fantasizing the incorporation of the love object that he craves yet is not capable of reciprocally engaging.[9]

6. Ibid., pp. 160–61
7. Ibid., p. 161.
8. Ibid., p. 162
9. This sentence and the one before it are developments of the implications of a sentence in

Thus, culturally speaking, the solipsistic fantasy state of a Hazlitt or a De Quincey represents a way of feeling and loving that has become more predominant as personal isolation—pathological loneliness and schizoid character structure—has become the sociocultural norm for the individual. In noting the connections that De Quincey makes between his separation from Ann and the labyrinthine isolation that life in London imposes upon its denizens, J. M. Hawthorn points to the link between such urban isolation "and the growth of human alienation and loneliness, and this latter seems to have encouraged many to create an alternative fantasy life to replace that which they lost by leaving the community of the country." Moreover, Hawthorn believes this link between urban isolation and the increase in alienation and loneliness accounts for "why it should be during the Romantic period in particular that the death-fantasy should flourish so healthily." Hawthorn concludes, after all, that it must be seen "that one's fantasy life bears a close relationship with one's social environment as well as with more personal aspects."[10] Hawthorn's examination of the Romantic period's use of imagined death, then, moves in the same general direction as Diamond's cultural critique. Hawthorn acknowledges that an increasingly popular fantasy state is and must be answerable to the social and cultural developments that help occasion it. In other words, romantic love and the Romantic death fantasy are by no means eternal or perpetual forms of the poetic "spirit." They constitute idealizations of love peculiar to modern, urban-oriented, civilized life and as such are open to critical and creative inquiry.

Hawthorn concludes his study with some tentative remarks on "the problem that so many critics of Wordsworth have fastened upon—'Why does Lucy die?'" Hawthorn, however, does not attempt to interpret any of the so-called "Lucy" poems. He quotes from a number of critical sources in order to show that

> . . . it is plausible that whatever the precise identity of Lucy, her death allows the lover to detach his image of her from a changing

---

Diamond, p. 168. The use of various kinds of violence in taking revenge on women is described as an achievement and a frustration for the American novel in Fiedler, pp. 291–336, especially pp. 310–36. See also Gershon Legman, *Love and Death: A Study in Censorship* (New York: Breaking Point, 1949), pp. 1–95, for this argument in a larger cultural context.

10. Hawthorn, pp. 76–77. See also Walter Benjamin's account of Baudelaire and the shock experience of urban crowds that Benjamin contends has become the norm for modern lyric poetry. Benjamin, "On Some Motifs in Baudelaire," pp. 162–96.

reality, to enjoy the satisfaction of an emotional relationship of a supremely private sort, with the independence and freedom of practical uninvolvement.[11]

In other words, Hawthorn sees Wordsworth's relation to the generalized figure of Lucy in the same terms as he sees Hazlitt's fantasy relation to Sally Walker or De Quincey's to Ann. Like so many other critics of Wordsworth, Hawthorn assumes that "Lucy" is fundamentally the same creature for all the poems in which the name appears.[12] On the contrary, Wordsworth's various figurations of "Lucy," as well as the "she" of "A slumber," cannot be granted the unity of character that Sally and Ann have in *Liber Amoris* and *The Confessions of an English Opium-Eater*. As has already been shown through my assessment of the work of Hugh Sykes Davies, there is no evidence to indicate categorically that the "Lucy" poems are to be taken as a cycle all about one and the same young woman. Yet Hawthorn commits the mistake of conflating all the poems in one integral cycle in order to advance the position that "the death of Lucy performs a specific function." We can then surmise the reason for her death; it is because Wordsworth imaginatively seeks to possess Lucy beyond the world of mutability:

In the poem "A slumber did my spirit seal," Wordsworth in fact shows Lucy's death as the means whereby she is removed from change and decay—from the real world to a dual existence in the grave and in Wordsworth's imagination.[13]

Of course, this reason fits well enough with the admirable explanations of the Romantic death fantasy that Hawthorn has detected at work in the prose of Hazlitt and De Quincey. However, this conclusion does not fit any one of the three ways of reading "A slumber" already developed from the possible ways of attending to the language of Wordsworth's text. Most

11. Hawthorn, p. 77.
12. See footnote 1, p. 16, and footnote 8, pp. 20–21. Hawthorn culls lines freely from various "Lucy" poems without acknowledging basic differences in the poetic functions of the different dead girls.
13. Hawthorn, pp. 77–78.

important, it does not correspond with the kind of death fantasies that emerge from Davies's line of interpretation as well as from the third, more subtle and integrative reading.

Wordsworth in large measure appears to have gone beyond the limits of Hawthorn's critical inquiry into the Romantic death fantasy by carrying out his own complex creative inquiry into the same fantasy. This creative inquiry is accomplished through the setting into one work of three intertwined strands of Romantic dreaming and fantasizing. These three strands are most intimately woven together in the words "my spirit" and "she" and their relations to one another in the first stanza of "A slumber." An initial confusion over the reference of "she" can lead a reader on two different paths of relating "she" to "my spirit," and attentive inquiry into the rationale for such a poetic strategy suddenly can disclose a third way of relating the same two terms. Accordingly, Wordsworth calls attention to certain possible plays on the relation of narrator to narrated, lover to beloved, male to female, self to other. Lyric identities are put into question, made problematic, so as to summon attention to problems in the interaction of human identities.

The initial confusion in the reference of "she" brings directly to awareness an ambivalence within the speaker or narrator, the voice or "spirit" of the lyric. In following out the logic of Davies's line of interpretation, the poem can become a private death fantasy; that is to say, it becomes for the speaker a vicarious experiencing of his own final and complete slumber. The narrator would seem to be a very self-involved, perhaps an even morbidly isolated solipsist. He has "no human fears" and his "spirit" seems to him to be unaffected by the passage of "earthly years." Indeed, he appears scarcely human at all; but he does not seem very disturbed or unsettled by his own inhumanity. From the stillness of the second stanza, the speaker covets the oblivion of his own total inertia; earth's course will bear the burden of what little is left. However, examined in the light of the conventional line of interpretation, the speaker—while still solipsistically self-involved—seems only imperceptive and insensitive. Here he awakes belatedly following the expiration of what seems a ghostly or unearthly girl; and the second stanza communicates a sense of pathos, of an intense feeling for lost love. "My spirit," then, seems to harbor both acute morbidity and benign insensitivity, two manifestations and extremes found within the purview of the solipsist. However, if both of the first two lines of interpretation are indeed possible and defensible, as was argued previously, then there is a curious ambivalence to be recognized in the character of the speaker.[14]

The same ambivalence occurs in the third way of reading "A slumber," but this time the morbidity and inhumanity of the speaker of the one interpretation coincide with the imperceptivity and insensitivity of the second. This "spirit" dreams the death of the other ("she") and, without a trace of "human fears," moves toward imaginative fulfillment of this yearning. The lifelessness of the lovely other is intoned in lines five and six, and the concluding image of diurnal movement now appears almost cold and inhumane. The speaker disclosed in this reading betrays an unconscionable insensitivity toward the other when he takes her for "a thing," an unearthly, disembodied, ghostly, or immortal object at his disposal. This narrator imaginatively conjures up the other in a guise of utter unearthliness and insubstantiality and then murders the object of his own fantasy. The speaker's unearthly victim has "no motion" and "no force" at all, but the course and power of the earth's strict movement and stark forms are evoked as the unwitting collaborators of her deadly fantast.

The complexity and power of "A slumber did my spirit seal" have been well attested to time and again by the attention its eight lines draw. At its most suggestive and instructive level perhaps the poem can give its readers a compact moment in Wordsworth's cultural critique of the inhumanity of modern man. Throughout the 1790s Wordsworth reveals a sustained effort at radical social criticism and even a marked interest in dramatizing the enticements and dilemmas of moral and intellectual solipsism. For instance, he mounts a critique of the French monarchy and aristocracy in *A Letter to the Bishop of Llandaff* (1793), meditates gloomily on the state of modern society in *Guilt and Sorrow* (1791–94), and produces an intensely wrought tragedy of political betrayal and murder in *The Borderers* (1795–96). All three of these works constitute early yet often

---

14. David Simpson has also argued in favor of the complexity and ambiguity of the speaker's character in "A slumber," in *Irony and Authority in Romantic Poetry* (Totowa, N.J.: Rowman and Littlefield, 1979), pp. 36–37, Simpson maintains that there are at least two ways that the poem can be read. He prefers the reading that fixes the speaker's state of mind upon a particular choice of identity for the woman: Annette Vallon and her child. Nevertheless, Simpson recognizes a general vagueness and ambiguity concerning the "spirit" and his "slumber," a state of affairs that draws attention to the curious difficulties of the character of the speaker or narrator of Wordsworth's lyric.

overlooked moments in Wordsworth's study of modern man's inhumanity and cruelty.[15]

The Borderers, especially with regard to the character of Oswald, appears particularly intriguing in connection with the notion of a Romantic death fantasy and the characterological purview of solipsism. To project a complete image of the speaker's character in "A slumber"— the speaker who emerges in the third way of reading the lyric—would yield an Oswald-like figure. Wordsworth has detailed the self-engrossed character of Oswald (initially named Rivers) in his "Preface to *The Borderers*," written sometime between spring 1797 and spring 1798 but not published until 1926. Oswald has been betrayed into murdering an innocent person, but his own pride and intellect in the aftermath of the murder generate a "morbid state of mind" that "requires constant provocations" and "is perpetually chasing a phantom." Moreover, his "powerful" "imagination" drives him on to the new crimes. The objects of his attention are included in his rather malignant solipsism: ". . . their colour is exclusively what he gives them; it is one, and it is his own" (*PW*, I, pp. 77–78). Oswald ruthlessly purifies himself of any feelings of compassion for his fellow beings, and his motives appear inhumane: "Power is life to him / And breath and being; where he cannot govern, / He will destroy" (p. 184). Oswald is one who can say "I had no human

15. These three works were not published until much later, though "The Female Vagrant" was extracted from *Guilt and Sorrow* and published in the 1798 *Lyrical Ballads*. *The Borderers* and *Guilt and Sorrow* were first published in 1842, and *A Letter to the Bishop of Llandaff* first appeared in *The Prose Works of William Wordsworth*, ed. Alexander B. Grosart (London, 1876). Nicholas Roe's *Wordsworth and Coleridge: The Radical Years* (Oxford: Clarendon Press, 1988) traces in rich detail the course of Wordsworth's radical political views, writings, and activities from 1789 to the composition of "Tintern Abbey" in 1798.

Insightful discussions of the possibilities of Wordsworth as a cultural critic of his own historical age and cultural developments has for the most part seemed seriously to lag behind the manifold enticements of his poetic practice. David Simpson, though, offers a broadly based and wide-ranging assessment of what he calls "Wordsworth's historical imagination." His argument presents a powerful portrait of the poet as a critic of his own society and culture, yet Simpson also claims that Wordsworth's complex cultural critiques tended to undermine or displace their polemical import because of the poet's own preoccupation with his personal anxieties and self-conscious construction of his own sense of selfhood. Accordingly, the poet's persona wavers and assumes a variety of social and intellectual positions. "Wordsworth is thus the poet of displacement or alienation" for Simpson—that is, he reclaims and persuasively reconstructs that image of Wordsworth as a cultural and historical "subject in conflict, a subject defined by a condition of acute alienation, both vocational and social." See David Simpson, *Wordsworth's Historical Imagination: The Poetry of Displacement* (London: Methuen, 1987), pp. 8, 2, and pp. 1–8 in passing.

fears: / She seemed a thing that could not feel." Oswald, though, before he was betrayed into murder, apparently had a beloved: "I had been, / And in that dream had left my native land, / One of Love's simple bondsmen" (p. 202). However, that innocent love in the past is now a "soft chain" gone "for ever." Oswald moves now as one of those awakened, self-conscious, "Restless Minds, / Such Minds as find amid their fellow-men / No heart that loves them, none that they can love" but must instead "turn perforce and seek for sympathy / In dim relation to imagined Beings" (p. 185). Oswald craves the sympathetic fellowship of a "Master" whom he actually fashions in his own image: "My Master shall become / A shadow of myself—made by myself" (p. 208). Solipsism becomes demonic here. This strange, unearthly prospect appears fully predicated upon a morbid, unfeeling isolation and an inhumane desire for power and control over others made demonically manifest.

Geoffrey Hartman has analyzed *The Borderers* within the context of an "intellectual murder." In a well-argued account that nonetheless has the effect of anesthetizing the act of murder in the drama and etherealizing the victim (the blind old man Herbert), Hartman intellectualizes the slaying in order to direct the discussion of the play toward the theme of the development of authentic consciousness of self as predicated upon a separation from nature.[16] The difficulty here perhaps stems from an inadequate understanding of the character of Oswald and the type of self-consciousness he possesses and into which he seeks to shock Marmaduke. Oswald is a proto-Nietzschean "Master" or "Intellect" separated from both nature and humankind as well as from the laws of the latter. His self-consciousness actually involves scornful pride and a compulsive dedication to the deception of innocence and kinship-based morality. He desires to corrupt personal innocence and social morality into personal suffering and the will to power over any collective expression of remorse and expiation. Wordsworth dramatizes but clearly abhors and admonishes such an immoral form of self-consciousness. It comprises a temptation, but it is not the kind of self-consciousness for which he struggles, for instance, in *The Prelude*. Quite similar to "A slumber," Wordsworth in *The Borderers* probes into a character that he seeks to expose. The poet recognizes, indeed lyricizes and dramatizes, the temptation, and in so doing lays it bare.

---

16. Hartman, *Wordsworth's Poetry, 1787–1814*, pp. 125–35.

Many poems in *Lyrical Ballads* also contribute powerful articulations of a cultural critique of modern man's insensitivity, cruelty, and self-closure. For example, "The Waterfall and the Eglantine" immediately follows "A slumber" in volume two of *Lyrical Ballads*. The poem portrays a natural and nurturing balance deranged through pride, tyranny, and strife. The waterfall boasts thunderously of its power and threatens complete destruction of the clinging eglantine that draws sustenance from the flowing waters. The narrator of the scene analogically connects these things of nature to a fearful agon of willful tyrant and distraught yet patiently reasonable child. "Ellen Irwin" immediately precedes the group of three "Lucy" poems in which "A slumber" appears in *Lyrical Ballads*, and in it Wordsworth satirically equates the rage and violence characteristic of warfare with the violence of chivalric love. A frustrated rival for the hand of Ellen Irwin spies upon the Edenic scene of her and Adam Bruce's lovemaking and "Sees them and their caressing, / Beholds them blest and blessing." This rival, "Proud Gordon, maddened by the thoughts / That through his brain are travelling," rises up in a strange fit of passion to take revenge on Bruce. Ellen is slain instead, and Bruce kills Gordon. Now solitary, Bruce rages in violence against the Moors, hoping for his own death:

> And Bruce, as soon as he had slain
> The Gordon, sailed away to Spain;
> And fought with rage incessant
> Against the Moorish crescent.
>
> But many days, and many months,
> And many years ensuing,
> This wretched Knight did vainly seek
> The death that he was wooing.
> So, coming his last help to crave,
> Heart-broken, upon Ellen's grave,
> His body he extended,
> And there his sorrow ended.
>
> (*PW*, III, p. 72)

Wordsworth mockingly draws attention to the violent excesses of chivalric love—where love breeds murder, and death in combat is wooed as a recalcitrant beloved. The poet satirically equates the rage of warfare and the violence of lover, two excessive modes of passion that he would have found separately depicted in the ballads of Bishop Thomas Percy's *Reliques of Ancient English Poetry* (1765), a book that Dorothy Wordsworth records that she and her brother purchased in Hamburg two days before their departure for Goslar (*Journals*, I, p. 31). Thus the two ballads that immediately frame the much-discussed threesome of "Lucy" poems in the 1800 edition of *Lyrical Ballads* mount lyrical critiques of cultural problems.

However, the first poem of the second volume of *Lyrical Ballads*, "Hart-Leap Well," may be even more telling. It concerns the gratuitous murder of a hart and the hunter's absence of sympathy. This lyric, moreover, is marked by various posturings and doublings by the narrator in order to bring his readers' "thinking hearts" to understand the "one lesson" of his "simple song" (*PW*, II, pp. 252, 254). In the first of its two parts (rhymes or tales, in the language of the narrator), the chase after the hart by an unusually determined Sir Walter focuses on the pleasure and triumph of the hunter. The second part of the ballad brings the voice and perspective of the narrator into full play. Here the somber origins of the purportedly exciting tale of part one become disclosed, and the desolation of the natural scene surrounding the pool of water where the hart expired call out for explanation. The narrator eventually settles upon a moral for this now dual tale of a hunter's murderous triumph and nature's loss and desolation: "Taught by what she ["Nature"] shows, and what conceals, / Never to blend our pleasure or our pride / With sorrow of the meanest thing that feels" (p. 254). Wordsworth toys with the narrative perspective of this poem, but he eventually permits the narrator to make his sympathies with the delicate fortunes of nature's various beings clear. A reader encounters the tale of the hunter and the hart at least twice, once from the perspective of the hunter and the chase and only secondly from the fuller perspective of the tale-teller, who witnesses the aftermath of the hunter's self-enclosing pride in the hunt and who himself hears the story first told by a shepherd dwelling nearby. The ballad mounts a telling critique of the egocentric and transumptive ethos of the willful Sir Walter, but it does so by orchestrating at least two perspectives on the one scene where the hart leaps and dies. Wordsworth's craft at narrative counterpoint and narratorial complexity work hand in hand to set a strong chord of social and cultural critique at the head of *Lyrical Ballads*, Volume II.

The foregoing remarks on *The Borderers* and various other lyrics first published alongside "A slumber" in 1800 may appear to divert attention onto peripheral matters, but the opposite is true. Such intertextual readings and linkages allow one to test the potential social and historical import of particular readings—in this case, the third way of reading "A slumber." As Jerome McGann has argued, "Romantic poems . . . tend to develop different sorts of artistic means with which to occlude and disguise their own involvement in a certain nexus of historical relations."[17] "A slumber did my spirit seal" can "occlude and disguise" its involvement with various other moments of Wordsworth's critique of the state of modern social conduct. However, "A slumber," for its own part—a part that it plays within a "nexus of historical relations" that circulates through many of Wordsworth's works of the 1790s—brings into sharp and striking poetic definition the solipsism of Romantic or modern man and his proclivity for fantasy states.[18]

Moreover, within this context of examining "A slumber" as a creative inquiry into and cultural critique of a Romantic death fantasy, what can be recognized as the greater significance of the experience of a referential confusion while reading the poem emerges. Confusion over the reference of "she" leads a reader unwittingly and abruptly into the center of the poem's most occluded and most suggestive line of interpretation. A reader

17. McGann, p. 82.
18. Solipsism and the Romantic death fantasy, however, do not exhaust the social and psychological resources of the poem. There are basic forces at work in "A slumber" that touch on the primal or mythic, and these forces should not go unmentioned. Joseph Campbell, in the first part of *The Masks of God: Primitive Mythology* (New York: Viking Press, 1959), "The Psychology of Myth," names and discusses five basic structuring forces of life on earth from primitive times. They are (1) the earth and its gravity; (2) diurnal alternation of dark and light; (3) the moon, its cycle, and the spectacle of the night sky; (4) male versus female; and (5) the normal progression through the stages of human growth, from birth through infancy and childhood to adulthood and old age and death (pp. 57–61). All of these basic socio-psychological structuring forces except for (3) are at work in "A slumber," and (3) can be seen at work in both "Strange fits" and "She dwelt." These structuring forces can help account for the enduring effect and sense of necessity about the images and operations of "A slumber." The underlying power of the image of the last two lines of the lyric involves the inherited, communal power of mankind's inseparable attachment to the earth. The specific transformation of that force in the case of "A slumber" yields the image of a corpse inseparably bound to the earth. F. W. Bateson, in *English Poetry: A Critical Introduction* (London: Longmans, 1950), pp. 33, 80–81, has gone so far as to interpret this final image as an expression of Wordsworth's supposed pantheism. As far as Campbell's fourth basic structuring force is concerned, the primal opposition between male and female still insists upon its reality and its pathos against the solipsistic Romantic death fantasy that attempts to incorporate the female within the fantasy life of the male. Campbell's five basic structuring forces of life on earth could be developed at length in an account that would pursue the cultural critique of the Romantic death fantasy and romantic love initiated above in the discussions of Hawthorn's and Diamond's work.

can initially become confused in attempting to trace the "she" back to a clear point of reference precisely because it is also the speaker's problem. The speaker's peculiar state of affairs is to be confused about his own identity and the identity of the woman purportedly referred to in the poem. The speaker solipsistically ingests the identity of the lovely other into his own awareness and identity. She resides for him in his own imagination, and she undergoes for him the fateful and fatal movements that his death fantasy decrees.[19] However, a reader consciously attains this knowledge of the speaker only when he or she has managed to break through to the third way of reading "A slumber." Strangely enough, the first hint of the actual problematic of the poem is given as the first piece of evidence. We can begin with an experience of confusion and can conclude with the clear knowledge that we have experienced a Romantic fantast at deadly play.

The burden of Chapters 5 and 6 will be to substantiate in more exacting detail the interpretive cogency and power of the way of reading and interpreting "A slumber" that I have constructed so far. Other readings as well as models of reading "A slumber" need to be engaged in order to test the mettle of the one that I have induced on the basis of a felt experience of referential confusion. This initial piece of problematic evidence has helped to direct the pathway of an inquiry into how Wordsworth's poem

---

19. Two articles in *Comparative Literature Studies* develop connections among the themes of solipsism, male narcissism, Romantic love, incest, and the destruction of feminine identity. Peter L. Thorslev, in "Incest as Romantic Symbol," *CLS* 2 (1965): 41–58, concentrates on the theme of incest in Gothic novels and in the poetry of Shelley and Byron but does provide remarks on the context in which incest has achieved intense interest: ". . . there is a very real sense in which the only love possible for the Romantic hero . . . is an incestuous love. First, it symbolizes perfectly this hero's complete alienation from the society around him; and second, it symbolizes also what psychologically speaking we can call his narcissistic sensibility, or more philosophically speaking, his predilection for solipsism" (p. 50). Incest, like murder, would be another way for the Romantic hero or lover to absorb or ingest the identity of the beloved into his own lonely, alienated, and all-consuming sensibility. This analysis is supported in greater detail by James D. Wilson, "The Romantic Love Object: The Woman as Narcissistic Projection," *CLS* 15 (1978): 388–402. Wilson examines the connections between narcissistic love and incest, between longing (*Sehnsucht*) and the chaste and inaccessible maiden-goddess, through the male hero's doomed infatuation with his own projection of the ideal beloved, his "sister soul." Works by Keats, Shelley, Chateaubriand, Hawthorne, and Hardy are considered; and Wilson concludes that "the ultimate result in all instances is a loss of feminine identity and a sterile, narcissistic love relationship which proves self-destructive" (p. 388). Neither Thorslev nor Wilson develops the Romantic death fantasy in connection with their materials; but perhaps it can be seen as a second, and a decidedly more drastic, manifestation of male narcissism and Romantic love. The remarks of Thorslev and Wilson also meld well with those of Stanley Diamond discussed above.

can be said to work. Three possible lines of interpretation have emerged, each with distinctive merits. The third one—occluded in the poem's syntax, its grammar, and the elliptical character of its speaker—does not so much supplant the other two as supplement them. It articulates what is lacking in both and turns squarely to address what precisely is at stake in a poetic work that appears at first to send its readers off along two divergent pathways of interpretation. However, other readers, other readings, other uses of the evidence of literary reading need to be brought to bear on the constructions of the foregoing chapters in order to test how well such constructions can stand up as a compelling account of the activity of reading and interpreting Wordsworth's "A slumber did my spirit seal."

5

The Problems of Context
and the
Determination of Meaning:
Reclaiming the Activity of Reading

The problem of solipsism and the Romantic death fantasy may very well provide the most adequate and inclusive general context for developing a full interpretation of "A slumber." However, it could be objected that to demonstrate three ways of reading the poem are plausible, even though each is developed and valued differently, may enhance the view that the meaning of the lyric is ambiguous or indeterminate. The threat of such indeterminacy may even seem to jeopardize the explanatory force and appropriateness of the preceding chapters. But, as David Ferry has indicated in his own inquiry into the power and art of "A slumber," careful probing into a complex and strange context for the poem is necessary, though initially declined or dismissed by some readers:

> The poem is difficult almost by reason of its apparent simplicity, which nearly prevents us from looking beyond the immediate impression of grief to the unsentimental sources of the grief's extraordinary power. One is inclined to say, "He loved her so much that he could not imagine that she could die," and let it go at that, content to marvel. But the poem is too complex for such mere admiration.[1]

---

1. Ferry, *The Limits of Mortality*, p. 77.

A certain complexity of context does not necessarily entail an ambiguity or indeterminacy in meaning. It would seem to demand an honest openness to a poem's "sources" of "power," however "unsentimental" they may be. It is my intention in this chapter to consider the problems of determinate meaning and poetic context in relation to the plausibility of the three ways of reading the poem for which I have already argued.

M. H. Abrams, of course, has most recently made "A slumber" a notable lyric touchstone for the problem of construing determinate meaning for a literary text. His appraisal of the critical task of construing the meaning of Wordsworth's poem does have some points in common with my own approach, especially with regard to the sort of expectations and presuppositions that particular grammatical constructions in English can be said to assume. Certain basic and unavoidable interpretive moves are involved in making meaning for Wordsworth's text, and Abrams stresses the acts of construing the "I" and "she" of the poem. However, he tends to elide the activity of reading the poem and some of its interpretive and cognitive complexities. For instance, though he briefly admits the possibility of construing "she" as referring to "my spirit," he finds this construal "extremely unlikely" because "the consensus of other competent readers" will not confirm it.[2] This prohibitive judgment, however, contradicts the mass of competently construed and assessed evidence in support of that distinct possibility. For Abrams the controlling context of his interpretive remarks seems not so much the lyric and cognitive complexities of Wordsworth's poem as his own struggle with such deconstructive readers as J. Hillis Miller, who transgress the bounds of careful and determinate construal of meaning in search of illicit and textually unconstrained meanings. Abrams reads Miller on Wordsworth's "A slumber" with strong insight and humor, yet he delimits the interpretive context of the poem too narrowly in the interests of combating Miller's own lack of interpretive constraint.[3]

2. M. H. Abrams, "Construing and Deconstructing," in *Romanticism and Contemporary Criticism*, ed. Morris Eaves and Michael Fisher (Ithaca, N.Y.: Cornell University Press, 1986), p. 145n. Abrams's entire argument on construing "A slumber" encompasses pp. 143–58. I will briefly return to Abrams's essay in Chapter 6, when I discuss J. Hillis Miller's reading of "A slumber."

3. The most notorious use of "A slumber" in recent discussions of theoretical controversy perhaps must be conceded to Steven Knapp and Walter Benn Michaels's polemical essay "Against Theory," *Critical Inquiry* 8 (1982): 727–29. Knapp and Michaels construct a hypothetical case in which the first stanza, and then later on the second stanza, appear upon the sands of a seashore.

A considerable amount of critical writing on "A slumber" has been preoccupied with selecting and defending various contexts for the poem and arguing for a particular, determinate interpretation on the basis of the context chosen. A case in point is Richard E. Matlack's major article "Wordsworth's Lucy Poems in Psychobiographical Context." The context Matlack develops ultimately derives from F. W. Bateson's contention that Dorothy is the emotional source of the "Lucy" poems. However, Matlack rejects Bateson's presentation of the relationship of Wordsworth and Dorothy as "being incestuously inclined."[4] Instead, Matlack works out in detail some suggestions made by Coleridge that Dorothy's presence in Germany and at Goslar caused Wordsworth social inconvenience and financial hardship. Coleridge, in a letter to his wife, speaks about Wordsworth's situation in Germany:

> His taking his Sister with him was a wrong Step; it is next to impossible for any but married women or in the suit of married women to be introduced to any company in Germany. Sister [here] is considered as only a name for Mistress. (Griggs, I, p. 459)[5]

Primarily on the basis of Coleridge's infrequent and scattered remarks about the Wordsworths at Goslar in letters to Thomas Poole and Sara

---

The example purportedly polarizes the choice of the interpreter: an attribution of these marks in the sand to chance mechanics or to human intention. The appearance of a submarine offshore and a crew of experimental scientists supposedly constitutes the answer: The marks can and must be attributed to human (Wordsworth's? the submarining scientists'? Knapp and Michaels's?) intention. Peggy Kamuf thoroughly and convincingly explodes the pretensions and unexamined theoretical assumptions of Knapp and Michaels's article in her review-essay, "Floating Authorship," pp. 3–13.

4. Matlack, "Wordsworth's Lucy Poems in Psychobiographical Context," p. 46. Matlack cites Bateson, *Wordsworth: A Re-interpretation*, pp. 151–54. See also footnote 9, p. 29–30. Matlack has developed this same psychobiographical context to embrace the whole of the Goslar period, including the "Matthew" poems and the two-part *Prelude* (1798–99), in "'That Melancholy Dream': Wordsworth's Goslar Experience and Poetry" (Ph.D. diss., Indiana University, 1976).

5. Matlack, "Wordsworth's Lucy Poems," p. 50. Wallace W. Douglas also notes Coleridge's remarks on the trouble caused by Dorothy's presence at Goslar; but Douglas, unlike Matlack, understands that the Wordsworths wanted to be together. Indeed, the majority of their correspondence with Coleridge indicates their mutual pleasure in that fact and in their single-minded concern to persuade Coleridge to live close to them when they should all return to England. Douglas notes that Coleridge's reaction to the infrequent but lengthy communications of the Wordsworths was perhaps "out of proportion to Wordsworth's dereliction." See Douglas, *Wordsworth: The Construction of a Personality* (Kent, Ohio: Kent State University Press, 1968), pp. 40–45.

Coleridge and a remark by Wordsworth on the pain involved in composition and revision, Matlack constructs "a comprehensive psychological and biographical ambience for the Lucy poems that will dispel the mystery of their genesis and account for their intriguing peculiarities; and to reach this objective, an important assumption must be made about the identity of Lucy." The assumption is that "Lucy" is Dorothy. Wordsworth's ambivalence toward "Lucy" and fantasies of her death are consequently expressions of his ambivalence and hostility toward Dorothy for keeping him penned up in their lonely rooms at Goslar "bereft of Coleridge's presence" and of the "company" that Wordsworth could have afforded if he had not burdened himself with "taking his Sister." Before the Wordsworths and Coleridge had left England for Germany, Wordsworth had enjoyed an annus mirabilis at Alfoxden from July 1797 to June 1798 in the company of Coleridge. Matlack contends that Wordsworth's pain and anxiety over composition and his hostility toward Dorothy "is no mystery if we consider the recent disruption he suffered and the risk it betokened, that is, the end of his blissful residence with Coleridge at Alfoxden and the likelihood that the creative experience of that year might never again be attained." At Racedown, Wordsworth's cohabitation with his sister "was dull and unpromising"; it was a life of "vegetative torpor"; and, "like a whirlwind, Coleridge entered this scene of sedentary retirement to arouse Wordsworth's genius."[6] While at Goslar Wordsworth is without Coleridge's inspiring presence and so is once again in the situation that he had endured at Racedown—alone with Dorothy and "the boredom, melancholy, and pain that were now his lot." In Germany "Wordsworth struggled to ward off his feelings of hostility toward his sister," yet "there was no way out: he both needed and resented her." Matlack claims, then, "that the Lucy lyrics began to form as an outlet for Wordsworth's ambivalence and frustration."[7]

---

6. Matlack, "Wordsworth's Lucy Poems," pp. 46–48.

7. Ibid., pp. 50–51. Matlack's account of the relationship of Wordsworth and Coleridge fails to concur with more detailed and circumspect descriptions of that important friendship. For example, in perhaps the most insightful study of Wordsworth's emotional experience and how it is reflected in his relationships and thought, Kenneth Eisold examines "Wordsworth's sudden intimacy with Coleridge" that began in June 1797. See Eisold, *Loneliness and Communion: A Study of Wordsworth's Thought and Experience* (Salzburg: Institut für Englische Sprache und Literatur, 1973), p. 62. Eisold draws upon a number of sources in order to hypothesize that Coleridge's "admiration for Wordsworth the man was connected with his sense of his own weakness, despite his assertions to the contrary" (p. 63). As Eisold sums up the situation,

The psychobiographical context that Matlack has constructed is riddled with difficulties. As I have already shown (see footnote 8, pages 20–21), no

---

> Coleridge's own friends worried at the time that there was something unwholesome and self-deprecating in his admiration for Wordsworth. Poole wrote to him in Germany . . . "The Wordsworths have left you—so there is an end of our tease about amalgamation, etc., etc." Coleridge's own letters confirm the idea that amalgamation is precisely what he was looking for in his friends, first in Poole and then more completely in Wordsworth: "I am sure I need not say how you are incorporated into the better part of my being," he wrote to him after their first prolonged separation. He seems to have sought a degree of identification he could probably never find. For a time, though, he seems to have thought he found it in Wordsworth. (p. 64; see also Griggs, I, pp. 419, 391, 453)

It would appear that Coleridge is the one who could not tolerate being "bereft" of the "Presence" of a beloved male companion. Matlack's account of Coleridge and Wordsworth at Alfoxden and in Germany, then, is a curious inversion of the thrust of Eisold's hypothesis and supporting remarks. Eisold's comments can lend support and credence to the contention that Matlack's "psychobiographical context" is at root a projection of Coleridge's psychic difficulties onto the figure of Wordsworth.

It is Coleridge, after all, who wrote these lines to William and Dorothy while the latter two friends were at Goslar:

> William, my head and my heart! dear Poet that feelest and thinkest!
> Dorothy, eager of soul, my most affectionate sister!
> Many a mile, O! many a wearisome mile are ye distant,
>
> . . . .
> Feverish and wakeful I lie,—I am weary of feeling and thinking.
>
> . . . .
> William, my head and my heart! dear William and dear Dorothea!
> You have all in each other; but I am lonely, and want you!
> (Griggs, I, pp. 451–52)

Wordsworth wants Coleridge's company, encouragement, and admiration. However, it is Coleridge who suffers intense loneliness and pain, who is alternately jealous of and heartfelt toward Dorothy and toward William, and who craves male intellectual camaraderie. It is also Coleridge who sees heterosexual and incestuous love and relations as counterfeits for the betrayed and now absent homoerotic love of boyhood. Coleridge's unrequited desire for amalgamation or incorporation with his male friends very likely has its origin and motives here. See his poem "The Pang More Sharp Than All" (especially section V) and Leoline's decision at the end of "Christabel" to choose Geraldine, who recalls his boyhood friend Roland.

Wordsworth, in the meantime, was enmeshed in an "emotional dialectic," a recurring "pattern of relationship and isolation," of communion and loneliness, that alternately offered him blissful, companionable participation or intimacy and reserved, isolated solitude (Eisold, p. 65). Eisold contends that Coleridge never really understood or could adjust to "the underlying pattern of duality in Wordsworth's thought" and emotional experience because "he probably craved too much affection himself to be able to understand the more contradictory demands of his friend" (pp. i, 65).

This alternative "psychobiographical context" garners more evidential support than Matlack's and consequently is more probable and cogent. It is also in substantial agreement with various

single person, including Dorothy, can be assumed to be "Lucy." At best, we can determine that the identity of "Lucy" is a composite of several historical personages and literary allusions. Therefore, Matlack's "important assumption" that "Lucy" is Dorothy is unsound; it discards considerable evidence, evidence that would demand a rather different context to account for it. The period of Wordsworth's stay at Goslar is itself an abbreviated *annus mirabilis*. Even though Coleridge was not present and Wordsworth once complained about the painful exertion of composition, Wordsworth did indeed write a considerable amount of verse, including a great deal of the new material for the 1800 *Lyrical Ballads* and various sections of *The Prelude*. Perhaps the task of composition was often painful, but Wordsworth's concern to be at work on his long poem *The Recluse* could account for such pain. He was continuing to author short lyrics, largely in imitation of the materials and meter of popular ballads; but the desire and need to compose a work of some permanence and range and his apparent difficulty in determining the proper materials and techniques to this end would have caused Wordsworth considerable anxiety and pain.[8] Then, too, Wordsworth was beginning at this time to plumb anxious and distressing childhood experiences. All these conditions of his actual work of composing are far more plausible sources of Wordsworth's pain than a hypothesis of an ambivalence and hostility toward Dorothy and Wordsworth's rupture and separation from Coleridge. Moreover, if Wordsworth actually felt so ambivalent toward Dorothy and so "bereft of Coleridge's presence," why does he permit Dorothy to write the far greater part of their *mutual* letters to Coleridge? Not only does she transcribe the poems that are supposed to be expressions of her brother's fantasies of being rid of her, but she is the one who communicates, mediates, her brother's (and her own) desire that Coleridge be near them and visit them often in England. Wordsworth, of course, never acquired an ease in letter writing; yet the direness of the psychobiographical context that Matlack presents would

---

studies of the Wordsworth, Dorothy, and Coleridge friendship. See especially William Heath, *Wordsworth and Coleridge: A Study of Their Literary Relations in 1801–1802* (Oxford: Clarendon Press, 1970), pp. 1–141. See also W. W. Douglas, *Wordsworth*; H. M. Margoliouth, *Wordsworth and Coleridge*; C. M. Maclean, *Dorothy and William Wordsworth*, pp. 33–58; and Stephen Gill, *William Wordsworth: A Life* (Oxford: Clarendon Press, 1989), pp. 156–63.

8. Kenneth R. Johnston, *Wordsworth and "The Recluse"* (New Haven, Conn.: Yale University Press, 1984), most fully explores Wordsworth's extensive labors and intensive desire to be at work on *The Recluse*, not only during the Goslar year but throughout the most productive period of the Wordsworth-Coleridge friendship—the years 1797 to 1806.

seem to indicate that Wordsworth would seek to correspond himself, and certainly more frequently, with the missing Coleridge.

It is curious that Matlack offers no readings of the so-called "Lucy" poems until he has fully stated the context in which they are to be read. The evidence for this psychobiographical context comes solely from sources and authorities other than the poems and the experience of reading them. Inferences about Wordsworth's state of mind and life as well as the meaning and significance of his poems are made on the basis of a handful of quotations from letters, and these documents are primarily written by someone else. Such inferences can be very useful and informative, but it is nonetheless curious that the evidence that one group of documents can provide is privileged over the evidence offered by the very texts one is attempting to understand and put in context. This privileging of one set of texts (letters) and evidence (psychobiographical deductions) over another set (the poems) and the evidence that they might have to offer (the particularities of the activity of reading) betrays an "important assumption" about Matlack's critical procedure: The activity of reading a poem cannot itself begin to specify the context in which the poem can be understood, its particularities drawn out and accounted for. Matlack admits that "it is one thing to acknowledge the plausibility of a biographical reconstruction but quite another to relate poems to an emotional milieu that does not seem to be operative in their form and content."[9] The "form and content" of poems cannot alone specify a context, "an emotional milieu"; but, according to Matlack's critical example, they can be related to a context formulated, presumably, from the form and content of sources outside them.

This methodological dilemma and its contradictory state of affairs is echoed in E. D. Hirsch, Jr.'s, well-known discussion of Cleanth Brooks's and F. W. Bateson's variant interpretations of "A slumber." Hirsch contends that Brooks's reading of the final lines of the lyric as an experience of despair and the bitter irony of death is irreconcilable with Bateson's interpretation of them as an expression of pantheism:

> While Bateson construes a primary emphasis on life and affirmation, Brooks emphasizes deadness and inertness. No amount of manipulation can reconcile these divergent emphases, since one pattern of emphasis irrevocably excludes other patterns, and, since

9. Matlack, "Wordsworth's Lucy Poems," p. 51.

emphasis is always crucial to meaning, the two constructions of
meaning rigorously exclude one another.[10]

10. E. D. Hirsch, Jr., *Validity in Interpretation* (New Haven, Conn.: Yale University Press,
1967), p. 229. Hirsch's discussion occurs on pages 227–30 and 238–40 of his text. These two
passages form not only parts of his argument but they also constitute Hirsch's main practical
application of his theory of interpretation in "Appendix I: Objective Interpretation," an essay first
published in *PMLA* 75 (1960): 463–79. Cleanth Brooks's interpretation of "A slumber" can be
found in "Irony as a Principle of Structure," in *Literary Opinion in America*, 2d ed., ed. M. D.
Zabel (New York: Harper & Row, 1951), pp. 735–37. F. W. Bateson's interpretation can be
found in his *English Poetry: A Critical Introduction*, rev. ed. (New York: Barnes & Noble, 1966;
orig. pub. 1950), pp. 29–30, 59.

Brooks's and Bateson's interpretations are actually far more insightful than Hirsch's summary
might lead one to believe. Both men notice conflicting or contrasting attitudes in their readings
of the entire poem. Hirsch's concentration on what they have to say about the final two lines of
the lyric constitutes an elision of the other halves of Brooks's and Bateson's perceived contrasts.
Brooks says that the first stanza yields "a context calculated to pull 'human fears' in opposed
directions": the lethargic insensitive nature of the speaker before learning of the loved one's death
and his "agonized shock" at "her utter and horrible inertness" (p. 736). The contrast pits the
speaker's former spiritual inertness against the humanization it undergoes when startled from its
slumber. Hirsch's selective emphasis leaves out the humanizing process and the complex context
in which it occurs. A similar act of selective emphasis on Hirsch's part conceals the "miniature
drama in which two 'sides' meet, come into conflict and are eventually reconciled" in Bateson's
interpretation. Bateson labels the two sides "humanism" and "pantheism." The pantheistic side
inhabits the final image of the poem, and the humanistic side resides in the sense that
"Wordsworth *ought* to have had 'human fears'" (p. 59). Bateson, then, shares with Brooks not
only the experience of opposed or contrasted attitudes in "A slumber" but also the perception that
the line "I had no human fears" harbors a humanistic side to the poem that Hirsch does not bring
into his own discussion. Recognition of this humanistic dimension to the experience of the poem
could have provided a way for Hirsch to appraise and adjudicate the differences in Brooks's and
Bateson's interpretations. There would appear to be more common ground than one would think.
Moreover, that common ground arises through attention to the activity of reading and not the
reconstruction of the most probable authorial intention.

David Ferry's interpretation of "A slumber" in *The Limits of Mortality*, pp. 76–79, would seem
to unite Brooks's and Bateson's. As a lesson in the limitations of mortality, the poem demonstrates
the "errors" of the speaker's insensitivity and shows him humanized "with a full realization of the
pain that change involves for human beings" (p. 78). Ferry adds, however, that "there is a
countercurrent in the poem": "Her death was right, after all, for by dying she was one with the
natural processes that made her die, and fantastically ennobled thereby. The poem is a distillation
of 'Three years she grew'" (p. 78). Here Ferry accepts the pantheistic interpretation of the final
two lines. Bateson's emphasis becomes a twinned and opposed "countercurrent" to the main
current of Brooks's interpretation. Ferry's analysis is admirable; but it depends far too much on
reading "She dwelt" and "Three years she grew" into "A slumber," the former lyric for its
expression of loss and the latter for its pantheism.

In the title essay of his book *Beyond Formalism* (New Haven, Conn.: Yale University Press,
1970), pp. 43–51, Geoffrey Hartman shows how the interpretations of Brooks and Bateson are
"nonhistorical" and how the "historical procedure" of reconstructing the "history of lyric style"
can salvage and validate certain observations of the two critics regarding Wordsworth's style in "A
slumber" and "She dwelt."

If one of the constructions of meaning is to be verified, "a deliberate reconstruction of the author's subjective stance to the extent that this stance is relevant to the text at hand" is necessary. "Such psychological reconstruction" is essential for Hirsch because it can develop the context needed to verify the relative probability of a construction of meaning:

> The best way to show that one reading is more plausible and coherent than the other is to show that one context is more probable than the other. The problem of adjudicating between Bateson and Brooks is therefore, implicitly, the problem every interpreter must face when he tries to verify his reading. He must establish the most probable context.[11]

Hirsch then asserts that "the most probable context" is the one that supports Bateson's interpretation. Since Wordsworth's "characteristic attitudes are somewhat pantheistic" and because "everything we know of Wordsworth's typical attitudes during the period in which he composed the poem" show that "inconsolability and bitter irony do not belong within its horizon," we are left with the conclusion that Bateson's reading is more plausible and coherent (verifiable) because it is more typical or characteristic (probable) of Wordsworth's attitudes at the time. Hirsch concedes that "Bateson overstates his case" and "fails to emphasize properly the negative implications in the poem"; yet,

> nevertheless, in spite of this, and in spite of the apparent implausibility of Bateson's reading, it remains, I think, somewhat more probable than that of Brooks. His procedure is also more objective. Even if he had botched his job thoroughly and had produced a less probable reading than that of Brooks, his method would remain fundamentally sound. . . . We shall never be certain what any writer means, [but] since Bateson grounds his interpretation in a conscious construction of the poet's outlook, his reading must be deemed the more probable one until the uncovering of some presently unknown data makes a different construction of the poet's stance appear more valid.[12]

11. Hirsch, pp. 238, 239.
12. Ibid., pp. 239–40.

And so Hirsch accepts an apparently implausible interpretation because the "procedure" involved is deemed to be "more objective" and "fundamentally sound." It can be recognized that what is at stake for Hirsch is not a fuller interpretation of the poem but a question of proper method or procedure, a question actually not even related to the particularities involved in reading the poem. Hirsch is transparently clear in accepting "the apparent implausibility of Bateson's reading" as "somewhat more probable" because to do so is an act in accord with the method he is proposing for "objective interpretation." Hirsch wants to secure theoretically the practice of Bateson, and by extension that of Richard Matlack, of reconstructing a psychological and biographical context so that the meanings of poems can be verified. Like Matlack, Hirsch assumes that the activity of reading a poem cannot specify its own context. However, Hirsch's critical project involves generalizing this assumption, despite its problems, as a critical procedure. He intends to institutionalize as critical methodology the approach to meaning and context that has just been recognized to generate implicit difficulties for Matlack and now would encourage the acceptance of implausibility in the name of "objective" and "sound" procedure.[13]

The difficulties in Hirsch's method have surfaced in other critics' remarks on Hirsch's presentation of Brooks's and Bateson's interpretations. Charles Altieri notes that "the full performance" of "A slumber" "depends on a critical description of what this poem is doing with possible general contexts" and that the alleged need to choose only one context as the most probable is an "instance" of "the unnecessary categorizing produced by an ideal of interpretive generality."[14] Louise Rosenblatt and

13. In *Interpretation: An Essay in the Philosophy of Literary Criticism* (Princeton, N.J.: Princeton University Press, 1980), P. D. Juhl produces an extreme extension of Hirsch's approach to meaning and intention and also applies it directly to "A slumber" (pp. 71–72, 199–202). Juhl's oversimplification of the problem of authorial intention has much in common with Steven Knapp and Walter Benn Michaels's controversial position on intentionality in "Against Theory," especially pp. 731–33, and their polemic against linguistic conventions in "Against Theory 2: Hermeneutics and Deconstruction," *Critical Inquiry* 14 (1987): 49–68. For an assessment of the critical possibilities and theoretical aptness of the typological (generic or conventional) aspects of Hirsch's approach to authorial intention, see Brian G. Caraher, "E. D. Hirsch, Jr.," in *Modern American Critics since 1955, Dictionary of Literary Biography*, Volume 67, ed. Gregory S. Jay (Detroit, Mich.: Bruccoli Clark Layman/Gale Research, 1988), pp. 151–61.

14. Charles Altieri, "The Hermeneutics of Literary Indeterminacy: A Dissent from the New Orthodoxy," *New Literary History* 10 (1978): 92.

Arthur Efron both object to Hirsch's slighting of the experience of reading "A slumber." Rosenblatt indicates just "how far removed Hirsch's typological defense of Bateson's interpretation is from any actual experienced meaning":

> The impact of the exact words of the total text has been overshadowed, thrust aside, in the preoccupation with extrinsic information about the author. Arriving at an interpretation thus becomes an exercise in the logic of evidence. The essentiality of both reader and text is ignored.[15]

In a much earlier critique of Hirsch's book, Arthur Efron presents the evidence of his own reading of "A slumber" to contest the probability of F. W. Bateson's pantheistic interpretation of the lyric:

> No talk about "probability" can alter the fact that each poem is a new utterance, and that as a new utterance it can only be assimilated into the old framework if there is evidence for doing so. Why would we analyze it as a separate entity at all were this not the case?[16]

Efron finds no evidence for Bateson's "pantheistic magnificence" in reading the poem, "and the critic who finds a celebration of pantheism in this poem simply cannot demonstrate that his hypothesis arose from an encounter with the parts [of the whole work]; all he can show is that he reads other Wordsworth poems into this one."[17] All three critics, with varying emphases and foci of contention, challenge Hirsch's notion of "the most probable context" and the logic of interpretive validation that goes with it. The context of "A slumber" is intimately connected with its "performance" (Altieri), "impact" (Rosenblatt), or "utterance" (Efron). The context of the poem arises in, comes with, the enactment of the poem, the activity of reading it. In addition, a hypothesis about the poem's

15. Louise Rosenblatt, *The Reader, the Text, the Poem* (Carbondale: Southern Illinois University Press, 1978), p. 117. Rosenblatt's full discussion of Hirsch can be found on pp. 115–18. The theory involved in Rosenblatt's book will be discussed in Part Two.

16. Arthur Efron, "Logic, Hermeneutic, and Literary Context," *Genre* 1 (1968): 222.

17. Ibid., p. 222.

meaning is grounded in what happens between reader and work. The evidence of the particular literary interaction is what will advance and verify the meaning (or meanings) of the poem.

Wordsworth himself concurs in this approach to the meaning and context of a poem in his well-known letter to Lady Beaumont of May 21, 1807. At great length, Wordsworth discusses the general reading public and various classes of readers, the special demands and difficulties of his poetic voice, and particular readers and the reading of his poems. The occasion of the letter and of Wordsworth's expression of principles is the troubled reception of his 1807 *Poems* and the inability of reviewers to read his poems and read them attentively. Wordsworth counsels his friend and reader:

> be assured that the decision of these persons has nothing to do with the Question; they are altogether incompetent judges. These people in the senseless hurry of their idle lives do not *read* books, they merely snatch a glance at them that they may talk about them. [18] (Wordsworth's italics)

Well over a third of the letter, however, yields an attentive reading by Wordsworth of one of his own sonnets, "With ships the sea was sprinkled far and nigh," from the 1807 *Poems*. Lady Beaumont had transcribed in an earlier letter to Wordsworth the response of a Mrs. Fermor, a mutual friend, to this poem. Wordsworth takes "the greatest pleasure" in this fact but feels that only a full description and explanation of the sonnet can elicit all that is in its "mere 14 lines" (*MY*, pp. 147, 149).

To begin his reading Wordsworth formulates "a general principle" that is operative in all his verse:

> There is scarcely one of my Poems which does not aim to direct the attention to some moral sentiment, or to some general principle, or law of thought, or of our intellectual constitution. (*MY*, p. 148)

With this principle made explicit and secured, Wordsworth directs Lady Beaumont to "take the case before us":

___

18. *The Letters of William and Dorothy Wordsworth, The Middle Years*, Part I (1806–1811), ed. Ernest de Selincourt, 2d rev. ed. Mary Moorman (Oxford: Clarendon Press, 1969), p. 150 (hereinafter cited as *MY*).

I am represented in the Sonnet as casting my eyes over the sea, sprinkled with a multitude of Ships, like the heavens with stars, my mind may be supposed to float up and down among them in a kind of dreamy indifference with respect to this one or that one, only in a pleasurable state of feeling with respect to the whole prospect. "Joyously it showed." (MY, p. 148)

Thus Wordsworth enacts the first two lines of the sonnet, and it should be clear that these words are not mere paraphrase. He is describing his stance as *observer* in and *also as author and as reader* of these lines. Wordsworth, at first, specifies his representation of himself as an observer of a scene; he is both cognizer (the "I" of the poem) and recognizer (author) of the prospect that stands before, and also includes, the "I" of the poem. However, it is neither the role of author nor of observer that is so predominant in the enactment of the first two lines of the sonnet above but Wordsworth's presentation of himself as a reader of his own movements as author and observer. We have the rare event of an author tracing out the activity of reading while describing himself in his capacity as originator of what he is reading. Reader and writer, for once, and quite intriguingly, coincide. When Wordsworth says "my mind may be supposed to float up and down," this supposal is phrased as a reader, and not as an author, would phrase it. Such a supposal is one that would occur to someone attempting to understand the passage and the situation of the observer in it. It is a reader, of course, who attempts to do precisely this. The phrases "a kind of dreamy indifference" and "a pleasurable state of feeling" express effects that a reader is to feel if the supposal concerning the "I's" mind is to achieve depth and vivacity. These effects, it must be said, are also the particulars of a mood of Wordsworth's own mind; but, again, Wordsworth in the passage above is foregrounding his role and activity as reader and not as writer. He describes his experience of reading what he has previously written. His "Joyously it showed" are the written words of the poem; but his apposite quotation of them above shows how he as a reader recognizes both the vivacity ("pleasurable") and the expansiveness ("whole prospect") of what they express—namely, a particular "state of feeling."

Wordsworth's reading of his own poem proceeds line by line in such manner until the final verse, where Wordsworth invites "the Reader . . . to rest his mind as mine is resting" (MY, p. 149). Again there is the doubleness of Wordsworth's activity as author-observer and as reader, but the implication is clear that the activity of reading a poem—in all its particularities and in its full course from beginning to end—is the procedure Wordsworth recognizes as the way to understand his poems. He does not render paradoxical the situation of a writer posing in and enacting the role of reader. The possibility of this situation, a possibility fully actualized in the reading of the sonnet, exists for all of Wordsworth's poems. The activity of writing for Wordsworth includes the determination of certain directions and limits for the activity of reading, just as Wordsworth the observer in and author of "With ships the sea was sprinkled far and nigh" includes certain directions and limits to which Wordsworth the reader of the same sonnet must pay full attention. These directions and limits also obtain for other readers of the sonnet, such as Lady Beaumont, Mrs. Fermor, or myself; Wordsworth, after all, presents himself in the letter as only one of his poem's readers.[19] Wordsworth can then be understood as encouraging the view that the context of any one of his poems arises in the activity of reading it and that the poem's meaning is grounded in the particularities of the interaction of reader and work. In the letter to Lady Beaumont, he instructs one of his readers in the pragmatics of just this sort of attention.[20]

19. It can be said that there is really no distinct and categorical difference between Wordsworth's activity of reading "With ships the sea was sprinkled far and nigh" and any other attentive reader's activity. Wordsworth, however, could be said to recall an image or memory in connection with his reading, while the reading performed by someone else involves learning to see or imagine some comparable scene or prospect. This situation does not collapse differences between writer and reader but allows for the activity of reading, *rather than anything else*, to be the frontier of contact, of meeting, of sharing, between the two roles.

In connection with this remark, see Frances Ferguson, *Wordsworth: Language as Counter-Spirit* (New Haven, Conn.: Yale University Press, 1977), especially pp. xiv–xv. In discussing "Poems of the Imagination," Ferguson notes that "Wordsworth is able to imagine his own writing as something to be read, by himself as well as by his audience" (p. xv).

20. The most often quoted passage from Wordsworth's letter to Lady Beaumont is a generalization and a justification of this point: ". . . every great and original writer, in proportion as he is great or original, must himself create the taste by which he is to be relished; he must teach the art by which he is to be seen" (*MY*, p. 150). Don H. Bialostosky has made a persuasive case for the way in which readers and critics of Wordsworth's poetry, especially the poems of *Lyrical Ballads*, can follow through upon the implications of this remark by Wordsworth. In *Making Tales: The Poetics of Wordsworth's Narrative Experiments* (Chicago: University of Chicago Press, 1984), Bialostosky strives to demonstrate the ways in which the reader of Wordsworth "must exert upon the poem . . . 'a co-operating *power*,' 'a corresponding energy' to those powers the poet has exercised in the production of it" (p. 6). Bialostosky's delineation of the poetics of Wordsworth's early experimental work also constitutes the tracing of a persuasive new art of taste whereby such poems can be read for and as the astounding experiments they yield.

Literary work, reader, and the activity of reading—that is, the temporal interaction of work and reader—these three literary terms that were briefly analyzed earlier as three of the four definitive features of having a literary experience occur again in discussing Wordsworth's letter on reading.[21] The fourth feature appears as well. The mood of the mind as it pleasurably attends to the movements of ships at sea, the delight in the multitude of possible local objects of attention as they are present in one capacious act of attention, is the quality or character developed and made distinct within and through the temporal interaction of the poem "With ships the sea was sprinkled far and nigh" and its reader.[22] And this reader may be Wordsworth, as it is in this instance, or someone else, as Wordsworth's letter to Lady Beaumont claims can be the case. Furthermore, Wordsworth speaks directly to this fourth feature of a literary experience through his statement of "a general principle" operative in all his poems. Indeed, he positions this statement, quoted above, at the beginning of his reading of the sonnet. His reading, in large measure, constitutes a demonstration of the way this principle operates in the poem. Wordsworth states that any one of his poems "aim[s] to direct the attention" to something of import; that is, the temporal interaction of a specific poem and an attentive reader involves the guiding or directing of the reader's attention to some recognition. The three features of work, reader, and their temporal interaction are all implied in this construction. However, what the poem directs the reader's attention toward is here made quite explicit: "some moral sentiment" or "some general principle, or law of thought, or of our intellectual constitution." "With ships the sea was sprinkled" directs attention to the latter, for the mental mood produced in a capacious act of attention can be seen as a "law of thought"—or, more specifically, as a "law" of "our intellectual constitution." The sonnet, then, engages a reader and directs his or her attention to a particular mood of the mind or

21. See the final two paragraphs of Chapter 1.
22. This ship is referred to as "She" no less than four times, and the "I" of the sonnet "pursue[s] her with a Lover's look." "She" passes north on her journey and "will brook / No tarrying." Her land-bound, distant "lover" himself passes no judgment of impatience or coldheartedness upon her. He makes only one calm inference from her own lusty behavior: "where She comes the winds must stir." The ship moves insistently and vitally in accord with the laws and properties of the winds and currents, just as his own loving and feelingful attention to her particular movements proceeds from the nature of his capacious act of attention. See *PW*, III, p. 18.

the intellect that can and does arise in accord with the laws and properties of the mind in general.[23]

Wordsworth's remarks on the reading of his poems, moreover, corroborate the critical position taken in faulting Richard Matlack's and E. D. Hirsch's critical procedures. The immediate context and meaning of a poem cannot be construed apart from the actual reading of it. That is to say, a critic cannot reach a particular, determinate interpretation through the construction of a biographical and psychological context external to the context or contexts that the poem and its reader develop in the course of their temporal interaction.

The interpretation of "A slumber" turns out to be a far more complicated task than that of "With ships the sea was sprinkled far and nigh." This interpretive complexity, however, stems directly from the fact that three ways of reading the poem and their corresponding contexts must be accommodated. "With ships the sea was sprinkled" does not serve to complicate the ways it can be read, nor does it confuse the identities and relationships of its speaker and the objects of his perception and feeling. The activity of reading "A slumber" has indeed already witnessed these complications. As a consequence, no single determinate interpretation can be argued for on the basis of the evidential particulars of reading. The two contexts and lines of interpretation of "A slumber" developed through the two ways of construing the relationship of "she" and "my spirit" are both possible, plausible, and coherent. However, precisely because they are both plausible and coherent and yet are so seemingly improbable in conjunction with one another, we can be guided into a discovery of that third way of reading and its terrifying and thoroughly—to use David Ferry's word—"unsentimental" context, the Romantic death fantasy. The activity of reading "A slumber did my spirit seal" offers a demanding probe into a problematic of confused perceptions, feelings, and identities.

---

23. Compare with Oscar James Campbell's idealist formulation of basically the same kind of activity:

> To transform the mental event from philosophical belief into esthetic experience, Wordsworth realized that his poetry must awaken some dominant emotion that would flood sensation, metaphysical affirmation, and spiritual aspiration with radiance. At the moment when the chosen feeling thus illuminates one's entire being, then poetry performs its essential function.

See Campbell, "Wordsworth's Conception of the Esthetic Experience," in *Wordsworth and Coleridge*, ed. E. L. Griggs (New York: Russell & Russell, 1962; orig. pub. 1939), p. 46.

Moreover, the struggle toward interpretive clarity is itself an experience, discovery, and analysis of the confusion. We can and, I would argue, should accept the complexity of context and meaning of "A slumber" as the way to a complex unraveling. We are not offered ambiguity, indeterminacy, or a textually unconstrained proliferation of meanings as M. H. Abrams fears, but a striking exercise in understanding.

6

The Problematic of "A slumber" and the Fate of Critical Reading

I have chosen the word "problematic" and have used it in the previous chapter in order to name the complex situation that reading such a poem as "A slumber" presents. Elsewhere I have proposed a general definition: "a 'problematic' is not a problem to be solved but a situation whose nature is problem-generating and is to be apprehended as such."[1] Reading "A slumber" is not like solving a mechanical-engineering problem—a situation where the symbols involved are purely instrumental, the parameters firmly established, and a definite goal sited on the horizon. The activity of reading Wordsworth's lyric generates a series of interconnected problems for a reader: a confusion in the reference of "she," a conflict of contexts in which to situate an interpretation, a confusion in the identity of the dead girl or woman, and an ambivalence in the character of the speaker. The progress of an interpretation of "A slumber" discovers, unravels, and clarifies each of these problems in turn. The entire network of problems, however, maintains its intimate interconnections; they arose together in the activity of reading and in the struggle toward clarity. The term "problematic," then, can be used to express the specific, integrated, temporal situation of reading and interpreting such a literary work as "A slumber."

1. Brian Caraher, "The Problematic of Body and Language in Sylvia Plath's 'Tulips,'" *Paunch* 42/43 (1975): 88. See also my essay "Construing the Knowledge Situation: Stephen Pepper and a Deweyan Approach to Literary Experience and Inquiry," *Journal of Mind and Behavior* 3 (1982): 385–89.

Put briefly, the problematic of "A slumber" is the question of how we are to understand the relation of an insensitive and solipsistic "spirit" and an insubstantial and dehumanized "she" through the widening problems and vicissitudes of their poetic copresence. This way of phrasing the poem's problematic embraces the various problems generated in reading, whether we are minutely concerned with the proper ascription of the antecedent of "she" or imaginatively fleshing out the ambivalent character of the speaker or narrator. In an unverbalized, in an unclarified, in a basically *unthought* way the problematic centers and guides reading and rereading of "A slumber." The full act of interpretation involves thinking through the evidences of our reading to discover (or to recover) the guiding problematic. Interpretation verbalizes and clarifies reading. Or, more precisely, an act of interpretation verbalizes and clarifies a particular instance of reading by discovering the specific problematic generating the problems that comprise the moments and movements of our reading.[2]

A major benefit of locating, determining, and justifying the problematic of "A slumber" is its possible pedagogical and heuristic value in addressing interpretations of the poem predicated on well-developed and different models of reading. Critical interpretations based on other sets of assumptions governing reading can be questioned in order to determine the shape and even the contortions the problematic of "A slumber" may be forced to undergo. As I hope to show, the assumptions and rhetoric of an interpretation, regardless of the sophisticated model of critical reading it may claim to depend upon, reveal the traces of a problematic of reading that the critic is ignoring or discarding or combating in order to promote his or her interpretation and its theoretical implications. As Cleanth Brooks remarked at the conclusion of his own, now famous interpretation of Wordsworth's poem:

> What is likely to cause trouble here is the intrusion of a special theory of composition. It is fairly represented as an intrusion since a theory as to how a poem is written is being allowed to dictate to us how the poem is to be read. There is no harm in thinking of Wordsworth's poem as simple and spontaneous unless these terms deny complexities that actually exist in the poem, and unless they justify us in reading the poem with only half our minds. A slumber

---

2. The term "problematic," as well as its important use in the work of John Dewey, will be discussed in the second part of this book.

ought not to seal the *reader's* spirit as he reads this poem, or any other poem.[3] (Brooks's italics)

If these remarks that seal Brooks's interpretation of the lyric can be taken in the right spirit, then his critical work on "A slumber" serves neither to advance merely a particular meaning for the poem nor strictly a general theory of ironical structure in modern English poetry. He calls attention, if only so briefly, to the fact that the rhetoric and assumptions of our theories of poetic composition tend to structure the terms and particulars of how we say we read poems. We must be alert to how we read, to the variety and complexity of the evidences of our specific readings. My notion of particular problematics of reading can serve to address critically and to clarify conceptually the theoretical assumptions that *dictate*—to borrow Brooks's word—particular interpretations. However, it can also draw attention to how we disclose and handle the evidence of our reading, especially troubling or confusing evidence that fully attentive readers often will allow to question and to help rethink their theoretical assumptions and already established habits of reading.

Norman N. Holland, in a fascinating and suggestive article, "Literary Interpretation and Three Phases of Psychoanalysis," presents three separate interpretations of "A slumber" as types of analysis representative of three distinct phases or stages in the development of psychoanalytic literary criticism.[4] Holland contends that the third phase of psychoanalytic literary criticism is an important advance upon the prior two. The juxtaposition and comparison of the three interpretations of "A slumber" is supposed to bear out this contention. The major failing of the two earlier phases involves a problem also shared by "formalist" or "objective" kinds of criticism: their "essential inhumanity."

> When critics are being "objective," they set the literary work in marmoreal isolation, apart from other kinds of experience; and they cast themselves as dispassionate observers (like scientists or computers) of a process located outside the self and in the text. The more intricate the process, the better the critic can perform. . . .
> I have to admit that this externalizing and complicating was for me—and perhaps for many others—reassuring. I did not have to

3. Cleanth Brooks, "Irony as a Principle of Structure," p. 737.
4. See *Critical Inquiry* 3 (1976): 221–33.

feel I was putting myself on the line—my real self—only my mind. I had, so to speak, no human fears. [5]

Holland here images the critic very subtly and suggestively as the speaker, the "spirit" or "I," of "A slumber." The formalist or objective critic is as sealed, insensitive, and slumbrous before experience, literary or otherwise, as Wordsworth's speaker seems to be before the other (the "she"). Such a critic becomes an ironic transformation of the ideal of the "dispassionate" observer. To admit no experience, no contact, to have "no human fears" in the task of interpretation smacks of the same "essential inhumanity" that marks the character of the "I" of Wordsworth's poem.

Holland's subtle insight actually carries throughout and emerges from his third way of interpreting "A slumber." Holland, in the unavoidable role of critic or interpreter, identifies with Wordsworth's speaker:

> I find in the first stanza a double denial: by giving up human touch and feeling and warmth, I escape human fear and the loss earthly time causes. Sneakily, for my own emotional well-being, I dehumanize another person. Yet, I want to say, *I* don't do this—the "I" of the poem does. Why should *I* feel guilty? Partly, I think, because I *do* tend to dehumanize people through systems and theories. Partly, I think, because I feel punished by the second stanza.
>
> The first stanza was mild. Everything was past. A simple "slumber" rid me of fears. To some extent, I imagine those reassurances of the first stanza continuing in the second, but I feel they have been exaggerated to an extreme and painfully mortal form. "She" is not just protected from the touch of years; she is completely obliterated:
>
> > No motion has she now, no force;
> > She neither hears nor sees.
>
> . . . I feel that my attempts at denial in the first stanza have been turned round into a monstrous universal indifference by the second. And throughout I feel, if I am being punished this way—retaliated upon—why then I must have been guilty of something. . . . As a theorist of personality, I have been guilty of

5. Holland, "Literary Interpretation and Three Phases of Psychoanalysis," p. 224.

just such dehumanizings as those the "I" of the poem finds in himself. . . .⁶

By identifying with the speaker, Holland allows his experience of the poem to be guided by the character of the narrator; it is this characterological aspect of the poem that interests him most. Holland questions his identification with the "I" of the poem at one point; he is somewhat ambivalent, perhaps wary of the implications of such an identification. The speaker is a denier of human feelings and the conditions of human temporality; he dehumanizes another person. Holland recognizes this situation and experiences its concomitant emotions of deceptive stealth ("sneakily") and guilt. Guilt wins out, though, by the second stanza, where "a monstrous universal indifference" and the feelings of retaliation and punishment overwhelm the denier and dehumanizer who sees that other person "completely obliterated." The inhumane ruthlessness of the solipsistic character of the speaker in my interpretation of "A slumber" reappears in Holland's explanation. He, too, senses a deceptive and monstrous dimension of the character of Wordsworth's narrator. Yet the feelings of retaliation and punishment for some guilty act imply that Holland does not and will not go all the way in identifying with the ruthless solipsism of the "I." One should have "human fears," and the complete obliteration of another person is too monstrous to allow. The recognition of some act of obliteration and the punishing guilt felt over it are strikingly similar to the speaker's death fantasy and the reader's terrifying apprehension of it in my interpretation of the lyric. Holland does not develop the Romantic death fantasy as the general context of the poem, but the rhetoric of his interpretation—especially concerning the character of the speaker—reveals that this context lies nascent.

Since I did not on the whole identify with the speaker in my moments of reading or in my full interpretation of "A slumber," I did not internalize a sense of guilt. As a reader of his character, my apprehension of the monstrous possibility of his solipsism was felt and developed as a sudden glimpse into the mind and motives of someone with whom I resist identifying. Yet to some degree I am tempted to identify because initially I want to read the poem as a vicarious death fantasy—the speaker's and my own—until the particulars of my reading deny me the offered fantasy.

6. Ibid., pp. 222–23.

However, Holland does happen to identify with the speaker in his interpretation. As a consequence, the resistance to and abhorrence of the speaker's character come to be felt personally as the sudden conversion of human denial into "monstrous universal indifference" and a sense of being "retaliated upon" for a guilty act. The character of the speaker and his "essential inhumanity" are shared recognitions in both Holland's and my own interpretations. The problematic of "A slumber" is indeed operative in the particular moments and movements of Holland's reading and interpretation. However, some of the differences that obtain between his and my interpretations involve quite unavoidable and expectable differences in attention, emotional interest, and sensibility. These differences might seem to construct considerable obstacles to a critical consensus; but I think it best to regard them as possible, though not equally plausible, divagations on a single problematic. Fundamentally, both interpretations share a similar sense of how crucial it is to understand the relation of a particular insensitive and solipsistic "I" to an insubstantial and dehumanized "she." I situate this crux in an elaborate linguistic play experienced between "my spirit" and "she," and Holland locates it in the travails of his emotional identification with the speaker. However, the shared problematic, once recognized, allows a sorting and adjudication of real differences. Thus the road to understanding the differences that occur in divergent interpretations begins with locating the guiding problematic that both interpretations share but may not equally or fully develop.

Holland's interpretation also shares another similarity with mine—namely, an awareness of how important the activity of the reader is to an interpretation of the poem. This awareness constitutes one of the major points of Holland's essay and, purportedly, the third phase of psychoanalytic literary criticism that the essay promotes. However, he unnecessarily psychologizes the role of the reader and the activity of reading.[7] Holland's reading of "A slumber," enacted before his "identity" theory of personality is brought to bear upon it, issues in a telling comment on his overall psychologizing project: "As a theorist of personality, I have been guilty of just such dehumanizings as those the "I" of the poem finds in himself." Holland's subsequent comments on his own "identity theme" might seek to defuse the powerful charge laid bare in these words, but I think it offers an appropriate warning.[8] Dehumanization is the very real risk all around.

---

7. See Chapter 8, pp. 139–48.
8. Holland, "Literary Interpretation and Three Phases of Psychoanalysis," pp. 229–33.

Wordsworth's speaker insubstantializes and fantasizes the death of "she"; his failure to interact humanely with her yields a peculiar case of murder, as it were. The personality theorist, even though usefully redirecting critical attention upon the reader and reading, may dehumanize himself or herself and other readers by channeling all the complexities of readerly and interpretive attention into a single "theme." The reader, the self, is obviously being "textualized." Moreover, the text itself suffers a peculiar fate. It appears insubstantialized and detextualized: a textual murder, one could say.

Paul de Man offers another curious sort of textual murder in his interpretation of "A slumber." He uses the lyric as a "demonstration" of the differences between "the temporal structure of allegory and of irony."[9] De Man asserts at the outset that Wordsworth's poem "clearly is not ironic, either in its tonality or in its meaning," yet the far greater part of his interpretation consists in the effort to undermine the insistence of the poem's third and fourth lines in being ironic. Abundant traces of de Man's own activity of reading the poem surface in the rhetoric of his critical interpretation, and these traces reinforce a temporal structure of reading that de Man is at pains to supplant with an allegorical structure. He would like to allegorize the lyric as a passage into "a stance of wisdom," with each stanza as an isolated yet successive stage of consciousness. The first stanza would belong to a mystified "past," the second to a demystified "now."[10] Yet the simpleness of this allegory of past "errors" and present "wisdom" and its successive temporal structure, one stanza discontinuous with yet following upon the other, can be unsettled by recovering some move-ments of de Man's activity of reading still present in the language of his interpretation.

De Man himself admits: "It could be said that, read within the

---

Holland contends that "[a]ll my acts, perceptions, and relationships are functions of my identity, including my relation to this lyric, for that is what identity is: my thematic sameness plus my variations on it" (p. 231). Moreover, he states: "My identity theme [has] to do with preserving a sense of the self and securing self-esteem by gaining power over relations between things, in particular, mastering them by knowing or seeing them from outside rather than being actually in the relationship" (p. 233).

9. Paul de Man, "The Rhetoric of Temporality," p. 204. All additional quotations from de Man in this and the following three paragraphs of the text will be drawn from pages 205–6 of his essay.

10. Or a "blindness" (first stanza) and an "insight" (second stanza), to use the terms de Man develops in *Blindness and Insight: Essays in the Rhetoric of Contemporary Criticism* (New York: Oxford University Press, 1971), especially pp. viii–ix, 102–11.

perspective of the entire poem, [the lines "She seemed a thing that could not feel / The touch of earthly years."] are ironic, though they are not ironic in themselves or within the context of the first stanza." A reading of the poem as a complete activity or experience, then, may allow it to manifest the kind of temporal structure that de Man is *not* interested in seeing. The context or "perspective of the entire poem" undermines and perhaps precludes the applicability of an allegorical structure for the lyric. Yet how and why? And why *must* those two lines, in order *not* to be ironic, be read "in themselves or within the context of the first stanza"?

De Man does not say but, instead, immediately *reasserts* that the poem is not ironic. He also claims that

> [t]he stance of the speaker, who exists in the "now," is that of a subject whose insight is no longer in doubt and who is no longer vulnerable to irony. . . . There is no real disjunction of the subject; the poem is written from the point of view of a unified self that fully recognizes a past condition as one of error and stands in a present that, however painful, sees things as they actually are.

The speaker or narrator of the lyric may very well have a unified character or self, but we do not actually see him or hear him expressing the indubiety of his conversion from "error" to "wisdom" in the "now" of the second stanza of "A slumber." The words of this stanza are the speaker's, but they clearly do not show that he "fully recognizes a past condition as one of error."[11] The "now" shows that "she" is dead, and the slumbrous "I" of the past *can now fully recognize this fact.* Only the dead "she" actually appears in the second stanza, and "the identity of the unnamed 'she' is not divulged." Unless "she" is somehow the speaker, de Man is forcing the second stanza to exhibit a self and a wisdom not actually present.

And indeed this is the case. The "stance of the speaker," the "stance of wisdom," that de Man wants to see is a "stance [that] has been made possible by two things: first, the death alluded to is not the death of the speaker but apparently that of someone else; second, the poem is in the third person and uses the feminine gender throughout." These "two things" yield further traces of de Man's activity of reading; they show that

---

11. Paul de Man, like so many critics, may be reading "She dwelt"—especially the final stanza—into the second stanza of "A slumber."

de Man initially must have experienced a confusion in the reference and identity of "she." To support his critical interpretation of the poem, however, de Man must affirm that: (1) it is the death of another, and *not* a vicarious experience of death on the part of the speaker, that the poem alludes to; and (2) the "I" is not to be confused with or seen cloaking itself in the identity of feminine third-person pronouns. But why would and should these "two things" surface? Why must they be said, unless they are what would turn the reading of "A slumber" ironic, in de Man's use of the word? If in the activity of reading the poem a confusion between the speaker's self and the feminine third-person pronouns was experienced, this "irony" would preclude the application of the schematic structure of allegory to the poem. Instead, the temporal structure of one's own reading would lead one to the insight that the speaker in Wordsworth's poem is undergoing a vicarious death fantasy. However, de Man seems to blind himself to the insight offered in the temporal structure of his reading, the temporal interaction of the poem and of himself as reader. Indeed he does not see a way to reconcile the feminine pronouns of the poem to the identity of the speaker. In other words, he does not see a way to probe into and come to terms with the experienced confusion in the reference of "she." Allegory, then, must supplant or suppress irony—the experienced confusion of identities. Interpretation must supplant or suppress the activity of reading. Yet it is de Man's brilliance, in a moment of blindness to his own reading, to offer immediately a true insight into "A slumber":

> If this were truly relevant, the question would remain whether Wordsworth could have written in the same manner about his own death. For the informed reader of Wordsworth the answer to this question is affirmative; Wordsworth is one of the few poets who can write proleptically about their own death and speak, as it were, from beyond their own graves. The "she" in the poem is in fact large enough to encompass Wordsworth as well.

This proleptic prospect of death is indeed "truly relevant" to the reading of "A slumber," as the discussion of Hugh Sykes Davies's interpretation and its implications shows. De Man's insight insists on speaking. Even though he may attempt to blunt its edge by generalizing about Wordsworth, de Man returns to the poem and its pivotal word, "she."

The problematic of "A slumber" can be recovered within de Man's interpretation just as it was for Holland's. Again, the question of how we are to understand the relation of the insensitive speaker and the insubstantial "she" occurs. Unlike Holland, though, de Man actually focuses on only one of the problems generated by the problematic of "A slumber"—namely, the confusion in the reference of "she." Nevertheless, since the problematic has been discovered centering and guiding several movements of de Man's reading and interpretation, the way is open for clarifying and adjudicating the differences between de Man's explanation of "A slumber" and my own. De Man's interpretation, however, can be faulted as inadequate because it does not confront all the problems generated in reading the poem. Moreover, de Man sacrifices crucial evidence of the activity of reading in the interests of an allegorical model of textual temporality. In a way, the reader dehumanizes himself and the temporality of his own activity of reading. It is as if the "now" of one's reading is laid asleep or murdered within the rhetoric of one's own critical interpretation. Another curious slumber or textual murder appears. The body or corpse of the reader, though, quickly turns up, divulging clues to its displaced temporality.

Some ten years after Paul de Man's allegorical reading of "A slumber" J. Hillis Miller performs another such reading of the text that has come to rival the earlier one for notoriety, even though Miller's pattern of reading is closely modeled on de Man's. The later reading, just like its model, issues in a curious textual murder. In "On Edge" Miller selects Wordsworth's poem as a "parable" for the relationship of deconstructive literary reading to logocentric metaphysics.[12] The initial stages of Miller's reading closely mime those of de Man, especially in conceptualizing the relationship between the poem's two stanzas as one of a "temporal allegory" in which the prior state of ignorance is supplanted by "the perpetual 'now' of a universal knowledge of death." Miller then passes on to elaborate what he calls "an obscure sexual drama"—namely, Wordsworth's "reenactment of the death of the mother" by "acting out" a death fantasy of "a surrogate mother, a girl who remains herself both alive and dead, still available in life and yet already taken by Nature." This fantasy, or rather its fulfillment, is impossible; but for Miller this impossibility is precisely the

---

12. J. Hillis Miller, "On Edge: The Crossways of Contemporary Criticism," *Bulletin of the American Academy of Arts* 32 (1979): 12–32. The essay was later reprinted with some additional commentary in *Romanticism and Contemporary Criticism*, ed. Morris Eaves and Michael Fischer (Ithaca, N.Y.: Cornell University Press, 1986), pp. 96–126. All citations from Miller's essay will be from pages 100–109 of the later version.

point. On one level, the terms of the fantasy reveal "a constant slipping of entities across borders into their opposites." For Miller "Lucy" seems "both alive and dead." Moreover, "the poet can be both the dead-alive girl and at the same time the perpetually wakeful survivor"; his knowledge of death also involves a loss of selfhood and becoming a "thing." On yet another level, Miller reads this perpetual slippage as emblematic of a perpetual parable, "a constantly repeated occidental drama of the lost sun." He associates the "she" of the poem with the "Lucy" of "She dwelt" and "Strange fits" and reads her proper name as meaning "light, the father sun as logos, as head power and fount of meaning." For Miller, then, "A slumber" holds the repeated parable or allegory of deconstruction: The loss of "Lucy" is the loss of the sun, the logocentric light of meaning. Wordsworth's poem perpetually wavers between the memory of light and life-giving power, on the one hand, and the knowledge of loss and death, on the other.[13]

Miller thus wishes to read the allegory of deconstruction's decentering of the vital power and light of logocentricism into the two counterposed stanzas of Wordsworth's lyric. The very terms of his desired interpretation nevertheless disclose an ambivalence, if not confusion, in the reference of "she." The death fantasy Miller speaks of seems localized one moment in the figure of a woman and then later in the poet or speaker. The speaker also seems forced to play two different roles—"the dead-alive girl and at the same time the perpetually wakeful survivor." The ambivalence of the speaker's character, as well as the experience of referential confusion—key moments in my articulation of the problematic of "A slumber"—are recuperable in the language of Miller's interpretation. Miller, though, seeks to allegorize the context of a death fantasy and the confused identities of the speaker and his "Lucy" in order to write a parable

---

13. Richard Posner has taken Miller's reading to task for the way in which it "disintegrates" the poem. See Richard A. Posner, "Interpreting Law, Interpreting Literature (I)," *Raritan* 7 (Spring 1988): 24–25. However, M. H. Abrams has mounted the most devastating appraisal of Miller's reading. In "Construing and Deconstructing," pp. 143–54, Abrams fully engages the overall patterns of Miller's interpretations. He shows the close dependency of Miller's deconstructive approach upon Paul de Man's earlier reading (pp. 146–47), and he itemizes at length the fairly standard interpretive moves that Miller makes before commencing his "obscure sexual drama" (pp. 143–46). Abrams's primary point of attack upon Miller's deconstructive reading of "A slumber" involves demonstrating the suspicious, if not illicit, forms of unconstrained intertextuality that the latter's reading manifests. For instance, the references and associations connected with the "I," the "she," and even the word "thing" appear without limit and without reasonable warrant (pp. 149–54). See also page 66 above.

regarding the loss of a central and centering light. His reading strives to deflect attention from the character of the speaker and the consequences of his perceived ambivalence and death fantasy. Miller, however, just like Paul de Man before him, momentarily discloses the terms of a strange textual murder. As Miller must concede, "knowledge is not guiltless. The poet has himself somehow caused Lucy's death by thinking about it." The "I" of the poem has "turn[ed] the other into [himself] and therefore [is] left only with a corpse, an empty sign." The speaker of the poem has dreamed the death of the lovely other, a figure of his own fantasy and solipsistic temperament. This death fantasy cuts across the grain of the one Miller initially propounds, and it reveals—if only momentarily—the solipsist and fantast at deadly textual play.

Like Holland, de Man, and Miller, Geoffrey H. Hartman has occasion to call forth "A slumber" as a crucial example illustrating the fate of critical reading. He turns to "A slumber" and the "Lucy" poems at strategic points in the texts of *Wordsworth's Poetry, 1787–1814* (1964) and *Beyond Formalism* (1970). Hartman recognizes that the relation of "spirit" and "she" is the real crux of "A slumber," yet his interpretations of the lyric are elegant circumscriptions and avoidances of the full implications of this recognition. For one thing, Hartman assumes "she" to be the "Lucy" of the other so-called "Lucy" poems in the 1800 *Lyrical Ballads*. Though he is primarily interested in discussing "A slumber," he alludes to the other lyrics to support points not apparent in that poem. As a result, Hartman's discussion of the "spirit" and "she" relation is cast in the more general and contextually inaccurate terms of "the poet" and "Lucy." Yet, what is more important, "she" or "Lucy" is characterized as a very ambivalent entity:

> Lucy is a boundary being, nature sprite and human, yet not quite either. . . . [She] is an intermediate modality of consciousness rather than an intermediate being. She is seen entirely from within the poet, so that this modality may be the poet's own, and Lucy the "inner   maiden."[14]

---

14. G. H. Hartman, *Wordsworth's Poetry*, p. 158. The full discussion occurs on pages 157–62. In "Wordsworth, Inscriptions, and Romantic Nature Poetry," *Beyond Formalism*, p. 226, Hartman expresses uncertainty over whether or not the "Lucy" poems can actually be read as a group: "I am not sure that all of the lyrics originated in the same impulse, and the cycle may have a life of its own which took over from Wordsworth's intentions." See my arguments in Chapters 2 and 3 and note 12, p. 31, and note 3, p. 41.

In "Evening Star and Evening Land," *The Fate of Reading* (Chicago: University of Chicago

So "Lucy" is something like, but not really, a human being. She seems to be a modality of "the poet's own" consciousness, a maiden of his own fancy and imagination. However, Hartman adds further to her character: "Except for this inwardness she belongs to the category of spirits who must still become human, and the poet describes her as dying at a point at which she would have been humanized."[15] This "inner maiden," then, somehow has the capacity for becoming human; she is a protohuman spirit who can still circumvent her location with the "inwardness" of someone else and nearly become "humanized." The closest she comes to humanization, though, is strangely and ironically an act far more characteristic of humans than of spirits—dying. Hartman's characterization of "she" apparently contains a contradiction. Even his summary phrasing of the predicament of the poem—"the most haunting of Wordsworth's elisions of the human"—cannot conceal this contradiction. "Lucy's" humanity, her personhood, is elided or omitted; but this happens in two contradictory ways. On the one hand, she is a "modality" of someone else's consciousness—an "inner maiden" without any human existence of her own. On the other hand, though, she is imagined as a "spirit" or being with the capacity of becoming human; and this capacity actually contradicts her previous status of "inwardness." She is a "boundary being" because she is forced to balance delicately two contradictory poles of existence: a fantasized or fictive maiden wholly possessed within another's consciousness and a separate but somehow strangely spiritualized or etherealized being not possessed by another. This separateness is emphasized when Hartman turns to discuss the impact of "Lucy's" death on "the consciousness of the survivor": The loss is deeply felt by someone awakened from "soft delusion" by the death of another.[16]

Press, 1975), pp. 158–63, Hartman ignores his own uncertainty and interprets "Strange fits," "She dwelt," and "A slumber" as lyric transformations of the evening-star theme, popularized and best represented by Akenside and Bion. I believe Hartman here reads an unsupportable thematics into "A slumber," as well as into "Strange fits."

15. G. H. Hartman, *Wordsworth's Poetry*, p. 158.

16. Ibid., p. 160. In a later reading of "A slumber" Hartman elaborates upon much the same kind of contradictory status for "Lucy" as in his earlier interpretations. In "The Interpreter's Freud," from his collection *Easy Pieces* (New York: Columbia University Press, 1985), especially pp. 145–54, Hartman employs a reading of Sigmund Freud's *Interpretation of Dreams* in order to speculate upon Wordsworth's "delusive daydream" in "A slumber did my spirit seal." Hartman contends that Wordsworth's "trance is linked to an over-idealization of the loved person." However, the recognition of the loved one's death provides no shock or rupture because of "an uncanny *displacement*": "in the initial stanza, the poet is sealed in slumber; in the second that

Perhaps the contradiction in Hartman's characterization of "she" originates in the need to handle an experienced confusion in the reference of the feminine pronouns of the lyric. Indeed, this seems to be the case:

> All Wordsworth can do is to emancipate the direction of the reference. . . . We cannot tell whether the poet is reacting to an imaginary thought or to an actual death, or which of the two came first.[17]

These remarks are from a subsequent discussion of Wordsworth's lyric style in "A slumber" and "She dwelt" in which Hartman contends that the "simple" or "natural style" of these two lyrics amounts to a parody and a purification of the highly mannered and pointed elegiac lyricism of the eighteenth century. Wordsworth's lyric style allows for a breaking of pointed and witty style and a loosening of reference.[18] Hartman beautifully locates and justifies Wordsworth's stylistic contrivance within a literary history of lyric style, but he does so without recognizing the full implications of the particular stylistic and grammatical contrivance found in "A slumber." However, what are the clear implications of a stylistic situation in which "[w]e cannot tell whether the poet is reacting to an imaginary thought or to an actual death, or which of the two came first"? Manifestly, there is a confusion in the reference of "she": The poet could

---

slumber has passed over, as if intensified, to the girl." Hartman also calls this displacement a rhetorical transference, or "an error of the imagination," but it does not reveal a death wish or a death fantasy so much as "an earthly euphemism." Wordsworth's poetic language resists psychoanalysis of its over-idealization and delusion because, by its very nature, it exposes the "sleep-walking" or daydreaming of ordinary speech or undemystified language. Wordsworth's poetic language, that is to say, exhibits not the cause but merely the occasion of a death-fantasy, of a dream state that troubles the properties of ordinary speech. Wordsworth's euphemistic power—displacing, for instance, "the word *grave* by an image of *gravitation* ("Rolled round in earth's diurnal course")"—mourns or elegizes in a "chastely fashioned inscription." Hartman strives, then, to displace the delusive daydream of a death fantasy away from the role of the speaker and onto the nature of ordinary discourse. Wordsworth euphemizes and eulogizes in his poetic discourse a haunting being, "a nature spirit in human form." His "epitaph does not record a disenchantment. The mythic girl dies, but that word seems to wrong her. Her star-like quality is maintained despite her death." In other words, the dead girl again appears as a strange "boundary being," at once the occasion for over-idealization and delusive daydreaming but also the chaste and liminal shape of a "eudemon," a benevolent spirit of nature who prompts *grave* thoughts, "thoughts that do often lie too deep for tears." This "Lucy" again bears two contradictory poles of existence, while the troublesome character of the speaker becomes elided.

17. G. H. Hartman, "Beyond Formalism," p. 50.
18. Ibid., pp. 43–51.

be "reacting to an imaginary thought" of the death of an "inner maiden" or he could be reacting to the death of a real woman. Furthermore, since we cannot tell "which of the two" references "came first," the implication is that they arose together or issued from the same circumstances. It seems quite possible, then, to recover traces of an experience of referential confusion in Hartman's activity of reading "A slumber." The evidence survives in his contradictory characterization of "Lucy," as well as in the dual reference that he recognizes as inescapably a factor in the lyric style of the poem. Just as in the cases of Holland, de Man, and Miller, evidence or traces of Hartman's activity of reading are discoverable within the procedures and rhetoric of his critical interpretation.

Again, the problematic of "A slumber" developed above appears central to a fourth major critical interpretation of the poem. As in de Man's and Miller's readings, the problem of a referential confusion eventually surfaces in Hartman's commentaries. The presence of this one problem indicates that the whole problematic could be brought to bear on Hartman's explanation, and the differences between my interpretation and his could be clarified and adjudicated accordingly. Suffice it to say here, though, that Hartman's interpretations of "A slumber" in *Wordsworth's Poetry* and *Beyond Formalism* do not confront all of the interlinked problems encompassed in my articulation of the problematic of "A slumber."

The character of the speaker, for instance, is not fully enough explored. Hartman calls him "the poet" but then does not draw out any connections between the "I" of the poem and Wordsworth himself.[19] The attempt at characterization is most fully directed at the "she" of the poem. However, it can be seen that the contradictory characterization of "she" or "Lucy" has a great deal to do with the transference or projection of aspects of the speaker's character upon her. His insensitivity and proclivity to solipsism insubstantialize, disembody, and dehumanize her. She is an "inner

19. Presumably, each interpretation, including that of "A slumber," in *Wordsworth's Poetry* is another moment in "the drama of consciousness and maturation" (p. xxiii) that Hartman delineates. I contend that "A slumber" can indeed be placed within such a drama, but it would be an unfortunate mistake to equate the speaker with "the poet." See Chapter 4.

In "The Interpreter's Freud," pp. 151–52, Hartman does, however, characterize the connection between the "I" of the poem and Wordsworth, "the poet." Hartman dwells upon Wordsworth's "eudemonic feelings" as expressed in the poem. These feelings of the presence and power of benevolent spirits "sustain and nourish him as intimations of immortality." As Hartman contends, nature "asks lover or growing child not to give up earlier yearnings—to die rather than become an ordinary mortal."

maiden" incorporated within his consciousness. His imagination is responsible, as it were, for the elision of her human nature. The etherealized being or "modality" still has a sense of humanity or personhood about her; she resembles a real maiden and can undergo death. Such an incorporeal yet humanlike being could be, *without contradiction*, a characterization of a fantasized love object. Hartman avoids this fuller probing into the problems of the identity of the "she" and the character of the "I." Instead, the problems are buried in silence, just like the nature of the death: "Lucy's death or the thought of her death . . . occurs in the blank between the stanzas."[20] Another textual murder discloses itself: Interstanzaic blankness is the final resting place of the mortal remains of confused identities. The problematic of "A slumber" is laid asleep there too, until awakened from its critical slumber by greater attention to the particular moments and movements of reading.

The foregoing detections of "textual murders" in the interpretations of Norman Holland, Paul de Man, J. Hillis Miller, and Geoffrey Hartman may seem excessive; but the excess of the phrase hopefully draws attention to a serious problem. The undermining, bypassing, or rejecting of the temporal interaction of work and reader and the complexities and particulars of the activity of reading yield critical fatalities: dehumanized and textualized readers, insubstantialized and detextualized texts, dehu-

---

20. G. H. Hartman, *Wordsworth's Poetry*, p. 159. Hartman briefly returns to the text of "A slumber" in the final chapter of *Saving the Text: Literature/Derrida/Philosophy* (Baltimore, Md.: Johns Hopkins University Press, 1981), pp. 147–49. Here he attempts to cope with the poem's would-be suspension at "the point-zero between curse and blessing." Such ironic suspension must eventually give way to what Hartman calls "a muteness close to mutilation." Silence and ironic suspension cannot be maintained, because death, or the thought of death, must be given its due. Wordsworth's lyric, however, seeks closure and "convert[s] a wounding thought of death into a beautiful irony"; it *seals* a sense of *unease* by rescuing itself from the recognition of a mutilating curse on the part of "the unquiet imagination." By implication, the "she" or the "Lucy" of the poem lies sealed, mute, mutilated, at some eerie point-zero in the poetic movement of the imagination. Wordsworth's imagination dreams the death of the lovely other—a dream at once anxious, unquiet, wounding, as well as hushed, sealed, fatefully rendered null.

In *Acts of Inclusion: Studies Bearing on an Elementary Theory of Romanticism* (New Haven, Conn.: Yale University Press, 1979), pp. 3, 53, 58–61, Michael G. Cooke offers several moments of reading "A slumber" that appear substantially indebted to Geoffrey Hartman's interpretive meditations upon the same poem. Cooke calls the lyric a "stunned elegy" (pp. 53, 58) because of the sharp contrasts in mood—from ecstasy to melancholy, from unearthliness to grave reality—and the paradoxical relationship of the speaker and the dead girl. In certain respects, though, the thrust of Cooke's commentary seems aimed at trying to integrate Hartman's general mode of reading the lyric with the line of interpretation that tends to read the tale of guilty forgetfulness and belated recognition from "She dwelt" and "Strange fits" into the poem (especially pp. 59–61).

manized and displaced temporality, and the sacrifice and burial of the evidence of the activity of reading. The lessons of reading "A slumber did my spirit seal" are manifold and resonant. As a consequence, the fate of critical reading seems best calibrated through judicious understanding and use of particular, text-focused, and reader-centered problematics of reading. Indeed, to echo the words of Cleanth Brooks a final time: "A slumber ought not to seal the *reader's* spirit as he reads this poem, or any other poem."

"two or three little Rhyme poems which I hope will amuse you"

The preceding investigation of the problematic of reading Words-worth's "A slumber" neither isolates the lyric from various con nections with other poems in *Lyrical Ballads* nor sequesters it from cultural and social questions regarding Wordsworth's art and work in general. The poem does have its place and function in the literary history of Wordsworth's thought and production in the 1790s as well as in the literary history of the Romantic lyric. However, the intensive exploration of various pragmatic and interpretive possibilities that the poem affords its readers offers a critical pathway toward resolving a local matter of literary understanding but also something more: the construction of a critical matrix in which the evidence of reading can have its due.

The foregoing discussion, nevertheless, does preclude an interpretation of the "Lucy" poems as a narrative cycle. Such a narrative cycle has been and is a fiction concocted by editors and critics.[1] Only one interpretation

---

1. See Chapter 2. A number of recent critics have proposed a wide variety of ways to read the so-called "Lucy" poems as a narrative cycle. Each critic constructs and rationalizes his or her own narrative order, using or discarding lyrics depending on their suitability to the narrative under construction. The most elaborate "Lucy" cycle is the one developed in the final and major chapter, "The 'Lucy' Poems," of Geoffrey Durrant's *Wordsworth and the Great System: A Study of Wordsworth's Poetic Universe* (London: Cambridge University Press, 1970), pp. 135–74. Durrant chooses five "Lucy" poems and links them in a sequence to tell the "story" of "the need to recognise and submit to the law which guarantees order and thus fosters life"—namely, natural law, "the great pattern within which we live and die" (p. 168). Helen Regueiro in *The Limits of Imagination: Wordsworth, Yeats, and Stevens* (Ithaca, N.Y.: Cornell University Press, 1976), pp. 49–55, takes the same sequence of poems that Durrant uses and interprets it as a narrative that shows Wordsworth's failed attempt "to pass into the child's vision of nature and death," to pass "from human time to natural time" (p. 49).

of the whole "Lucy" group manages to allow each poem its separate
complexity and important differences in context and meaning. In a very
careful and thoughtful essay, Spencer Hall weighs the evidence for and
against the "unity" of the "Lucy" poems. Even though the lyrics tend to
"form their own context, in and of themselves," Hall "doubt[s] that a
specific order can be determined which would correspond in any critically
meaningful fashion to a plan or perspective in Wordsworth's mind during
the period of composition."[2] Thus a narrative cycle, a "Lucy" "tale" or
"story," is not an issue. Various "common features—tonal, thematic,
conceptual, imaginal, verbal, metrical—which set them apart from other
poems by Wordsworth" helps "the reader . . . to approach [the "Lucy"
poems] in at least a tentatively contextual way."[3] The poems obviously

---

Three other critics interpret the "Lucy" poems as a cycle primarily concerned with a
developing relation of lover to love object. In "Poet and Lover in Wordsworth's 'Lucy' Poems,"
Modern Language Review 61 (1966): 175–79, James G. Taaffe argues that the poems are all one
"elegy," "a meaningful lyric progression" that carries poet and lover through tragic bereavement
"to see gain in loss, to imagine life in death" (pp. 175, 179). Terry Otten in "Action in
Wordsworth's 'Lucy' Poems: A Reading," *Illinois Quarterly* 34 (1971): 18–29, claims that the
lyrics make "a dramatic whole"; "they form a unified action beginning with one particular poem
and evolving logically through the other four poems" (pp. 18–19). The "unified action" is the
"ontological realization on the part of the poet"—his "victory"—that his "spiritual potential" can
only be aroused through loss of the love object (pp. 18, 28). Thirdly, and by far most interestingly,
Frances C. Ferguson offers a deconstructive interpretation of the "epistemological uncertainty"
involved in the "negative quest romance" of "the poet-speaker" for a love and poetic object:

> Read as one quasi-continuous whole made up of the five separate poems, the Lucy poems
> figure in little a variety of problems about poetic representation and naming, ultimately
> calling into question the very possibility of locating an object of representation or a
> signified. Through the course of these poems, Lucy is repeatedly and ever more decisively
> traced out of existence; and it is this progressive diminishment of Lucy's existence in the
> poems which suggests that they may serve as paradigmatic cases in coming to terms with
> Wordsworth's elusive notions of poetic language.

See "The Lucy Poems: Wordsworth's Quest for a Poetic Object," *ELH* 40 (1973): 532–33, 536.
The essay is reprinted, with a few minor changes and a new concluding paragraph, in F. C.
Ferguson, *Wordsworth: Language as Counter-Spirit* (New Haven, Conn.: Yale University Press,
1977), pp. 173–94.
    Two more recent interpretations of the "Lucy" poems as a narrative cycle are carried out
through the construction of rather specious contexts. See J. R. Watson, "Lucy and the
Earth-Mother," *Essays in Criticism* 27 (1977): 187–202 (the *terra genetrix* myth as the
"mythological mode" of the cycle), and Richard E. Matlack, "Wordsworth's Lucy Poems in
Psychobiographical Context" (discussed above).
    2. Spencer Hall, "Wordsworth's 'Lucy' Poems: Context and Meaning," *Studies in Romanti-
cism* 10 (1971): 162–63.
    3. Ibid., p. 162.

share poetic uses of the lover and his dream, sleep, or slumber and his relationship to nature and a beloved. They also share moments of sudden awakening, recognitions of death and mortality, English Common Meter, and so on. These "common features" constitute the measure of "unity" that the "Lucy" poems can be said to show. I differ with Spencer Hall on several particulars of his interpretations. However, I admire the sensitivity and balance of his critical procedure, especially his overt use of "A slumber" "as a point of reference" for drawing out the finer differences in tone and complexity among the poems.[4]

In this chapter I will offer readings of two other so-called "Lucy" poems, "Strange fits of passion have I known" and "She dwelt among the untrodden ways." As discussed above, "A slumber" was first published in a threesome with these two lyrics. My intention is to garner some intertextual support for my claim that "A slumber" involves a highly imaginative use of personal pronouns. As I shall demonstrate, the pronominal linguistic play within "Strange fits" and "She dwelt" also has consequences for the way in which two different speakers express the nature of their relationships to their beloved Lucys.

Every time I read "Strange fits" the same peculiar dilemma occurs: Is Wordsworth presenting a moment of sublime experience or is he allowing his lyric to slide into the comical or comically pathetic? I experience this peculiar contradiction in Wordsworth's tone and the poem's mood and then want to reread in order to discover how this could happen: What in the language of the poem would permit such an incongruous confluence? Or what is it that I am misconstruing or misreading? In reviewing the critical writings on "Strange fits," one can catch instances of this mismatching in tone and mood also occurring in the remarks of various critics. Anthony Conran considers "Strange fits" to be a poetic failure because it "is a poem that has lost its way": The lover's sudden panic does not match the ballad style or the story being developed.[5] A second critic, John Speirs, notes that the poem is "precariously balanced between the sublime and the ridiculous or at least the banal, such is its extreme reduction to simplicity of expression."[6] In his "Retrospect 1971" Geoffrey Hartman supplements or adjusts at some length his earlier "halted

---

4. Ibid., pp. 163, 168–73.
5. A. Conran, "The Goslar Lyrics," in *Wordsworth's Mind and Art*, ed. A. W. Thomson (Edinburgh: Oliver & Boyd, 1969), pp. 162–64.
6. J. Speirs, *Poetry Towards Novel*, p. 140.

traveler" interpretation of "Strange fits" in *Wordsworth's Poetry*. Hartman's self-revision discloses:

> The lyric has more *error* (anticlimax, illusion, mismatching of event and meaning) than *center*. The action is now too slow and now too fast, now overstated (first stanza) and now understated (last stanza). . . . The rider too is strangely displaced. Is he man plus horse, or a becalmed knight from Romance? He is certainly not the conventional hotspur of ballad tradition, and his night ride has a touch of parody. Instead of sparking hooves and a charged message, a gentle distractable trot. [7]

Conran, Speirs, and Hartman experience some measure of mismatching or incongruity in reading the poem, though each critic phrases and values this experience in slightly different terms.

In rereading the lyric, I initially located, and still do locate, my sense of incongruity in such lines as "I to her cottage bent my way," "Upon the moon I fixed my eye, / All over the wide lea," and "My horse moved on; hoof after hoof / He raised, and never stopped" (*PW*, II, p. 29). The comical oddity of the speaker's serious and severe overdetermination with regard to the object of his journey first arises in the phrase "bent my way"; it calls to mind, and perhaps prefigures, Ichabod Crane's ride through Sleepy Hollow in quest of his Katrina. The line "Upon the moon I fixed my eye" carries forward the sense of concentrated determination, yet the next phrase is strangely indeterminate and diffuse. It is not clear what is "All over the wide lea;" perhaps it is the moon shining "all over" the open field or meadow, or the supposedly "fixed" eye sweeping "all over" it. Only after scrutinizing the phrase does the possibility arise that the speaker's line of vision could be arcing across "the wide lea" to the moon above. The words "all over" misdirect and diffuse attention and thereby comically undercut the fixity of the "I's" determination to attend only to the moon. And then the lines "My horse moved on; hoof after hoof / He raised, and never stopped" seem to elevate mundane and exacting observation to a moment of comic redundance. Indeed, Chaucer's "Tale of Sir Thopas" from *The Canterbury Tales* comes to mind as an implicit model and pretext for the comic aspect of the questing horseman that seems lurking

---

7. G. H. Hartman, *Wordsworth's Poetry*, p. xix. See also pp. xviii–xx, 23–25.

in the language of the poem. One critic, Frances Ferguson, also makes this connection between Chaucer and Wordsworth. The metrical forms of "Strange fits" and the other "Lucy" poems, she remarks,

> are all cast into the meters of ballad or romance, tonally ambig-
> uous forms (in potentia) from at least Chaucer's day, when the
> re-Englishing of these forms to accommodate continental ro-
> mances sometimes yielded humorous results (as Chaucer himself
> demonstrated in the playful miscomprehensions of his *Tale of Sir
> Thopas*).[8]

Wordsworth, appropriately enough, had studied some Chaucer while at St. John's College, Cambridge. By 1800–1801 he was reading and "modernizing" selected tales and poems of the earlier author.[9]

Quite aside from any direct matter of influence, critics generally recognize that the poems of *Lyrical Ballads* exhibit great humor and playfulness as well as various experiments in comic tone.[10] However, the mark of Chaucer and the "Tale of Sir Thopas," I contend, is clearly upon Wordsworth's "Strange fits." This claim, moreover, becomes quite instru-mental in thinking through the confluence of "the sublime" and "the ridiculous," to use John Speirs's terms, in the poem. It is mentioned frequently that Dorothy and William Wordsworth purchased a copy of Bishop Thomas Percy's *Reliques of Ancient English Poetry* in Hamburg,

8. Ferguson, "The Lucy Poems," p. 534. See also p. 539.

9. See Moorman, I, pp. 100–101, 513, 515; and *PW*, IV, pp. 209–33.

10. See, for example, R. F. Storch, "Wordsworth's Experimental Ballads: The Radical Uses of Intelligence and Comedy," *Studies in English Literature: 1500–1900* 11 (1941): 621–39, and T. H. Helmstadter, "Wayward Wisdom: Wordsworth's Humor in *Lyrical Ballads*," *Mosaic* 9 (Summer 1976): 91–106. Storch points out that such ballads as "Simon Lee" and "The Idiot Boy" are experiments in comic tone and that Wordsworth's playfulness allows him to annex new and unusual characters and fields of experience to serious lyric poetry. Wordsworth's humor involves a mocking of the reader's sense of decorum and urges one to expand both literary and social sensibility. Helmstadter similarly contends that Wordsworth's humor in *Lyrical Ballads* is a "wayward wisdom," a means to mount criticism of bad custom, routine and set forms of behavior.

Wordsworth's humorous lyrical balladry also emerges from, parodies, and criticizes the large mass of sentimental magazine poetry and popular ballads of the time. See especially Paul G. Brewster, "The Influence of the Popular Ballad on Wordsworth's Poetry," *Studies in Philology* 35 (1938): 588–612; Robert Mayo, "The Contemporaneity of the *Lyrical Ballads*," *PMLA* 69 (1954): 486–522; and Mary Jacobus, *Tradition and Experiment in Wordsworth's "Lyrical Ballads" (1798)* (Oxford: Clarendon Press, 1976), especially chapters 8, 9, and 10.

two days before their departure for Goslar.[11] However, it has not previously been noticed that Percy's *Reliques* contains a brief essay on the word "fit," elucidating its uses as a term throughout the history of balladry and its use in Chaucer's "Tale of Sir Thopas." It is quite possible that Wordsworth read this essay and that it had some measure of influence on his revising, if not his original drafting, of "Strange fits." Bishop Percy says that "the word *fit*"

> . . . seems at one time to have peculiarly signified the pause, or breathing time, between the several parts [of "our ancient ballads and metrical romances"]. . . . By degrees it came to signify the whole part or division preceding the pause. . . . This sense it had obtained so early as the time of Chaucer: who thus concludes the first part of his rhyme of Sir Thopas (writ in ridicule of the old ballad romances):
>
> > "Lo! lordis mine, here is a fitt;
> > If ye woll any more of it,
> > To tell it woll I fonde."
>
> The word fit indeed appears originally to have signified a poetic strain, verse, or poem; for in these senses it is used by the Anglo-Saxon writers. . . . So in Cedmon . . . *Feonðh on fitte* seems to mean "composed a song," or "poem." The reader will trace this old Saxon phrase, in the application of the word *fond*, in the foregoing passage of Chaucer.[12]

Here Percy points out the ridiculing effect of Chaucer's tale in the context of a discussion of the use of the word "fit." If he had not previously made the connection himself, Wordsworth, in reading this passage, would have had his attention drawn to the comic effect that an admired author could produce through playing with the elements of ballads and metrical romances. Within the history and general context of balladry, a peculiar use of the word "fit" would have offered itself. In addition to the sense of a sudden, sharp, or uncontrollable bout or spell of feeling or violent activity—actually a use or meaning of the word common in Chaucer's day

11. See *Journals*, I, p. 31; Moorman, I, p. 411.
12. Thomas Percy, D.D. (Bishop of Dromore), *Reliques of Ancient English Poetry* (Philadelphia: Porter & Coates, 1869; orig. pub., 1765), pp. 231–32.

as well as Wordsworth's and our own[13]—"fit" can also mean "verse," "poem," "song," or perhaps "canto." Both meanings would seem to be operative in Wordsworth's lyric because both the context of a sudden, passionate feeling and the context of metrical balladry are present. Thus the phrase "strange fits of passion" can mean strange verses of passion as well as strange bouts or spells of passion. The first line of Wordsworth's poem contains this overplus or overdetermination of meaning, as if it also were too passionate to restrain itself to one calm and clear meaning. The speaker's "fond and wayward thoughts," then, begin with the first line; they slide into and out of the phrasing of the poem during its entire course, comically undercutting his romantic quest and severe act of mental fixation. And if a reader follows Percy's instruction to "trace" "in the foregoing passage of Chaucer" "the application of the word *fond*" from Caedmon's own earlier phrase, as perhaps Wordsworth himself did, one can see the words "fond and wayward thoughts" moving in two directions, just as the words "strange fits of passion" do. The speaker's thoughts can be tender and affectionate in their waywardness; or they can be contrived, devised, or invented, as a rhymer would contrive tender and adventurous thoughts in composing a fit. "Fond," for Chaucer, could mean foolish or foolishly tender or could be the past participle of "finden," the Middle English form of the verb "to find," which also includes the sense of "to devise" or "to invent."[14]

Bishop Percy's brief essay, then, provides external evidence to lend plausibility to an interpretation of "Strange fits" that would promote a comic undercutting of romantic questing. The initial experience of an incongruous or mismatched tone and mood is, consequently, not a misconstruing or misreading of the poem but is, instead, the first bit of evidence toward a literary understanding. The activity of reading, and the evidence it has to offer, is once again the necessary ground for interpretation. Just as in the case of "A slumber," the most telling clue to the interpretation of the lyric may well be the peculiar quality encountered in the act of reading the poem.

"Strange fits" begins in a bold manner with two lines of rather confident declaration: "Strange fits of passion have I known: / And I will dare to tell." However, the speaker's bold voice seems to diminish quickly to a

---

13. See *The Works of Geoffrey Chaucer*, 2d ed., ed. F. N. Robinson (Boston: Houghton Mifflin, 1957), p. 950.

14. Ibid.

suggestive whisper, enticing the reader on with a promise of confessing some passionate act: "But in the Lover's ear alone, / What once to me befell." This first stanza does not appear in the first extant version of the poem, a version that is found in the letter Dorothy and William wrote to Coleridge from Goslar in December 1798 (*EY*, p. 237; *PW*, II, p. 29). Yet Wordsworth's addition of the stanza, sometime between December 1798 and the publication of the 1800 *Lyrical Ballads*, amounts to placing a preface or "exordium" before the ballad or fit of passion that follows. Bishop Percy notes that many old metrical ballads have such an exordium and so "begin in a pompous manner, in order to captivate the attention of the audience."[15] Indeed, the first stanza does so captivate the reader's attention: "the Lover's ear alone" is not pricked in curiosity, but almost all occasional lovers and readers would seem to be likewise anxiously attendant upon the speaker's promised tale of passion. Besides the archaicism and doubled sense involved in the word "fits," the last word of the first stanza ("befell") seems also to draw attention to its use. Its slightly archaic inflection, though still quite functional and comprehensible, effectively evokes the atmosphere and language of the old ballads. However, in the sixth stanza, where the speaker sees the moon drop behind the cottage, the action involved in the word "befell" pathetically and comically becomes literalized. The moon falls and a fit of passion abruptly befalls the speaker. The language of the first stanza, then, exhibits a comic playfulness with the form, manner, and diction of the older metrical ballads.

The next three stanzas of the poem commence the ballad proper and develop a peculiar love triangle. The speaker is on his way to the cottage of his beloved, but their separateness or the difference in their identities is initially conflated in the line "When she I loved looked every day." The personal pronouns "she" and "I"—both in the nominative case—are juxtaposed in the syntactic order of the line. For a brief moment it is possible to confuse the two and take "she" rather than "I" as the subject of the predicate verb "loved." Wordsworth has introduced this more troublesome word order in place of the simpler line found in the earlier manuscript version of the poem—"Once, when my love was strong and gay" (*EY*, p. 237). This earlier line is syntactically uncomplicated and forceful, but the revised line doubles up pronouns and predicates and

15. Percy, *Reliques*, p. 232.

allows a brief syntactic fit. That is, the syntax can be said to suffer fitfully the expression of the speaker's passion or love. He narrates the tale of a passionate fit, and the words and phrases of his narration incarnate and express his emotional state.[16] Indeed, the speaker's passion seems to blend his beloved's identity into his own: "she I loved" lets one pronoun and one identity slide too easily into the other.

However, there is also a third term in this love relation—namely, the moon. The speaker "bent [his] way, / Beneath an evening-moon"; he can be imagined as assuming an almost crescent-shaped appearance, as if in strange imitation of a phase of the moon.[17] Nevertheless, he fixes his eye "Upon the moon" as he journeys across "the wide lea" or open meadow, past "the orchard-plot" and up the hill upon which "Lucy's cot" sits. The moon lights the way for the speaker, and he rivets his attention upon it. Both speaker and moon come "near, and nearer still," to the beloved's cottage. The moon appears as a third term in this relationship because the light it provides allows the lover to seek out his beloved at evening time. Moreover, the speaker's visual fixation on the moon works to bring it subtly and strangely into his relationship with his beloved. The speaker's bent posture recalls a phase of the moon; and, like himself, the moon seems to be journeying to Lucy's cottage. These circumstances, together with the speaker's otherwise unmotivated yet forcefully determined fixation on the moon, convey the sense that the identities of moon and lover are subtly and hypnotically blended. The forcefulness of the speaker's visual fixation on the lunar orb, though, also communicates the sense that this source of the evening's light is taken as a substitute object of attention and desire in the absence of Lucy, a mortal and earthly source of light and visual delight. Lucy's name itself, after all, derives from the Latin name "Lucia" and noun "lux," meaning "light." The speaker's passion, then,

16. Language as incarnate thought and feeling was a frequent metaphor used by Wordsworth, as in this sentence from "Essays upon Epitaphs, III": "If words be not (recurring to a metaphor before used) an incarnation of the thought but only a clothing for it, then surely will they prove an ill gift; such a one as those poisoned vestments, read of in the stories of superstitious times, which had power to consume and to alienate from his right mind the victim who put them on." See *The Prose Works of William Wordsworth*, ed. W. J. B. Owen and Jane Worthington Smyser, 3 vols. (Oxford: Clarendon Press, 1974). (The volumes of this edition will hereinafter be cited parenthetically as *PWWW*, I, *PWWW*, II, and *PWWW*, III; the quotation above is from *PWWW*, II, pp. 84–85.)

17. The Latin word for moon (and for crescent) is taken from the Latin verb "lunare," "to bend into a crescent." Perhaps a subtle etymological play on "bent" and "moon" is operative here—the word "bent" recalling a specific shape of the moon itself.

allows a crossing of boundaries among the identities of lover, moon, and beloved. His strong passion and quest propel him into a strange love triangle in which "she," "I," and "the moon" slide into one another—both in the syntax and diction as well as in the action of stanzas two through four.

The final three stanzas bring the ballad to its fitful climax. The speaker has fallen into reverie as he rides toward Lucy's home: "In one of those sweet dreams I slept, / Kind Nature's gentlest boon." This dreamy state recalls "A slumber," but this sleep is a sweeter and a gentler one: a lover's reverie rather than a death fantasy. Besides, the speaker records that "all the while my eyes I kept / On the descending moon." His eyes are open, focused, and intent upon one object. He does not actually slumber or sleep except in a rather hyperbolic and pathetically comic fashion. The comic dissonance felt in the juxtaposition of dreaminess and fixated attention, though, is perhaps answered and kept mollified by the particularly acute and telling enjambment: "And all the while my eyes I kept." At this line break there is a slight hint that the speaker's vision is really a self-enclosed, blinded, and solipsistic kind of sight and attention. Though staring at the moon, he actually keeps his eyes to himself, seeing only the figures of his daydream while moving like a somnambulist toward the "cot" of his beloved. And so withdrawn is he into his own reverie that the motion of his horse goes mechanically onward as if without him. The "I" and his "eyes" are enthralled in daydream while "he"—the horse—plods onward, no longer the "we" of an earlier stanza. Then suddenly and climactically "the bright moon dropped" behind the roof of Lucy's cottage. The loss of light imperils the speaker's reverie, and the shock of this loss leaves him open to the "fond and wayward thoughts" that "slide / Into a Lover's head" when the object of his fixation unexpectedly disappears. The lover is caught unawares, and the tender yet contrived ("fond") thoughts characteristic of his passionate reverie welcome an equally daydreamed, contrived yet strangely tender thought to them—the unexpected death of his beloved earthly light, Lucy.

This thought of death slides into the speaker's head as though through his own ear: He cries out to himself, " 'O mercy!' . . . / 'If Lucy should be dead!' " This lover exclaims fitfully to himself what has befallen him, just as he said he would in the first stanza: "And I will dare to tell, / But in the Lover's ear alone, / What once to me befell." Wordsworth here has tenderly contrived a strange fit of passion that captures a lover speaking into his own ear while at the same time delivering his tale to the ears of other lovers. This comic doubling melds with and rounds out the whole series of comic doublings and dissonances already described. As one critic has put it:

> Wordsworth deliberately articulates a humorously unfounded thought in order to show the irrational way of love. At the same time, he has taken us within the mind of the dreaming lover so completely that we see with his eyes, hear the thoughts with his ears, feel the same mixture of bafflement, embarrassment, and genuine fear that he does. For a reader who would find a tale in everything, "Strange fits of passion" is a warm comic vision into the nature of love.[18]

It is the *character* of the speaker of "Strange fits," ultimately, that must bear the brunt of the criticism implied in this "comic vision into the nature of love." His fit of passion is finely delineated in the syntax, diction, and action of the poet's deliberately articulated lyrical "fit."

Wordsworth's interest in and emphasis on character in poetry, of course, can be traced in numerous passages in his work and correspondence. An especially crucial remark for the interpretation of "Strange fits," as well as "She dwelt," occurs in a letter Wordsworth wrote to Coleridge in late November or early December 1798. Wordsworth posted it from Goslar two or three weeks before sending the letter containing the first versions of "Strange fits" and "She dwelt." In the first letter, Wordsworth vigorously objects to the lack of "character in [the] personages" of Bürger's poems.

> I see everywhere the character of Bürger himself. . . . But yet I wish him sometimes at least to make me forget himself in his creations. It seems to me, that in poems descriptive of human nature, however short they may be, character is absolutely necessary. (*EY*, p. 234)

At the time Wordsworth wrote this letter, or soon thereafter, he also composed "Strange fits"—indeed, a short poem that can be said to

18. Helmstadter, p. 100.

describe an aspect of human nature in which not Wordsworth's character but the character of some persona was of chief interest. Nevertheless, in the work of many critics, as one writer has pointed out, "the character of the narrator . . . has been much misunderstood"; the speaker or narrator "was never meant to be taken as Wordsworth, but as a much more limited 'persona.'"[19]

The narrator of "Strange fits," to be precise, is one given to "a 'mistaken' association of ideas (mistaken or 'wayward' in the sense that it has no rational justification) in which natural law is seemingly overruled by the emotional intensity of some psychic transaction."[20] The "I" of "Strange fits" is prone to mental delusion. He confuses himself, "she," and the moon in his progress toward a climactic fit of passion in which the sharp decline and disappearance of the moon at night is mistakenly and unjustifiably confused with a thought of the beloved's death. Kent Beyette has developed the psychological context for understanding this mistaken association and mental delusion. In so doing he draws heavily upon Erasmus Darwin's Zoönomia (1794–96), a book that Wordsworth was well acquainted with and that influenced the composition of numerous poems in Lyrical Ballads.[21] Darwin notes that a "great source of error" in perception and in understanding lies in

> the vivacity of our ideas of imagination, which perpetually intrude themselves by various associations, and compose the farrago of our dreams; in which, by the suspension of volition, we are precluded from comparing the ideas of one sense with those of another, or the incongruity of their successions with the usual course of nature, and thus to detect their fallacy.[22]

19. Kent Beyette, "Wordsworth's Medical Muse: Erasmus Darwin and Psychology in 'Strange fits of passion have I known,' " Literature and Psychology 23 (1973): 96. Beyette also discusses the speakers or narrators of "The Thorn" and Peter Bell in similar terms.

20. Ibid.

21. Ibid., pp. 93–101. Perhaps the best essay on Wordsworth's use of Erasmus Darwin is J. H. Averill, "Wordsworth and 'Natural Science': The Poetry of 1798," JEGP 77 (1978): 232–46. With special attention to the first volume of Lyrical Ballads, Averill traces the career of Wordsworth's attitudes toward natural philosophy and scientific inquiry, as well as toward Darwin's case histories of psychological extremes.

22. Erasmus Darwin, Zoönomia: or the Laws of Organic Life, Vol. II (Philadelphia: Edward Earle, 1818; orig. pub. 1794–96), p. 351. The quotation is taken from a section that discusses perceptual errors caused by ignorance, credulity, and the mistake of taking "the fictions of fancy" for reality.

Incongruous associations of vivacious ideas "compose the farrago of our dreams," and in this context reverie would seem the best way to read Darwin's use of the word "dreams." Such associations, powerful as they are, are delusive and fallacious with regard to "the usual course of nature," the usual course of our perceptions, associations, and understanding. The speaker or narrator of "Strange fits" goes against "the usual course of nature" and deludes himself by erroneously associating the perceived movement of the moon with the fate of his wayfaring for the beloved. Rapt in his wayward reverie, the speaker fails to attend to the perceptual triangulation that is about to waylay him. Even though he is focused on the moon and Lucy's cot, the "I" himself becomes the crux of focal attention in the course of the poem. His "bent" shape forms quite ironically an *acute* angle in a triangle of visual attentions that locates its other two angles at the moon and at Lucy's cottage.[23] While riding across "the wide lea," the speaker's line of vision is riveted on the moon. In the meantime, he is intent on gaining his way to "those paths" that lead to "Lucy's cot." As the narrator begins his ascent of "the hill" toward his destination, it becomes clear that the cottage is on the hilltop and the moon appears somewhere in the night sky just above it. The moon, of course, slowly descends in "the usual course of nature," as Erasmus Darwin might phrase it. However, because the speaker is ascending a hill the moon will appear to him to drop much faster until it is quickly blocked from view behind the roof of the cottage. Since the speaker, apparently, is not very far from the cottage—indeed quite "nigh"—the roof will appear large enough to accomplish this optical delusion. The speaker's own physical movement toward the house of his beloved, then, causes the moon to drop so abruptly out of sight. As a consequence, the speaker's own effort leaves him lightless in the night shade cast by Lucy's roof and fitful with the strange passion that befalls him there.

The progress of the "I's" self-deluding optical trick can thus be graphically represented (see illustrations 1 to 4 on p. 114). This delusion reveals how "the unconscious identifying trick of the narrator's mind," to borrow F. R. Leavis's phrase, can actually work.[24] While lost in a reverie

23. In Euclidean or plane geometry an "acute angle" is one that has an angularity of 0 to 90 degrees—that is to say, smaller than a right angle or a perpendicular. The opposite term is "obtuse angle"—one that has an angularity of 90 to 180 degrees.

24. F. R. Leavis, "Wordsworth," *Revaluation: Tradition and Development in English Poetry* (London: Chatto & Windus, 1936), p. 202. Donald Davie, in "Dionysus in *Lyrical Ballads*," in *Wordsworth's Mind and Art*, ed. A. W. Thomson, p. 124, seems to come close to this idea in

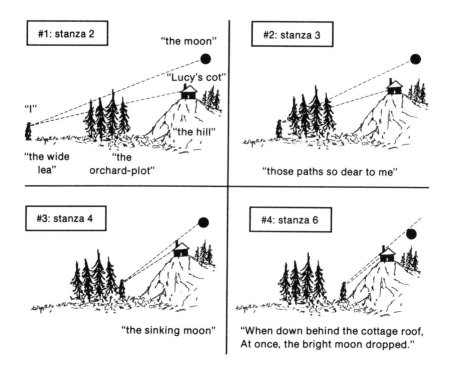

This four-panel illustration schematizes the optical trick that the speaker of Wordsworth's "Strange fits of passion" perpetrates upon himself.

involving a triangle of lover, moon, and beloved, the narrator pays no attention to a perceptual triangulation involving the same three terms. When the latter triangle suddenly collapses into a straight line, the "I" of the poem mistakenly and waywardly lets Lucy and his quest for her plummet to the zero degree. We can alternately empathize with and find mocking humor in the mistaken association into which the narrator's emotional intensity and self-blinding inattention have precipitately led him. However, the character of the narrator and the syntactic and perceptual "fits" characteristic of his narration are the focal points of

---

a remark on "Strange fits": ". . . the movements of the poet's body astride his horse make the moon drop out of sight and therefore (by Berkeleyan logic) out of existence." Davie, however, does not go on to develop this remark.

Wordsworth's lyrical ballad and a full interpretation of it. The reader of "Strange fits" ultimately reacts to the narrator and his narration much like the "her" and the "I" of the canceled final stanza of the first version of the poem once did:

> I told her this; her laughter light
>   Is ringing in my ears;
> And when I think upon that night
>   My eyes are dim with tears.
>   (EY, p. 238)

In concluding with these lines, the earliest version of "Strange fits" revealed a different audience for the lover's tale of passion—not "the Lover's ear alone" but the beloved herself, quite alive and responsive. The lover's fit of passion is comic and provokes fond laughter, and the beloved's tender laughter—clearly not a strange fit—fills his ears. The lover also concurs in this response. He too laughs when thinking upon that evening, though with a hint of sadness or melancholy: "My eyes are dim with tears." Such laughter fills both the ears and the eyes of the speaker-lover with the sound and memory of the lovely other, his "Lucy." She has found his perceptual error and his passionate excess touching perhaps, but surely foolish and wayward.

Wordsworth, of course, deleted this final stanza in revising the poem. His development of "Strange fits" in comic imitation of older metrical ballads, as a consequence, leaves the burden of understanding the character of the narrative persona entirely with the reader. The revised "Strange fits" concludes abruptly, without any indication that the speaker himself sees the humor and self-delusion of his situation. His character remains uniform, unitary, and limited.[25] The reader, though, must work through to a full description and explanation of Wordsworth's poem by attending to the initial experience of mismatched tone and mood and by following through on its numerous implications. The foregoing interpretation of "Strange fits" has performed precisely that activity.

---

25. In general my account of Wordsworth's revisions of "Strange fits" is at variance with the consciously "modernist" emphasis on Wordsworth's "writing" as an obsessive process of "revision," as an attempt to substitute composed "harmonies" for initial imaginative "excesses," developed in R. F. Carney, "Strange Fits of Passion: Wordsworth's Process of Poetic Composition" (Ph.D. diss., Rutgers University, 1978).

"She dwelt among the untrodden ways," the constant companion poem to "Strange fits" in all groupings since their first publication and even in the first extant versions of both (EY, pp. 236–38), actually has only a few things in common with the latter poem. Like "Strange fits," "She dwelt" employs the Common Meter, involves a first-person speaker and a "Lucy," and expresses the nature of their relation, in great part, through the pronominal linguistic play of the lyric. For the first nine lines of this twelve-line poem, the reader encounters a "She" who has not yet been named, whose identity remains unclarified. The antecedent of the pronoun, though, is provided before the poem ends; but the disclosure of her identity is ironically the moment in which her death is disclosed. The knowledge of identity, in this instance, is allowed only at the moment in which the difference such naming makes is lost to death.

In a lengthy and careful interpretation of "She dwelt," Roger L. Slakey offers several remarks bearing on the function of the pronouns in the lyric. These remarks, moreover, are set in the context of readerly attention to the "evolving grammatical and rhetorical artifice" of the poem—what Slakey, borrowing a term from Coleridge, calls the "proceeding" of a poem.[26] Such "proceeding" I have been calling the activity of reading a poem, with full attention to the evidential particulars that come into play during the activity. Though the greater part of Slakey's interpretation involves determining distinctions and differences among the propositions and appositions used in the poem, he attends closely to the way in which the structure of such statements actually works for a reader:

> Grammatically, the first two lines are a proposition, a simple statement of fact; the next six are three parallel phrases, in apposition with the subject "She." The change here from the one grammatical form to the other is more than a change from an explicit to an implicit proposition. For one thing, while the predication moves us from the subject "She" to whatever will be said of her, the appositive thrusts our attention back to the girl, that still unidentified "She."[27]

Syntactically and semantically "She" dominates the reader's experience of the first two stanzas of "She dwelt." The two lines "She dwelt among the

26. R. L. Slakey, "At Zero: A Reading of Wordsworth's 'She dwelt among the untrodden ways,' " *Studies in English Literature, 1500–1900* 12 (1972): 630.
27. Ibid., p. 631.

untrodden ways / Beside the springs of Dove" (*PW*, II, p. 30) yield the basic statement and situation of the first two-thirds of the lyric. The three pairs of lines that follow insistently turn and direct the reader's attention back upon the subject and first word of these two initial lines. An unidentified "She" lived in an unvisited and peaceful spot, unmarried, unpraised, and all but unloved: "A Maid whom there were none to praise / And very few to love:" (lines 3–4). The colon that punctuates the end of the first stanza signals that the negative state of affairs—the dearth or virtual absence of human relationship that marks the life of this unknown woman—is to be characterized further. Two metaphors attempt to evoke substance and specificity for the life of this unknown "She":

> A violet by a mossy stone
> Half hidden from the eye!
> —Fair as a star, when only one
> Is shining in the sky.
>   (lines 5–8)

Scarcely noticeable and fleeting natural events appear to qualify her identity. They offer ways to visualize or imagine her in less "untrodden" and more familiar or *known* spots. The attempt, though moving and touching, verges on the pathetic. "She" is a violet and the evening and morning star, the planet Venus. Emblematic of passion, these natural entities would suggest a passionate, feelingful, and forward nature for her. However, the violet is hidden away, left "untrodden," in a place, perhaps dark and damp ("mossy"), dominated by a stone. The planet Venus, though "fair" and seasonably bright, is not "a star": It only reflects light and does not emit its own. The moment of its unaccompanied appearance before dawn or after dusk is fleeting and evanescent. These metaphors actually work to keep hidden any substantial or concrete knowledge of the woman referred to as "She." Such metaphors are affecting but not really satisfying because their efforts at vitally qualifying who "She" is only lend pathos and not enough specificity to her. Indeed, the third and final stanza of the lyric opens quite appropriately: "She lived unknown, and few could know" (1. 9). *Few could know* her. "She" dwells concealed, hidden, evanescent, however variously imaged.

The last three lines of "She dwelt" yield a sudden change in the development of the poem. "She" is finally and abruptly identified and placed in relation to someone else. "Lucy" and the speaker of the lyric emerge as the two human figures implicated. However, "She" is identified as "Lucy" only at the moment in which the speaker acknowledges that she has "ceased to be." She is completely hidden now. Her name marks powerfully this fact, for the effect of delaying clarification of the antecedent of "She" is resoundingly felt when the resolution of identity coincides with mortal dissolution. The reason for this effect emerges in the final two lines of the poem: "But she is in her grave, and, oh, / The difference to me!" (lines 11–12). As Roger Slakey has put it, "the full force of the poem here presses down on the speaker himself."[28] Up until these final lines the poem had seemed to focus completely on some unknown girl, but now it is clear that the speaker is at least equally present throughout its course. A general sense of the speaker's relationship with the "Maid" is recovered in rereading the lyric—that is, once it is understood that the speaker knew and felt strongly toward the woman he is evoking. While Lucy had been alive, he paid her little or no attention; he left her unvisited, unpraised, and essentially unloved. Though it can be said that he may actually have loved her while she was yet living, he did so in his own peculiar fashion: He scarcely allowed her a separate and independent identity and existence. Consequently, the speaker does not feel the need to clarify or specify the identity of "She" for others, and perhaps even for himself. He recounts and imagines her in thoroughly isolated environs. Her identity made no difference to him, and the pronominal organization of the first ten lines of the lyric reproduces and embodies the narrator's neglect and lack of relationship. Who "She" is is not really important—that is, at least not until the moment he loses her irrevocably. Only in verbalizing such loss does the narrator intone her name, belatedly granting her a single identity and satisfying the reader's delayed expectation of learning or knowing it. However, at the moment of mortal loss of identity, the futile yet pathetic difference that human identity painfully makes now is registered in grieving despair: "and, oh, / The difference to me!" Difference and its ground in human identity finally emerges. The speaker belatedly recognizes Lucy as a being whose separateness and humanity is and was crucial to him. Now, however, she is lost to him, and his deferred recognition of difference stings him in final helplessness. The last word of the poem, the pronoun "me," is what this belated recognition leaves him with: the abject loneliness and despair of the self hopelessly estranged from another. Another's living yet fleeting difference now yields knowledge of love and love's lack.

28. Ibid., p. 636.

"She dwelt among the untrodden ways," then, involves a play on identities. In its brief course it evokes the failure of the speaker or the narrator to differentiate Lucy as another living human being with whom he can interact. The first stanza evokes her isolation and social impoverishment, and the second stanza offers two metaphors that pathetically augment this sense of a hidden or concealed person. The pronominal organization of the lyric, moreover, immediately focuses the reader's attention on the way in which the speaker himself more directly denigrates or diminishes Lucy's identity. The reader's expectation of learning who "She" refers to goes unsatisfied until the final stanza. At this point the revelation of identity falls suddenly and with shock: The woman's identity, focused now so belatedly in a name, succumbs to extinction. "She" is gone and the "me" of the poem, the speaker, declares himself in a powerful, personal outburst of grief. The last word of the poem, "me," has revealed a second person implicated in the action of the lyric; that is, the lyric has concealed that it is to be taken as a narration in the first person until the very end. The narrator or speaker does not show himself until the admission of loss, as though involuntarily and from a deep source, forces personal grief from him. However, in the course of the poem prior to this final confession, his narration strives to keep hidden and depersonalized the identity of the "She" he purports to describe. Seemingly, he would wish her still "among the untrodden ways," offering the "hope" but not the differentiating and specific demands of a relationship between two people.[29] "She dwelt," then, can be understood in great part as an affecting play on the possibilities of identity and interaction offered by its first and last words, "She" and "me."

There exists also an intriguing bit of unusual "textual" support for developing the pronominal linguistic play of "She dwelt" as a major aspect of an interpretation of the lyric. In a late manuscript version of the last stanza, dated July 20, 1848, Wordsworth offers the following variation on the final two lines of his poem: "But She is in her grave—and oh / The difference to Me.!"[30] In this singular occurrence Wordsworth has capi-

29. In the earliest extant version of "She dwelt," the poem began: "My hope was one" (*EY*, p. 236). The "she" of this version (the name "Lucy" does not appear) seems to be the speaker's "hope" or human potential for relationship, but her death from "slow distemper" (p. 237) only belatedly shocks him into this awareness.

30. I discovered this manuscript in the second volume of a copy of the 1800 edition of *Lyrical Ballads* deposited in the Poetry and Rare Books Collection at the State University of New York at Buffalo. The text of the full manuscript, various comments and conjectures concerning its

talized the initial letters of the two pronouns. This alteration in the orthography of the pronouns "she" and "me" is remarkable here because Wordsworth is at pains, in this variation on the final stanza of his lyric, to remove a whole set of typographically designated textual emphases that his 1800 text contained. I discuss these changes in the appendix to this book and conjecture that they amount to a clarification and channeling of textual emphasis toward stressing the sudden difference the irrevocable loss of the woman means for the speaker. Now in this instance of pronominal capitalization, Wordsworth would appear to be emphasizing or stressing a suddenly realized and incontrovertible difference in yet another way, one quite obviously unique and unprecedented.[31] Without undue insistence, and with full cognizance that the poet was consciously and selectively making changes in the typography of "She dwelt" so as to indicate better his desired emphases, this singular use of "She" and "Me" would also seem to lend support to my contention that Wordsworth placed interest and significance in the character and fate of the relation between the two pronouns. They represent and evoke two different identities, but their linguistic play constitutes the poem's specific way of presenting in such a brief course the personal and fateful difference of two human figures.

The foregoing readings of "Strange fits" and "She dwelt," on the whole, offer intertextual support for my contention that "A slumber" involves a highly imaginative use of personal pronouns. Although the full interpretations of the three poems show that they differ with regard to the type of incident and mood as well as the character of the speaker or narrator involved, each of the three is grounded in the relationship of a first-person speaker to a woman generally referred to as "she." The pronominal linguistic play within each poem thus constitutes and imparts, to a considerable degree, the specific quality of the interaction of speaker and "she" in each of the lyrics. This situation would ultimately seem to be a major rationale for the publication of "Strange fits," "She dwelt," and "A slumber" as a threesome in the three editions of the second volume of *Lyrical Ballads* during Wordsworth's lifetime.

---

particulars, and its dating with regard to the events of Wordsworth's life at the time are all discussed in my essay "Lucy in Retrospect: A Late Wordsworth Manuscript of 'She dwelt among th'untrodden ways,' " *The Wordsworth Circle* 10 (1979): 353–55. A slightly revised version of the essay appears as an appendix to this book.

31. Ibid., p. 354.

Another lyric almost always grouped with the so-called "Lucy" poems, "Three years she grew in sun and shower" (*PW*, II, pp. 214–16), was also published in the same volume but not in sequence with the three poems under discussion. Even though this lyric too involves a speaker and a "she," the former allows "Nature" her own lengthy narrative justification for taking back to herself a very young "Child." Essentially, the mortal (and presumably male) speaker listens to and stoically accepts these words of another—a nonsolipsistic attitude clearly not evinced by the various speakers of "Strange fits," "She dwelt," and "A slumber." Then too, the "Lucy" of "Three years" is lovingly and lavishly described and praised, as a mother would her daughter or Demeter would Kore or Persephone.[32] The "she" in any one of the three other poems scarcely has her identity so acknowledged or developed. Instead, "she" or "Lucy" is faintly limned as a figure in a death fantasy, or in a self-deluding reverie, or as a "half hidden" and unpraised "Maid."

Wordsworth, however, separated "A slumber" from "Strange fits" and "She dwelt" in his collected *Poems* of 1815. He inserted the latter two poems under the rubric "Poems Founded on the Affections," and he placed "A slumber" with "Poems of the Imagination."[33] This separation reveals what is arguably a fundamental difference in the way they are to be read, most specifically in the different ways their linguistic contrivances are to be experienced and understood.

"Strange fits" and "She dwelt" are aptly said to be "founded on the affections" because their syntax, diction, and action present particular movements of the sensibility and passions of two distinct speakers who in the course of their narrations reveal much more about their own emotional lives than they do about their Lucys. Or rather, to phrase the same point in a more Wordsworthian idiom, the emotions or affections of these two speakers help structure and impart verisimilitude to the language and action of their narrations. The activity of reading these two poems

---

32. In "Little Girls Lost: Problems of a Romantic Archetype," *Bulletin of the New York Public Library* 67 (1963): 579–92, Irene Chayes links Wordsworth's poem "Lucy Gray" to the Persephone archetype. I think this archetype would have even greater explanatory force if addressed to the poem "Three years she grew in sun and shower." More pointedly, "Lucy Gray," like "The Thorn" and "The Idiot Boy," involves an untrustworthy narrator, who tells a tale of sentimentalized suspense, anguish, and superstition but leaves evidence that he is forcing the limits of credibility. For instance, after a night filled with the ravages of a snowstorm, Lucy Gray's mother is still able to espy her daughter's footprints the next day!

33. See note 1, p. 16.

likewise is "founded on the affections"—namely, on the reader's affections or feelingful attention to the mood, movement, and content of the poem. After all, in the long letter sent to Coleridge from Goslar in December 1798, Wordsworth initially prefaced the transcription of the earliest versions of "Strange fits" and "She dwelt" with the remark: "She [Dorothy] will copy out two or three little Rhyme poems which I hope will amuse you" (EY, p. 236). The pathos evinced by these two poems, indeed quite comic in the first one, is supposed to amuse the reader, to entertain but also to engage the attention pleasurably and direct it toward an affecting awareness.

"A slumber," though, would appear to do far more than amuse. As a work "of the Imagination," it depicts "operations of the mind upon . . . objects" such that the latter are either modified or composed. This "activity" affords both the poet and his readers "gratification" in contemplating such objects and the processes by which they are transformed (PWWW, III, pp. 30–31). Rather than merely disclose an affecting moment, the language and action of "A slumber" depict a powerful and transforming event in the mental and perceptual activity of the lyric's speaker. There is a sense of deliberateness and willfulness about the speaker's death fantasy and its operations upon its "she," and the activity of reading leads to a discovery and contemplation of this fantasy's specific operations in the poem. The pronominal play of "Strange fits" and "She dwelt" evokes pathos, but that of "A slumber" depicts the movement of a terrifying act of the Romantic imagination.

Coda and Ricorso:
Coleridge as Reader, Interpreter, and Fantast

Our talk gets its meaning from the rest of our proceedings.
—*Ludwig Wittgenstein*, On Certainty

Paul Magnuson has recently examined in superb detail the "lyrical dialogue" carried out by Wordsworth and Coleridge in their poetry. He attends closely to an unfolding itinerary of what Coleridge's good friend, patron, and interlocutor Thomas Poole called in October 1798 "our fears about amalgamation" between Coleridge and Wordsworth.[1] Poole's phrase articulates the concern that Coleridge was merging, indeed sublimating, his own personality and conception of the "poet" in the stronger personal presence and poetic power of Wordsworth. Magnuson, though, exhibits an ongoing dialogue recuperable in the work of the two poets; each friend, collaborator, and conversant helped shape and direct the poetic practice of the other. However, in looking at the "Lucy" poems written in Goslar and posted to Coleridge by Wordsworth and Dorothy late in 1798, Magnuson contends that they embody gloomy moods and anxious fears concerning the budding poetic project *The Prelude* and the sources of Wordsworth's imaginative power. That is to say, these lyrics reproduce many of the fears of personal loss and poetic silencing that

1. Paul Magnuson, *Coleridge and Wordsworth: A Lyrical Dialogue* (Princeton, N.J.: Princeton University Press, 1988), pp. 3–4.

Coleridge underwent.[2] The lyrical dialogue of that winter in Goslar perhaps can be articulated and attended upon in yet another manner. Coleridge read, interpreted, appropriated, even amalgamated Wordsworth's lyrics in ways that disclose the troubled relation of self to other and the eerie consequences of the failure of the Romantic imagination to interact humanely, fully, and self-reflexively.

Coleridge's remark that "A slumber" is "a most sublime Epitaph" and one in which Wordsworth "fancied the moment in which his Sister might die" is usually taken as Coleridge's interpretation of the poem (Griggs, I, p. 479).[3] However, it has not previously been noticed that this comment is actually only one moment in a far more extensive as well as emotionally intensive appropriation of the three short lyrical poems that Wordsworth sent Coleridge in late 1798 or early 1799. To judge from evidence found in three lengthy letters that Coleridge wrote between April and May 1799, he seems to have read and reread the early versions of "A slumber," "She dwelt," and "Strange fits" with considerable personal interest. The language and action of Wordsworth's three lyrics would appear to have helped Coleridge verbalize a time of loss and pain in his own life. His good friend Thomas Poole had written to him in March 1799 with the news that his second son, Berkeley, still in infancy, had died of consumption. Coleridge tried to come to terms with this loss in two letters to Poole and in an oddly distant letter of consolation to his wife, Sara. Each letter in turn seems to draw upon Coleridge's reading of one of Wordsworth's three lyrics in order to interpret and structure his feelings about the early and unexpected death of Berkeley.

The first of the two letters to Poole falls in two parts or half-letters markedly different in tone and concern. The first part, dated April 6, 1799, yields Coleridge's first reaction to the news of his son's death. Poole's letter makes Coleridge "suffer . . . over again" the "mass of Pain" that "was brought suddenly and closely within the sphere of [his] perception" when his wife wrote him earlier about "the miseries" their child was undergoing (Griggs, I, p. 478). Coleridge feels this pain because his "bodily frame is an imitative Thing, and touched by the imagination gives the hour that is past, as faithfully as a repeating watch" (p. 478). In effect, Coleridge is attempting to be empirically precise in stating the nature of his sensitivity; his body seems a thing that can feel the touch of an earlier

2. Ibid., pp. 199–205.
3. The full comment is discussed near the beginning of Chapter 2.

earthly hour. Launching into a discourse on "Consciousness" and "immortality" (or, "future Continuance"), Coleridge then speaks of "that force" which his motion in skimming a stone across water imparts to "that Stone" (p. 479). Force or motion does not "perish" but goes on, immortal in a moving and movable stone if not in a body. Familiar words and notions occur here. Coleridge calls them "fancies," but they would appear to originate in a subtle preoccupation with "A slumber." Coleridge has his own loss to grieve; yet he says, quoting from his own *Osorio*, that "Grief" "Doth love to dally with fantastic thoughts, / And smiling, like a sickly Moralist, / Finds some resemblance to her own Concerns / In the Straws of Chance, & Things Inanimate!" (p. 479). Seemingly, Coleridge's grief would rather "dally with fantastic thoughts" found in "some resemblance to her own Concerns." Coleridge feels and acts this way because he "cannot truly say that [he] grieve[s]": He has "*not* wept," as he himself confesses. He has been kept from real grieving by "this strange, strange, strange Scene-shifter Death! that giddies one with insecurity, & so unsubstantiates the living Things that one has grasped and handled!" (p. 479). The figure and power of Death fascinates Coleridge here, and the "fantastic thoughts" involved make insubstantial what formerly was so real and touchable. Thoughts on death and immortality, then, are Coleridge's present "Concerns"; and it is perhaps understandable why he would be disposed to interpret "A slumber" as an epitaph and as a moment in which Wordsworth could fancy that a loved one, Dorothy, might die. Wordsworth's "most sublime Epitaph" would consummately express for Coleridge the thoughts or fancies he feels moved or driven toward in his moment of griefless pain. Wordsworth's expression of an unfeeling and insensitive narrative persona perhaps allows Coleridge to admit his inability to grieve his son's death, while using the occasion for "fantastic thoughts" on consciousness, death, and immortality. Coleridge, however, does feel the pain that his son's suffering and death brings, and he acknowledges this fact by saying that his own body must be a thing that feels the touch of time. Coleridge is thus freely using his reading of Wordsworth's poem to help phrase the language and to structure the feelings and movement of his response to young Berkeley's death. Significantly, Coleridge places the full text of Wordsworth's poem at the end of his letter of April 6. The letter draws from it as from a source and slowly moves toward its consummate expression.

On April 8, 1799, Coleridge wrote to his wife Sara to express consolation. His moving evocation of Berkeley is strangely reminiscent of the girl in the poem later to be known as "She dwelt":

> Dear little Being!—he had existed to me for so many months only in dreams and reveries, but in them existed and still exists so livelily, so like a real Thing, that although I know of his Death, yet when I am alone and have been long silent, it seems to me as if I did not understand it.—Methinks, there is something awful in the thought, what an unknown Being one's own Infant is to one! (Griggs, I, p. 481)

"For so many months" Coleridge had been in Germany, apart from his wife and his children, and his son Berkeley had to exist for him "in dreams and reveries." Even though the child is now dead, Coleridge confesses that there are moments, apparently intense ones, in which he does not understand the change or difference in his child's state of being. Just as in Coleridge's former "dreams and reveries," his son even now "still exists so livelily, so like a real Thing." However, Coleridge still registers the sudden and powerful difference the death means for him. It undermines the more or less complacent solipsism of his reveries that, understandably and movingly, would insist on imaging the child now as before, alive and "real." Death and loss are now what is real, and the knowledge of the difference involved brings on the recognition of how "unknown" Berkeley had actually been to him. The Lucy of "She dwelt" is a similarly unknown being,[4] and the knowledge of her death abruptly unsettles the complacency and dreamlike distance of the speaker of that poem. Wordsworth's lyric on the sudden loss of a scarcely known yet loved person has evidently helped to structure Coleridge's expression of unsettling loss.

In the second letter to Thomas Poole, an emotionally mercurial one written on May 6, 1799, Coleridge bursts into two moments of passion that recall strongly the climactic moment in Wordsworth's "Strange fits of passion." Indeed, the letter contains other moments of excessive passion as well, as though to provide a general context of rather overwrought feelings. Coleridge opens with an impassioned and rhetorically profuse

---

4. The word "unknown," though, is not used in the early version of "She dwelt" that Wordsworth sent to Coleridge in 1798. That version, however, dwells on how far away the girl had been from the poem's speaker and on the slowness of her illness and sufferings (*EY*, pp. 236–37).

declaration of his homesickness and yearning for Poole's company, and he fancies the moment of their affectionate reunion. This projected affection quickly slides through associations to spring and roses and nightingales to a sudden thought on Hartley, Coleridge's firstborn and remaining son:

> I thought of Hartley, my *only* child!—Dear Lamb! I hope, *he* won't be dead, before I get home.—There are moments in which I have such a power of Life within me, such a conceit of it, I mean—that I lay the Blame of my Child's Death to my absence—*not intellectually*; but I have a strange sort of sensation, as if while I was present, none could die whom I intensely loved— (Griggs, I, p. 490).

Suddenly, and without any intellectual connection to what has gone before it, Coleridge fearfully anticipates the death of Hartley. The thought slides into his mind, as it were, on the crest of forcefully affectionate thoughts about home and wishing himself there. Moreover, he also thinks about the actual death of his other child, Berkeley. That death happened, so it appears in certain moments, because Coleridge was absent from the scene. The "power of Life" within him makes Coleridge feel, at least occasionally, this odd conception to be true. If he had been present, the "intensely loved" Berkeley *could not* have died.

The speaker of "Strange fits," of course, has a similar "strange sort of sensation." It is because he is still absent from "Lucy's cot" that the "conceit" of such "a power of Life" within him makes Lucy's fancied death imaginable and credible. He has usurped the whole scene, and his fit of passion inordinately merges all within his all-consuming consciousness. Curiously later on in this same letter, Coleridge says that "in all violent states of *Passion* the mind *acts & plays a part*, itself the actor & and the spectator at once!" (Griggs, I, p. 493). Here Coleridge aptly describes the malady that befalls the speaker of "Strange fits," as well as himself in the first part of his letter to Poole. In a fit of self-deluding passion, the self (or, more restrictively, "the mind") collapses interaction with things and with others outside itself and, instead, takes up and performs the two roles of actor and spectator on its own. Coleridge gives a far more severe example of this kind of blinding and delusive passion in his letter (a murder-suicide of two lovers in Germany), but his own failure to *interact* marks his falling so precipitately into self-delusion and solipsistic consciousness.

Coleridge's letter concludes with a brief repetition of the excessive and fearful fantasy of his remaining son's death: "My dear Poole! don't let Hartley die before I come home.—That's silly—true— & I burst into tears as I wrote it" (Griggs, I, p. 495). The second half of this exclamation, though, reveals Coleridge's awareness of how foolish and perhaps how "wayward" his thought is. He breaks into tears at the realization, and his weeping may also communicate the grief he now truly feels over Berkeley's death. Yet it also recalls the final line of the canceled last stanza of "Strange fits": "My eyes are dim with tears" (EY, p. 238). With this line and with a touch of sadness, the speaker of Wordsworth's lyric—as it originally appeared in the letter of 1798—revealed his recognition of his own error. Such recognition can lead one away from the condition of solipsistic consciousness, fantasy, and error toward recovery of a balanced interaction between self and others.

Ultimately, it is impossible to determine how great an impact Wordsworth's three poems may have had on Coleridge. The three letters that have been discussed here would seem to indicate that Coleridge's readings of his friend's poems helped him to interpret an awareness of loss. It may be that Coleridge himself did not consciously recognize this state of affairs—even when quoting the early text of "A slumber" in full. Even if one is persuaded that he did not, the marked appearance of the language and action of Wordsworth's poems in Coleridge's letters still cannot be dismissed as merely fortuitous. Perhaps it indicates how basic and important a problem Wordsworth was addressing in his three lyrics: the nature and quality of the interaction of a speaker—a self—and another being. Solitude without relationship is the problem. Solipsistic consciousness, consciousness without conscience and careful acts of attention, marks the personas of Wordsworth's poems.

> Solitude is fine when relationship is possible, but the possibility of relationship—indeed its very nature—had first of all to be established. Solitude without relationship is isolation and radical loneliness. That is what Wordsworth feared and fled.[5]

The fear and the flight, however, are not irrational and erratic. "A slumber," "Strange fits," and "She dwelt" explore the problem of solitude

---

5. Frederick Garber, *Wordsworth and the Poetry of Encounter* (Urbana: University of Illinois Press, 1971), p. 27.

without relationship, each in its own specific way and from within a specific experience or manifestation of the problem. By dramatically exhibiting the failures of human figures to interact with one another, the three poems that have been studied in Part One of this book clearly tend to undermine a defective form of consciousness and attention—that of the fantast or the solipsist.

In a way, these three poems serve as brief preludes to a more thoroughgoing poetic and philosophical exploration of the same problem. Wordsworth's eventual masterwork, *The Prelude*, was begun during that same, intense winter in Goslar that witnessed the composition of the first forms of these three "Lucy" poems. For many years the unpublished drafts of Wordsworth's long poem bore the title "The Poem to Coleridge" among the Wordsworth domestic circle. The poet's fullest exploration and critique of the dilemmas and delusions of a self-focused and self-troubled consciousness was, significantly, addressed to his most cunning, ingenious, and appropriate reader. These three lyrics, though, can serve us here as exemplary preludes to a careful and attentive theoretical exploration of the problematics of reading and to the development of a model of reading fully attuned to the exigencies of interaction.

The first part of this book, then, has served to pose in practical terms and in thick descriptive detail the problems that the second part will address in more distinctly theoretical terms. A complete case study of the particulars, problems, and history of the reading of such a central and canonical poem as "A slumber did my spirit seal," as well as two additional so-called "Lucy" poems with which the former has so often been connected, can generate enough practical difficulties and insights to merit and warrant theoretical elaboration. Conceptual generalizations concerning literature are not necessarily tied to literary works and attentive readings of them. However, in the way of proceeding exemplified in this book, the particulars of the activity of reading serve as facts that theorizing must continually take into account. Indeed, theory should be recognized as emerging from the cases that it is called upon to help explain. The construction of theory, that is to say, follows the progressive elaboration of cases.

During the course of the foregoing discussion of Wordsworth's "A slumber," moreover, several basic terms were used and some briefly defined: experience, attention, evidence, work, reader, the activity of reading, interaction, quality, context, and problematic. These terms served to advance a full description and explanation of Wordsworth's

poem. In Part Two of this book, these conceptual and critical terms will
be more fully developed and interrelated. This theoretical elaboration will
proceed inductively, drawing upon and occasionally yet insistently return-
ing to the particulars encountered and articulated in an already full act of
interpretation. My inductive argument will also be at pains to indicate and
clarify the shareable patterns for this kind of literary inquiry—namely, the
recurrent structural features and evidential bases of literary experiences
and inquiries. These shareable patterns constitute the perceptual and
cognitive foundations for the critical and institutional viability of my
notion of the problematics of reading.

PART TWO

REALIGNING LITERARY READING AND CRITICAL INQUIRY:
Interaction and the
Problematics of Reading

. . . *neither the organicism of the extreme biological analogy nor that of the* a priori *or transcendental absolute assertion is likely to encourage superior readings of poetry, but rather that homelier and humbler sort of organicism, in the middle . . . empirical, tentative, analytic, psychological, grammatical, lexicographic.*
> —*Wm. K. Wimsatt, "Organic Form: Some Questions about a Metaphor."*

. . . *good criticism is . . . criticism based on a good philosophy. For a good philosophy is simply the best disposition of all evidence available.*
> —*Stephen Pepper,* Concept and Quality

. . . *we are heirs to a cultural situation particularly unsuited to produce art and likely to encourage the wrong kind of thinking about it. Our experiences and ideas tend to be common but not deep, or deep but not common. We are neglecting the gift of comprehending things by what our senses tell us about them. Concept is split from percept, and thought moves among abstractions.*
> —*Rudolf Arnheim,* Art and Visual Perception

Overt intelligent performances are not clues to the workings of minds; they are those workings.
> —*Gilbert Ryle,* The Concept of Mind

I did not realize at the time of writing how deeply interpretation was rooted in the need to reconcile past and present, letter and spirit, self and other. If the modern tendency is against a reconciling mediation, is it also against interpretation?
> —*Geoffrey Hartman, "Prefatory Note" (1966),* The Unmediated Vision

I found a new hermeneutic;
I found a new paradigm;
I found a plan just to make you mine.

    —Green & Scritti Politti, "Lover to Fall," Cupid and Psyche '85

There, when new wonders ceased to float before,
And thoughts of self came on; how crude and sore
The journey homeward to habitual self!

    —John Keats, Endymion (Book II, lines 274–76)

. . . the construction of an empirically informed critical theory of society might be a legitimate and rational human aspiration.

    —Raymond Guess, The Idea of a Critical Theory

8

Experience, Authority, and Theoretical Ideals: A Preliminary Methodological Caveat

To begin with a practical case study and thereby draw attention to a specific experience of reading eventually, if not immediately, brings into the foreground the kind of authority and theoretical qualifications that experience in general can be said to have. Four general, shared features of experience were sketched in Chapter 1 and will be elaborated in Chapter 14. First of all, however, two broad strategies for displacing the nature of experience and for constructing peculiar models to control the reading of literary works need to be discussed. These two strategies constitute interpretive paths with which my own model of literary reading, developed over the course of the second half of this book, will stand in fundamental disagreement.

The first strategy involves a reification and privileging of beginnings. In order to answer the question concerning the origin of textual meaning, a possible course of critical thinking can lead one to posit the authority of a pure or unqualified beginning. An original and pristine first reading or experience of reading, for instance, could be assumed. The trouble with this procedure is that such a first reading can easily be or become too precious, too private, and perhaps even fictionalized in retrospect. If a reading does not appear to recur or repeat itself on a number of occasions, then the act of privileging a unique first reading incurs the real danger of fictionalizing that reading. The underlying motif here would be the desire for a pure and unqualified beginning for an experience of a text; it would be a beginning that could *authorize* that particular experience. It would be a beginning in need of no other authority or verification than the claim that *it came first.*

A more powerful and persuasive instance of this first strategy can be found in Edward Said's *Beginnings*. Said completely displaces the actual experience of reading a text in favor of reifying and privileging a beginning intention: *"The beginning, then, is the first step in the intentional production of meaning."*[1] As a consequence, in meditating on beginnings, Said places great emphasis on their anteriority or "anterior authority": "To identify a beginning . . . the mind prefers contemplating a strong seminal figure to sifting through reams of explanation," for here "the creation of *authority* is paramount" (pp. 22, 32). The identification of a beginning, then, since it is a preference or even a creation of the mind, actually involves the fictionalizing of a beginning. The originary power of an "anterior authority" fascinates and monopolizes attention, but it may yield no more than a clever fiction. Even though Said himself might be seen as an apologist for a rhetorical strategy that privileges authoritative beginnings throughout Modernist thought, the question still should arise whether this conceptually deceptive rhetorical strategy merits more than historical explanation and critical apologetics. Basically, Said also appears to desire the authority of a pure and unqualified beginning and avoids confronting the consequences of that beginning's being too precious, private, or even arbitrary.

As a case in point, Said chooses Freud as an exemplary instance of "the necessary creation of authority for a beginning." As Said contends, "Freud's lonely discoveries originate what Foucault calls a discursivity— that is, the possibility of, as well as the rule of formation for, subsequent texts" (pp. 33–34). Yet Freud's "authority"—his "lonely," anterior "discoveries"—can be undone. Freud, in the guise of an authoritative beginning for "a discursivity," actually has a number of predecessors whose influence on his work unravels Said's fiction of his being a "lonely" and "strong seminal" beginning. Henri F. Ellenberger, for instance, discusses earlier discoveries and explorations in the notion of the unconscious and proposes Mesmer and hypnosis as the wedge that opens up the

1. Edward Said, *Beginnings* (New York: Basic Books, 1975), p. 5. Italics are Said's. Additional quotations from Said in this paragraph and the next will be followed by the appropriate page numbers in parentheses.

field of modern psychology.[2] Odo Marquard, moreover, traces the roots of the notion of the Freudian unconscious back through a number of nineteenth-century German philosophers of the unconscious, including Nietzsche, E. von Hartmann, C. G. Carus, and Schelling. Marquard claims that the origins of psychoanalytic concepts are to be found in a receding line of philosophical writings and Romantic poets.[3] Contrary to Said's meditations, when a fuller historical view of a conceptual "discovery" is carried out more than likely the historical development or the *temporality* of that notion will eventually steal the interest away from a fascination with putative origins or beginnings. Such beginnings can only be reconstructions *after the fact*. Indeed, any potential history of a notion seems radically compromised or silenced once a fictionalized beginning is permitted the undue power to *authorize* "subsequent texts."[4]

The second broad strategy that displaces the nature of experience and constructs a peculiar model for governing the reading of literary works is the attempt to promote controlled experiments with the responses of readers. Such experiments, however, may not yield normal or authentic responses to a literary work at all. Instead, they may only reveal evidence of the motivation and extent of the experimenter's control and desires in what is an ineradicably contrived and highly selective situation. This

2. H. F. Ellenberger, *The Discovery of the Unconscious: The History and Evolution of Dynamic Psychiatry* (New York: Basic Books, 1970).

3. See Odo Marquard, "Zur Bedeutung der Theorie des Unbewussten für eine Theorie der Nicht Mehr Schönen Kunste," *Die Nicht Mehr Schönen Kunste*, ed. Hans R. Jauss (Munich: Fink, 1968), pp. 376–79. Friedrich von Schiller in his *On the Aesthetic Education of Man, in a Series of Letters*, ed. and trans. E. M. Wilkinson and L. A. Willoughby (Oxford: Clarendon Press, 1967) psychologizes Kant's conception of the transcendental subject by initiating the use of the term "drive" (*Trieb*) to name the three fundamental drives or functions of human nature—sense, form, and play. Schiller's conception and usage of these drives appears to constitute a major pretext and prefiguration for Sigmund Freud's conception of unconscious psychic drives.

4. In a wider view, Said's meditations on beginnings are powerful and moving, perhaps because of his covert presentation of "beginnings" as a term for "God," for an authoritative and ineffable absolute:

> Its existence cannot be doubted, yet its persistence is wholly to itself. Because it cannot truly be known, because it belongs more to silence than it does to language, because it is what has always been left behind, and because it challenges continuities that go cheerfully forward with *their* beginnings obediently affixed—it is therefore something of a necessary fiction. It is perhaps our permanent concession as finite minds to an ungraspable absolute. (p. 77)

The rhetoric of this passage is disturbingly transfused with theological content and constructions.

condition appears frequently, if not unavoidably, in controlled experiments in general. Basically, the very principles an experiment attempts to establish or verify are already present within the operational procedures the investigator has chosen. In other words, controlled experiments attempt to test the usefulness or applicability of a proposed system of measurement solely by using or applying the essentially uncriticized terms and procedures of that system.

This state of affairs in the methodology of science and the conditions of experimentation is recognized and examined by Stephen Toulmin. He observes that an experimenter needs guidance in all aspects of his experiment even before he enters the laboratory in the first place. "This guidance," Toulmin avers, "can come only from a careful statement of his theoretical problem, and if one looks at the conditions of the experiment he performs one will find that they are tailor-made to suit this theoretical problem."[5] An experimenter's theoretical problem, then, dictates the parameters—the pattern, the cut, and the fit—of the experiment. A scientist, or a researcher employing a standard scientific methodology, determines from the beginning the very conditions he or she will be observing and testing in order to clarify or verify the problem posed. Toulmin notes that this "limited scope" of experimental method and techniques necessitates "other methods." Indeed, "it remains to be discovered from experience how far [a] theoretical ideal [proposed in the self-closed terms of the experiment] can be realized."[6]

Toulmin's observations on the *solipsistic* nature of uncritical and uncriticized scientific experiments and their theoretical ideals should serve as cautionary remarks as well as for humanists who seek to apply experimental method and techniques to the study of readers' response. The results of such systematic application will probably not yield "authentic" responses at all but should eventually reveal an overall imposition of the response critic's "theoretical ideal" upon his or her respondents. The complexities and diverse discoveries involved in the experience of reading will often be forgotten or displaced when only certain conditions of "response" are selectively sought out and formulated according to predetermined theoretical ideals.[7]

---

5. Stephen Toulmin, *The Philosophy of Science* (London: Hutchinson University Library, 1953), p. 66. See also pp. 63–73 for Toulmin's full analysis.

6. Ibid., p. 69.

7. In his commentary on the *New Literary History* issue on "Readers and Spectators," A. R.

Some examples of controlled experiments with readers' response can help to illustrate their general methodological difficulties. For instance, in a special issue of *New Literary History* devoted to "The Language of Literature," Gillian Cohen addresses the skills and strategies of the reader of literature.[8] Her theoretical problem is to achieve a reliable statistical sample of reading comprehension. The conditions of her experiment, however, can accommodate only an extremely selective and contrived version of this problem: a reading speed versus comprehension accuracy "trade-off." The skills and strategies of the reader are supposed to be reflected in statistical mappings of the quantity of "material" retained against the quantity of time consumed in its "uptake." The chosen "material" consists of prose passages that possess an even texture and that place a minimum demand on readers. Needless to say, such texture and demand may help in talking and thinking about ordinary newspaper, popular magazine, and pulp novel comprehension; but then again such material also can be attended to and used in a wide variety of ways. The conditions of Cohen's controlled experiment, though, presuppose a certain homogeneity of material so that the variables of reading speed and comprehension can be singled out and calibrated. The single "theoretical ideal," to use Toulmin's phrase, of a speed versus accuracy ratio thereby imposes from the start significant restraints on the kind of "literature" and varieties of response involved. Furthermore, the conditions and procedures of this experiment in reading comprehension actually already delimit and promote a very restricted model of reading: Readers are just so many types of vacuum cleaners that can be run over the same or similar surfaces at varying speeds and with proportionally varying suction and retention. The conditions, the procedures, and the resultant statistics all assume and reinforce this one model of the reader as a variously efficient consuming machine. Human skills and strategies here atrophy or, rather, become the motions and built-in features of that theoretically ideal machine.

In another and longer study of readers, James R. Squire statistically patterns and assesses the verbal reactions of fifty-two ninth- and tenth-

---

Louch points out that the writers in the issue collectively manage to avoid readers and the particulars of reading and emphasize only theory. See "Criticism and Theory," *NLH* 8 (Autumn 1976): 171–81.

  8. "The Psychology of Reading," *New Literary History* 4 (Autumn 1972): 75–90.

grade students to four short stories from popular magazines.[9] Squire categorizes and charts the progress of his respondents' reactions, associations, and judgments in the course of their actual reading. At several points the adolescents are stopped and asked to summarize their responses to what they have read so far. The stories themselves use adolescent characters, problems, and fantasies in a generally unreflective and undemanding way. The stories, then, are available for and indeed encourage an easy emotional transfer and identification on the part of their adolescent readers. Because the reading selections present no significant challenge or departure from the expected behavior of their adolescent readers, Squire could just as well have statistically patterned and assessed stories and fantasies produced by the adolescents themselves. His conclusion about his respondents' reading reactions could also just as well suit their reactions to almost anything: "The results suggest that although certain group tendencies are observable in the reading reactions of adolescents, individual variation is caused by the unique influence of the abilities, predispositions, and experiential background of each reader."[10] That is, their reactions all exhibit certain characteristics common to their stage of intellectual, social, and emotional development, *as well as* behavioral particulars caused by the fact that each respondent is an individual with his or her own unique abilities, predispositions, and background. The conditions of Squire's experiment, therefore, do little more than guarantee a statistical reinforcement or confirmation of the sociologically obvious: A person's typical and uncritical behavior exhibits both group tendencies and individual influences. This observation is not to say that statistical reinforcement or confirmation is not without its uses. Squire's choice of material and his procedure of interrupting readings and soliciting summary responses, however, guarantee that his experimental results will not depart very much from those that a psychosocial or cultural analysis of his adolescent respondents would easily produce. His theoretical ideal, then, is much the same as that which a quantitative psychologist or sociologist would frame in attempting to measure and categorize the standard behavior of this group of adolescents: How *regular* is the *behavior* I have chosen to measure, and can I account for or dismiss as insignificant any irregularities that may occur? This theoretical ideal, as it

9. J. R. Squire, *The Responses of Adolescents While Reading Four Short Stories* (Champaign, Ill.: NCTE, 1964), pp. 1–65.
    10. Ibid., p. 50.

can perhaps now be recognized, is thoroughly and redundantly mirrored in the conditions and procedures of Squire's controlled experiment. Essentially, this single theoretical ideal dictates the conditions, procedures, and results of this quantitatively biased form of experiment with readers' response.[11]

Not all studies of readers' response to literary works, however, are quantitative or rigidly experimental in the usual scientific sense. The works of Norman Holland and David Bleich constitute more holistic and seemingly less rigidly controlled investigations of readers responding to what they have read.[12] Careful analysis, however, can reveal experimental control and manipulation of response in their work that appears every bit as epistemologically suspect as that which readily surfaces in the projects of Gillian Cohen and James Squire. For all their discussion of the psychological complexities of readers and their responses, Holland and Bleich resolve on their separate theoretical ideals and, as a consequence, displace a great deal of the complexities and diverse discoveries involved in the actual experience of reading a literary work. Through the remainder of this chapter, I will examine in some detail Holland's and Bleich's variations on the second broad strategy under discussion—the displacement of experience through controlled experiments with the responses of readers.

The general epistemological problem that marks their attempts at a broad psychological explanation of the divergences in the responses of readers can be formulated as an objection to a summary statement made by Norman Holland in *Poems in Persons*: "The plain fact of the matter, however, is: no one, until quite recently, knew what went on in the mind of the reader because no one had a psychology adequate to the

---

11. For a survey of predominantly quantitative studies of readers' response, see Alan C. Purves and Richard Beach, *Literature and the Reader: Research in Response to Literature, Reading Interests, and the Teaching of Literature* (Champaign, Ill.: NCTE, 1972).

12. The works under review here are N. N. Holland, *Poems in Persons* (New York: W. W. Norton, 1973) and *5 Readers Reading* (New Haven, Conn.: Yale University Press, 1975), and David Bleich, *Readings and Feelings* (Champaign, Ill.: NCTE, 1975) and *Subjective Criticism* (Baltimore, Md.: Johns Hopkins University Press, 1978). I will not discuss Holland's earlier work on response, best represented by *The Dynamics of Literary Response* (New York: Oxford University Press, 1968) and "The 'Unconscious' of Literature: The Psychoanalytic Approach," in *Contemporary Criticism*, ed. M. Bradbury and D. Palmer (London: Edward Arnold, 1970), pp. 131–53. The earlier position on response taken by Holland is perhaps best appraised by Wolfgang Iser, *The Act of Reading: A Theory of Aesthetic Response* (Baltimore, Md.: Johns Hopkins University Press, 1978), pp. 38–45.

problem."[13] Holland assumes that one must have a theory before one can know anything about what the theory is supposed to explain. That is to say, a response critic must stipulate a set of psychological conditions for readers before he or she can know what happens to readers psychologically. The conditions here will dictate the results. However, one can at least object that the diverse facts and complexities of readers and readings have been with us a long time, showing us movingly "what went on in the mind of the reader." The Greco-Roman writer Longinus's intelligent and emotional response to the invention ("inventio") of Sappho's ode "Peer of gods he seemeth to me, the blissful," in the tenth section of *On the Sublime*, Coleridge's insightful and imitative response to *The Prelude* in his ode "To William Wordsworth," Wordsworth's own sensitive and instructive attentions to his poem "With ships the sea was sprinkled far and nigh" discussed in Part One of this book, and a reflective reader's cognizance of his or her own history of reading are just a few examples of a bountiful *foreknowledge* of what goes on in the minds of readers. Indeed, theories of reader response need "other methods," in Stephen Toulmin's words, to keep them responsive and attentive to the experience of reading. The prior and authoritative positing of "a psychology" is ultimately only an *assertion* of adequacy to the problem of reading and response. A history of readers and readings is actually already available to question such a psychology's "adequacy," its "priority," and its "authority."

The theoretical ideal that governs Holland's work on readers' response is a concept that he borrows from the psychoanalytic psychiatrist Heinz Lichtenstein:

> When we describe the "character" or "personality" of another person, Lichtenstein shows, we abstract an invariant from "the infinite sequence of bodily and behavioral transformations during the whole life of the individual." That is, we can be precise about individuality by conceiving of the individual as living out variations on an identity theme much as a musician might play out an infinity of variations on a single melody. We discover that underlying theme by abstracting it from its variations.[14]

13. Holland, *Poems in Persons*, p. 60
14. Holland, "Unity Identity Text Self," *PMLA* 90 (1975): 814. This essay is a general statement of Holland's "identity theme" approach, which is developed at length in *Poems in Persons*, pp. 45–59, 76–78, and *5 Readers Reading*, especially pp. 53–62, 113–29. Heinz

Holland assumes that the "personality" or "character" of a reader can be graphed by abstracting an invariant "identity theme" from among all his or her *supposed* behavioral variations or transformations. He claims that "there is *one* style that operates in *all* the ego's activities."[15] It is established in infancy "out of the 'fit' of mother and baby," and it is mandated as "a zero point which must precede all other mental developments."[16] Holland cites a number of remarks by psychoanalytic clinicians and theorists as support for this invariant "identity theme," yet none of them are so rigorously reductionist and theoretically ambitious. Even Lichtenstein himself, as David Bleich points out, is far more careful and thoroughgoing in the development and generalization of a patient's identity theme than Holland is in articulating the identity themes of his paid reading subjects. Holland's undergraduate-student respondents are not undergoing long-term and circumspect therapy; and the full "array of interpersonal relationships and personal history—parents, siblings, friends, lovers, vocational aspirations, religious and ethnic backgrounds, and so on"—is scarcely brought into account. Thus "there is no context that can establish the generality of the identity theme and hence its explanatory authority over a reader's response." Indeed, as Bleich concludes, "unless a personality style is carefully developed in the full way described by Lichtenstein, it cannot be a principle of explanation in the study of response."[17]

This "principle," or, rather, this theoretical ideal, nonetheless becomes the notion through which Holland can experimentally control the minds and responses of his reading subjects. He assumes beforehand that a single identity theme can be found for each of his readers. He assumes that this theme *can be found by examining* their various elicited responses and that this theme *can then be used to explain* all the variations manifested in these responses. Again, a familiar methodological predicament surfaces: The conditions, the procedures, and the results of a managed experiment in response are all dictated by a single theoretical ideal preselected by the experimenter.

Lichtenstein develops his concept of a person's "identity theme" in " Identity and Sexuality: A Study of Their Interrelationship in Man," *Journal of the American Psychoanalytic Association* 9 (1961): 179–260.

15. Holland, *Poems in Persons*, p. 48.

16. Ibid., p. 49. The last phrase is Lichtenstein's.

17. Bleich, *Subjective Criticism*, pp. 118, 119. For Bleich's full critique of Holland's use of the concept of the "identity theme," see pp. 116–19.

Holland, moreover, strives to assert his assumed authority in the very face of this methodological predicament:

> In the developed adult, I can assume an invariant identity theme (whether or not it coincides with an actual primary identity imprinted in infancy), and by means of it grasp an unchanging essence, a "personality" or "character," that permeates the millions of ego choices that constitute the visible human before me, ever changing and different, yet ever continuous with what went before. I can abstract, from the choices in the life I see, facts as visible as the words on a page, various subordinate patterns and themes until I arrive at one central, unifying pattern in that life which is the invariant sameness, the "identity theme" of the individual living it.[18]

Holland boldly asserts what amounts to his own *myth* of the human mind. Indeed, if he can assume access to "an invariant identity theme," "one central, unifying pattern," regardless of *"whether or not it coincides with an actual primary identity imprinted in infancy,"* then Holland simply manufactures the psychology that he feels he must have in order to explain response. Such a project clearly approximates mythmaking. It is curious, and I believe illuminating, that Holland in a number of passages quotes with approbation William Butler Yeats's offhand "fancy" of an all-informing personal "myth": "I can, in fact, achieve Yeats's 'fancy that there is some one Myth for every man, which, if we but knew it, would make us understand all he did and thought.'"[19]

The myth of the human mind that Holland here propounds *generally* is that any human mind possesses a definite and definitive "organic unity." Holland notes that Freud took such unity as a singularly basic assumption of psychoanalytic explanation and that Lichtenstein, among later psycho- analysts, is "the one who has best grasped the organic unity in the

---

18. Holland, "Unity Identity Text Self," p. 815.

19. Ibid., p. 820. See also Holland, *Poems in Persons*, pp. 9, 48, and 5 *Readers Reading*, pp. 51f. The sentence from Yeats can be found in his "At Stratford-on-Avon," *Ideas of Good and Evil* (London: Bullen, 1903), p. 162. The context of Yeats's fancy is a series of impressionistic reflections on Shakespeare and the "myth" that might unify his stories and characters. Yeats's "myth" and Holland's "identity theme" resemble the "cogito" of an author that George Poulet's literary criticism strives to locate.

psyche."[20] Organic unity, however, is a notion based on an analogy. If the analogical basis is not understood or interpreted adequately, the notion itself will misleadingly (if not erroneously) be taken as precisely transcribing the human mode of mental organization.[21] The analogy itself merely allows us to think of the mind as structured like an organism whose parts and functions all contribute to that organism's spatio-temporal existence and subsistence. A single "identity theme," "character," "personality," "personal style," "ego identity," "lifestyle," or "myth"—to use all the terms that Holland invokes[22]—is not a necessary structural feature of the analogy of organic unity.[23] It is, though, a frequent and contingent feature of the uses to which organic unity was put by many of the so-called New Critics. Holland actually employs "organic unity" in much the same way that such literary formalists used the notion in theorizing the mode of organization of literary works. And he is aware of this similar use:

> What is surprising to me—and troubling—is the discovery that my critical method, disciplined, professional, accredited, also acts out my identity theme. I *like* examining the verbal surface of a text, looking for an "organic unity" in the way the parts all come together. From the very first evening I encountered it, the new criticism has exerted almost a spell on me. I found compelling and attractive the idea of analyzing the words on the page and them alone. The demand that one treat the poem as a thing in itself referring only to itself and hence that one pay no more attention

20. Holland, *Poems in Persons*, p. 49.
21. As Roy Schafer has argued at great length in *A New Language for Psychoanalysis* (New Haven, Conn.: Yale University Press, 1976), Freud's metapsychology and the metapsychological language of many of his disciples are plagued with mechanistic and organismic metaphors and analogies. These "unsuitable, confusing, unnecessary and meaningless metaphors and meta-phorical preconceptions that are inherent in Freud's eclectic metapsychological language" can be examined and eliminated; and, "to be internally consistent, the evolving theory of the psychoanalytic process requires a thoroughly non-mechanistic, non-organismic language" (pp. 123, 120).
22. Holland, *Poems in Persons*, pp. 48–50 and elsewhere.
23. See James Benziger's excellent essay "Organic Unity: Leibniz to Coleridge," *PMLA* 66 (March 1951): 24–48, especially pp. 33–34. See also Jonathan Culler's remarks on the relevance of organic unity to the work of Holland in his "Prolegomena to a Theory of Reading," in *The Reader in the Text*, ed. I. Crosman and S. Suleiman (Princeton, N.J.: Princeton University Press, 1980), p. 55.

than absolutely necessary to historical background, evaluation, or author's biography or intention suits me exactly.[24]

A sense of full control over another entity seems paramount here, and the notion of "organic unity" is the means to that end. The "identity theme" of the critical analyst must separate the analysand from social and historical contexts, values, and individual intentions and analyze the isolated texture or surface of what remains in search of that which unifies it. Many of the New Critics reduced the text to "a thing in itself referring only to itself" and sought out the central or governing theme that would show how "the parts all come together." In a similar, indeed in an analogical fashion, Holland's "critical method" reduces the person to a textlike thing and seeks out the "identity theme" that would show how all the (behavioral) "parts" of that person coherently and organically converge on it:

> Precisely because I came from a tradition of New Criticism, I found I could translate Lichtenstein's concept into operational terms: we can arrive at someone's identity by interpreting their behavior for an underlying thematic unity just as we would interpret a literary text for a centering theme.[25]

Holland's myth of the human mind implies that the mind must be understood as a text, must be understood as structured and organized as the kind of text favored by many New Critics for rigorous and controlled analysis. "*Identity* is the *unity* I find in a *self*," he states, "if I look at it as though it were a *text*."[26] Here the appended *conditional clause* cannot and should not be overlooked. Unemphatic syntactically, this clause still

24. Holland, *Poems in Persons*, pp. 112–13.
25. Holland, "The New Paradigm: Subjective or Transactive?," *New Literary History* 7 (Winter 1976): 337.
26. Holland, "Unity Identity Text Self," p. 815 (Holland's italics). Holland's two most recent books carry on this concern for taking unity as the measure of identity for the self. See especially pages 1–82, "The Aesthetics of I," of Holland's most ambitious projection of a psychology of personal identity, *The I* (New Haven, Conn.: Yale University Press, 1985), and pages 8–42 of *The Brain of Robert Frost: A Cognitive Approach to Literature* (New York: Routledge, 1988) in which Holland models personal identity psychology upon research into the holistic architecture and biochemistry of the brain. Generally he makes the claim: "I *can* read Robert Frost as a theme and variations. I *can* phrase a theme against which I can interpret his poems and his opinions as variations" (pp. 41–42). (Italics in original)

carries a resounding sleight of hand. Holland's myth frequently discloses itself troubling the verbal surfaces that express his most basic and well-shared analogy. That is, the dehumanizing textualization of persons (readers) is semantically cognate with the rhetoric of New Critical "organic unity" and governing "theme."

This dehumanizing textualization of readers was found in Part One of this book to be a danger of Holland's critical method as it applied to his reading and theorizing of "A slumber did my spirit seal." This state of affairs connects clearly enough with his narrowly conceived personality psychology, his sense of the way in which an individual (a self, a person) relates to others, be they things, poems, or people:

> The individual (considered as the continuing creator of variations on an identity theme) relates to the world as he does to a poem or a story: he uses its physical reality as grist with which to re-create himself, that is, to make yet another variation in his single, enduring identity.
>
> . . . people take in the "other" by building up from it their structure of defense and adaptation. The physical reality of the other, be it literary text or the real world or what someone else says, serves as building blocks.[27]

Holland does not image the individual here as a being who interacts in different ways and at different levels with various types and levels of others in the world. Instead, all others are imaged as the same sort of entity for the self who relates to them. Others are "grist" or "building blocks" that the self can "take in" and use to "re-create" itself. Metaphors of eating and growing (or self-construction) converge here; and, of course, the image of an infant feeding at a mother's breast can be detected informing their choice, appeal, and power. Holland admits that he builds a great deal of his psychology out of the oral fantasy,[28] but he never questions whether this one fantasy and the corresponding emphasis on the so-called oral or

27. Holland, *5 Readers Reading*, pp. 128–29, and *Poems in Persons*, p. 143. Both of these statements appear as important and summary conclusions of the two books. The first is a "basic principle" of what would be "a general account of the relation of personality to the perception and interpretation of experience" (pp. 128–29), and the second is "a general law of human psychology" (p. 143).

28. Holland, *Poems in Persons*, pp. vii, 139.

infantile phase of human development is adequate to explain the whole of human psychology. The risk here, I think, amounts to an infantilizing conception of human beings or a conception of personality that, for all intents and purposes, arrests it at an infantile stage of development. This situation resembles the conception of the Romantic lover derived from J. M. Hawthorn and Stanley Diamond discussed in Part One. Never really satisfied emotionally in his earliest stages of development, the Romantic lover is transfixed by the desire to incorporate the other. The Romantic lover's oral fantasy usually and quite morbidly takes the form of a death fantasy. In the imagination of the beloved's death, the lover has the illusion of utter control. Imaginatively and satisfyingly and, more than likely, repeatedly, he incorporates or ingests the insubstantialized other into his own psyche. With Holland's conception of human psychology, it can be said, the individual is similarly emotionally unsatisfied and unsatisfiable. Fixated at the so-called oral or infantile phase, the self is transfixed by the desire to incorporate or ingest the other—the mother or the mother's breasts, as the psychoanalytic fantasy would have it. The self, then, continually takes in and feeds on others in its self-involved re-creation of itself. Because they are not attended to in a mutually responsive and attentive way, others become either denatured or dehumanized in this consumptive process. Others are incorporated—absorbed—in the solipsistic and narcissistic project of the re-creating self.

Holland's readers, consequently, incorporate or absorb texts into themselves: "Reading provides us with a potential space in which the distinction between 'in here' and 'out there' blurs as we ingest the external world into our ongoing psychological processes."[29] Readers denature—detextualize—texts during this process of ingestion: "the reader treats the text as a treasure of words, images, episodes, characters, sounds, and the like, from which he draws to construct within himself his own fantasies and defenses, those that satisfy his unique personality and character structure."[30] Readers reading, in effect, utterly undo the texts before them and take in selected items as so many gleanings from a thesaurus. In

29. Holland, 5 Readers Reading, pp. 287–88.
30. Holland, "Letter to Leonard," Hartford Studies in Literature 5 (1973): 22–23. This attitude toward the text would generally seem to encourage inattention, disregard, and narcissistic fantasy. Richard W. Noland, "The Future of Psychological Criticism," Hartford Studies in Literature 5 (1973): 100, cautions against such readerly and critical irresponsibility: "What the text establishes" is "a useful limitation, since it blocks [psychological critics] from inventing childhood fantasies and events not given in the text."

essence, they construct their own "texts," "texts" that re-create their personal identity themes. The response critic, in turn, reads these "textualized" selves. He dehumanizes his reading subjects as he incorporates them into his own identity theme.[31] That is to say, readers reading detextualize texts yet textualize themselves. Response critics interpreting dehumanize and textualize readers while self-consciously textualizing themselves. Texts serve merely as pretexts for the reader-as-text.

Perhaps a brief examination of one of Holland's practical examples, which collectively are supposed to justify the need for his psychological and critical theorizing and procedures, can demonstrate pragmatically the inadequacy of his theoretical ideal to the actual problems of reading a literary work and understanding texts as texts and readers as readers. Holland begins the first chapter of *5 Readers Reading* ("The Question: Who Reads What How?") by logging the different responses of his five reading subjects to a tableau description of Miss Emily from William Faulkner's "Rose for Emily."[32] The five readers—Sam, Saul, Shep, Sebastian, and Sandra—all respond to this description and apparently say markedly different things about it. Such differing responses are supposed to justify the ensuing quest for that principle or theoretical ideal of personality psychology that will explain them. By looking closely at the summaries of how these five readers responded, however, one can see that only two of them are actually reading and attempting to interpret this tableau description with some measure of attention to it and its place within the story. Sam singles it out quickly, responds articulately and precisely, and integrates it with what else he knows and thinks about the character of Emily. Sandra, who is very familiar with the story and has written on it, also brings up the tableau description, though a little inaccurately, and integrates it in her sense of Emily, a sense of her character really quite similar to Sam's more articulate response. The three other readers do not single out or bring up the description. Holland had to prompt two of them— Saul and Shep—to respond to the passage; Saul

---

31. Taped interviews provide the texts of these textualized selves in *Poems in Persons* and *5 Readers Reading*. In a variation on this response format—the "Delphi seminar"—students write out their responses to literary and critical works and then assist in eliciting or abstracting one another's identity themes from these documents. See Holland and Murray Schwartz, "The Delphi Seminar," *College English* 36 (March 1975): 789–800, and English 692 (with Norman Holland), "Poem Opening: An Invitation to Transactive Criticism," *College English* 40 (September 1978): 2–16.

32. Holland, *5 Readers Reading*, pp. 1–14.

had to look it up and Holland had to read it aloud to Shep. Saul's and Shep's elicited and rather diffident responses are fragmented, halting, free associations to an uncontextualized image. Whatever they may be doing, I think it unreasonable and misleading to call it reading or responding to "A Rose for Emily." Sebastian, meanwhile, does not mention the tableau description but does cynically and unattentively stereotype the character of Emily. Clearly, Sam and Sandra are the *better* readers of this passage and, probably, of the entire story. They are interested and engaged in and by the particulars of the tale. They attempt to understand, even empathize with, Emily as if she were a person and not a type. The nature and quality of their attention and interest and their need and ability to articulate an integrated response justify the judgment of them as the "better" readers of the passage and story in question. The five responses and their differences are not all equally adequate, as the drift of Holland's presentation would have it. They are responses *to* a situation, either an experience of reading or a prompting to associate freely. Accordingly, the responses can be assessed as to the quality and appropriateness of the performance. Differences occur but not ineluctably. They can be judged knowingly and successfully, and Holland at one point confesses an awareness of this fact: "some of these differences involve outright misreadings."[33] The theoretical ideal of the identity theme has not been necessary here in order to sort out and make some initial sense of a group of readers and their responses. Holland's work on readers' response very usefully draws attention to readers and their role in understanding literature, but it fails to be adequate to the full complexities of actual experiences of reading literary works.

David Bleich also dwells on the role of personality in readers' response. In general, he comes up against many of the same problems that Holland's work has already been shown to encounter while employing psychoanalytic psychology and the theoretical ideal of the identity theme. Bleich does not draw upon psychoanalysis or identity theory but still, in a number of places, critiques Freud sympathetically. He does, however, emphasize the motivational theory of individual psychological development, especially as it relates to the acquisition of language.[34] Bleich's conception of an individual or a person yields a portrait of a subjectively and aggressively motivated member of a clearly designated community

33. Ibid., p. 4.
34. Bleich, *Subjective Criticism*, pp. 38–67.

who seeks out and needs a consensus from the other members of that community for the validation of his or her opinions or judgments. With respect to reading, Bleich contends that readers create the meanings and importance that literary works have for them. Like Holland, Bleich promotes the case for the reader's role in the "re-creation" of literature, but he does so in a much more thoroughgoing way. Holland waffles on whether or not he is proposing a subjective paradigm for literary studies; Bleich straightforwardly admits and campaigns for the subjectivity that both of their stances imply.[35] If Holland's stress on psychoanalytic identity theory is placed in abeyance, then Bleich's work on readers' responses can be recognized as aggressively following out the logic of their *mutual* insistence on the primacy of the reader's personality or "subjectivity" in responding to literature.[36]

Bleich proposes a whole program for the controlled eliciting and manipulation of adolescent student responses to literature. The classroom becomes the chosen scene for this program and appears to function as a laboratory for the production and conversion of "feelings" or "emotional responses" or "reactions." This program is not as rigorously controlled an experiment as quantitative and statistical studies of response characteristically are, but it is nonetheless supposed to be carefully managed and directed by "an enlightened teacher."[37] The idea is to achieve written statements or documents of individual student responses to a particular work under class consideration. Guidelines for doing this are developed by Bleich and will be discussed shortly, but what is important here is that individual or personal responses are being documented by the respondents themselves. This is a very important and informative strategy for understanding response and has good precedent in the "protocols" of I. A. Richards's *Practical Criticism*. Richards, however, evaluated his student respondents by a more or less normative psychology. In clear contradis-

---

35. Bleich, *Subjective Criticism*, pp. 10–37, where Bleich gives his fullest statement of "the subjective paradigm." She also pp. 110–16 for his critique of Holland's waffling on subjectivity, objectivity, and transaction. Bleich and Holland squared off over "the subjective paradigm" in two articles in *New Literary History* 7 (Winter 1976): 313–46, and in two letters to the editor in *College English* 38 (November 1976): 298–301.

36. Holland's work on the "Delphi" seminars foregrounds written, subjective response statements and classroom (seminar) discussion of them. These are important features of David Bleich's overall method of "subjective criticism." See also footnote 31, p. 147.

37. Bleich, *Readings and Feelings*, p. 17. Pages 7–19 of this book outline the program that teachers are to follow in eliciting and managing student responses. Bleich carefully differentiates his program from statistical studies of response in *Subjective Criticism*, pp. 101–7.

tinction, Bleich formulates a theoretical ideal that foregrounds the
personal, and even the idiosyncratic, rather than the normative features of
response.[38] Essentially, he claims that "feelings" or "emotional responses"
are the source of and, what is more, *authorize* knowledge. Bleich states
that "the aim in class is to understand how people respond emotionally
and then translate these responses into thoughts and judgments."[39] The
assumption here is that feelings, which are personal and apparently prior
to anything else, can be converted after the fact of their occurrence into
a shareable language:

> The practice of formulating response statements is a means for
> making a language experience (hearing, speaking, reading, or
> writing) available for conversion into knowledge.[40]

The value accorded feelings and the attempt to integrate them with what
we call knowledge are, I believe, extremely important and commendable
goals in literary theory and criticism. These goals should be recognized as
positive and strong features of Bleich's work on response. However, he
does tend to streamline a complex interaction of feelings and types of
knowledge into a single uniform model: The self and its feelings are prior
to anything intersubjective or interactive, and this self's *subjectivity—and
nothing else—authorizes* whatever counts as *knowledge*. The "subjective
authorizing of knowledge," then, can be said to be Bleich's theoretical
ideal. It guides the attention being paid to personal feelings, to the
planned eliciting of individual response, and to the formulation of
individual response statements. That individuals have feelings or emotional responses becomes singled out as that which alone can originate or
authorize knowledge and guarantee its authority for whatever intersubjective or communal exchange may ensue.

The written response statement constitutes a very important fulcrum in
this model of response. First of all, it reifies feelings, makes them more or
less precise yet clearly present to the respondent. If they were initially too
fleeting, haphazard, or halting, now they are established and formed, if

38. Bleich sets out his differences from Richards in *Readings and Feelings*, p. 111, and in
"The Subjective Paradigm in Science, Psychology, and Criticism," *New Literary History* 7
(1976): 330–31.
39. Bleich, *Readings and Feelings*, p. 15.
40. Bleich, *Subjective Criticism*, p. 132.

not in part forged, as the facts of a particular individual's response.[41] Second, these documents then become available for the *negotiation* of subjective responses into some type of communally agreed-upon knowledge. Bleich states this twofold importance of the response document in these terms:

> But no matter what sort of symbolic objects are under scrutiny, it is not likely that the development of subjectively grounded knowledge can proceed without a verbal document and its verbal negotiation. . . . The response statement is a symbolic presentation of self, a contribution to a pedagogical community, and an articulation of that part of our reading experience we think we can negotiate into knowledge.[42]

The "verbal document," the response statement, then, stands between and links the responding subject and the community that he consents to present himself to and to which he seeks to contribute knowledge via negotiation.

The concept of negotiation is crucial for Bleich's theory of subjective criticism. It adds the necessary communal or intersubjective dimension to the discussion of response, while reining in possible excesses in response, excesses that would be subjectively grounded but may not offer knowledge that would be of use or significance to a particular community. Bleich develops some roughly generalized anthropological facts of belief and public authority, of social and institutional control of language and meaning. Summarizing, he claims:

> The use of language, even by all of us who are now literate, depends on the *belief* in meanings. I stress that the handling of language and literature depends not on certain knowledge of meanings, but belief in them. These beliefs have no other source

---

41. The issue of forging response for classroom, and ultimately graded, use is a potentially endless one. I do not want to bring it up as something that can significantly fault Bleich's pedagogical techniques because the same issue can and will recur for any method using *oral or written* responses to reading. All responses should not be taken at face value. Some respondents will and do *forge* (or counterfeit) responses: Some overmake, form, or *forge* them as a smithy works over raw materials; some fake, falsify, or *forge* them as a confidence man might do with a credulous yet enthusiastic naif (e.g., the response-oriented teacher).

42. Bleich, *Subjective Criticism*, p. 167.

> than the accumulated social uses of language. . . . It is not
> possible [for instance] to separate the meaning of words and of
> literature from the way language and literature are handled by
> speakers and readers.[43]

Since belief and "the accumulated social uses of language" serve to secure
whatever counts as knowledge in and for a community, and no single
individual has privileged or intuitive access to certain knowledge of
meanings (Cartesianism or rationalism), new knowledge must be communally negotiated into acceptance and credence. We believe in and use
knowledge within social groups and must assimilate new knowledge by
means of some form of public negotiation. The social uses to which
speakers and readers put language and literature thus cannot be divorced
from the kind of knowledge that language and literature can be said to
provide. New uses, of course, require a communal struggle toward
understanding, assimilation, and readiness for further social use.

Remarkably, there would appear to be an interactional and context-
oriented speech-act model implicit in Bleich's application of his concept
of negotiation. It remains, however, an implicit model that is continually
undercut by his recurrent emphasis on the prior authority of subjectivity.
At one juncture, for instance, Bleich dismisses the interactional possibilities of the social uses of language by strangely opposing language to
personal feelings:

> It is not simply a matter of habit and tradition to avoid speaking of
> one's own feelings; our linguistic forms of discourse seem espe-
> cially to facilitate speaking of what we perceive to be outside
> ourselves before speaking of what we know to be inside.[44]

Even Bleich's diction here—"what we perceive to be outside" versus "what
we know to be inside"—uncritically but insistently supports his privileging
of subjectivity over against socialization and the resources that language
provides for individuals. Language and the interactions it facilitates with

43. Ibid., pp. 6–7. Bleich's appeal to anthropological considerations is not altogether helpful
or credible. His generalizations about the institution of religion, his interpretation of the first
verse of the Gospel of John, and his account of the function of the literate in so-called illiterate
societies (pp. 4–6) amount to questionable social anthropology.

44. Bleich, *Readings and Feelings*, p. 9.

what is outside ourselves is needed, but it is wholly posterior to the self's private knowledge of itself.

Negotiation, then, becomes a concession to the unavoidable. Individuals clearly must and manifestly do deal with other individuals, and so discrete subjectivities must negotiate toward what they all agree to accept as mutually known and regulative. Belief and the social uses of language *accumulate* as so many laws and regulations and precedents pile up in codes of law and their commentaries. The law analogy, along with its situations of legislative assemblies and law courts, is not an idle one. The term "negotiation" and the way Bleich puts it to use certainly bring the analogy into play. In a way, Bleich images the individual as much like a lawyer (or legislator) whose client (or constituent) is his or her own subjectivity and its feelings and motives. In order to secure public acknowledgment of one's private needs and rights and to protect one's self-interest and property claims (e.g., these ideas, opinions, and contributions are *mine*), the individual prepares and files his or her own legal brief (response statement) and negotiates for its amendment and acceptance among peers (students) and a higher judicial authority (the teacher). The classroom is the assembly or courtroom element of this analogy, and negotiation moves toward the amendment and passage of various bills or the adjudication and settlement of various cases. This analogy has a very definite and instructive appeal, I believe. The adjudication of literary cases pragmatically has many points of similarity with legal cases.[45] However, it is fair to say that in *Subjective Criticism* Bleich inhibits the conceptual and epistemological power of the concept of negotiation by emphasizing its distinctly secondary status and by concentrating on the *authoritarian* features of its institutional practice. Indeed, how authoritarian these features are is perhaps best recognized through the law analogy that I have already introduced. Bleich's frequent mentions of power and authority and his characteristic presentation of instances of love, dependency, and emulation in terms of dominance and subordination all stress the control one subjectivity asserts, wins, or achieves over others.[46] For instance, in discussing the regulation of meaning, he says:

45. In "Against Formalism: The Autonomous Text in Legal and Literary Interpretation," *Poetics Today* 1 (Autumn 1979): 23–34, Walter Benn Michaels compares and contrasts the interpretations of the meanings of words in formalist criticism and contract law. He indicates structural similarities in the procedures of court cases and critical controversies.
46. See Bleich, *Readings and Feelings*, pp. 16, 98–99, 102, and *Subjective Criticism*, pp.

In an illiterate society, the regulation of verbal meanings lay in the hands of those who could read; the regulation of meaning is thus bound up with the exercise of power. It was just as Carroll's Humpty Dumpty said: meanings are utterly subjective, and what counts is who is master.[47]

If the terms "regulation," "exercise of power," and "master" here are taken along with their legal and political implications—and not merely as harmless or clever overstatements of a priestly or scribal role—negotiation becomes a power game, becomes the struggle of aggressive and contending subjectivities (or personalities) for assertive control and mastery.[48] In this context, Bleich's theoretical ideal of the subjective authorizing of knowledge turns into an authoritarian ideal. In the classroom or in the courtroom, the stronger personalities will bull through and prevail, displaying or performing their feelings and opinions most forcefully and masterfully.[49] Such assertion of subjectively and aggressively motivated

---

3–9, for just a few instances of an almost obsessive or fixated interest in the exercise of power and the location of authority.

47. Bleich, *Subjective Criticism*, p. 6.

48. If Bleich had interested himself in *Subjective Criticism* in carrying out a cultural critique of such uses of power in (American) pedagogy, then his statements might yield descriptive analyses of aggression and power politics in education. It is precisely this new direction and perspective on the uses of power in the academy and in pedagogy that mark out the domain of Bleich's theoretical discourse in his recent *Double Perspective: Language, Literacy, and Social Relations* (New York: Oxford University Press, 1988). In this book Bleich examines various aspects of student-teacher relations as they bear upon the understanding of the uses of language and literature in the classroom and upon the lives of undergraduate students.

49. Compare Bleich's statement: "I am therefore viewing negotiation as the fundamental practice in the growth of intellectual and pedagogical communities. Such growth proceeds on Darwinian principles, where persuasion is the index of strength of any one person or subgroup." See Bleich, "Negotiated Knowledge of Language and Literature," *Studies in the Literary Imagination* 12 (Spring 1979): 75.

Bleich significantly ameliorates this perspective on the nature of negotiation in *The Double Perspective*. Indeed, he examines practical and theoretical ramifications of what he calls "the ideology of individualism"—the often racist, sexist, and class-biased authoritarianism based upon a sociocultural tradition of individual privilege and subjective power. As Bleich asserts generally:

I do consider the ideology of individualism that is responsible for the unfair distribution [of wealth] also responsible for the rigidity of our language use habits, the inertia of our pedagogical mores and traditions, and the isolation of large-scale public injustices of gender, race, and class from our teaching of language and literacy. By teaching these subjects under the ideology of individualism, we are lying about what these subjects really are. (p. ix)

behavior, part and parcel of Bleich's conception of the individual, constitutes an excessive valuation of self-projection. Moreover, it amounts to an authoritarian demand for the recognition of the undisciplined authority of the individual.

In order to bear this last point out it is best to examine the guidelines that Bleich prescribes for eliciting emotional responses and authoring response statements. Instead of initially asking the class to report freely on readings and feelings, Bleich states that

> . . . it is easier and more convincing to provoke the class into an emotional response. Most students are fairly shy at first. A class may be significantly provoked in a relatively safe way by writing an inflammatory proposition on the board. One of my favorites is a statement like, "Men are smarter than women," or if you prefer, "Women are smarter than men." Or writing a mild smutty term like "son of a bitch!" in big letters. These have never failed to elicit responses strong enough to create a prolonged discussion.[50]

Such is Bleich's recommended technique for "getting an emotional response." It can quickly break the initial silence of the classroom, usually with laughter, catcalls, outrage, or the like as the immediate reactions. Admittedly, this situation is quite removed from literary response; but the idea, supposedly, is to explore "the nature of feelings."[51] What appears to be taking place, though, is a controlled attack upon students by the authority figure, the teacher. Women, especially, may feel the most assaulted and offended by this technique—a point that Bleich confesses yet dismisses as unproblematic.[52] Such basically callous and rather adolescent provocation does challenge students to inevitably confused and anxious *reactions* because, more than likely, they will perceive the teacher toying both with their feelings and with his or her assumed authoritative role. Bleich's "inflammatory proposition[s]" may strike one as scarcely more "relatively safe" than the sexual humor that Gershon Legman analyzes so insightfully in *Rationale of the Dirty Joke*:

50. Bleich, *Readings and Feelings*, pp. 9–10.
51. Ibid., p. 5.
52. Ibid., pp. 14, 17. On pages 121–315 of *The Double Perspective*, Bleich offers half a dozen different aspects of attending to the ramifications of gender issues and social responsibilities of teachers and students in the literature classroom. Collectively these aspects reveal Bleich's current sensitivity to and thoughtful focus upon the implications of gender and authority in literary pedagogy and research.

> Under the mask of humor, our society allows infinite aggressions,
> by everyone and against everyone. In the culminatory laugh by the
> listener or observer—whose position is often really that of victim or
> butt—the teller of the joke betrays his hidden hostility and signals
> his victory by being, theoretically at least, the one person present
> *who does not laugh.*[53]

The teacher, who may be covertly anxious about his or her own authority,
can aggressively assert subjective control over a potentially ambiguous and
embarrassing classroom situation by victimizing others. Bleich seems to
recommend that the teacher play at a type of adolescent and anxious
authoritarianism, with feeling as the lure not for thought but for callous
self-assertion.

An "adolescent orientation," as Bleich himself terms it, runs through
virtually the whole of *Readings and Feelings.*[54] Supposedly, this orientation derives from the fact that the students whose responses are being
studied are themselves adolescents—ages 12 to 22. Accordingly, Bleich
claims to choose his examples in order to fit his subjects. He states the
"principle" guiding his choices: "an adolescent student—ages 12 to 22—is
intensely preoccupied with his own person—physically, psychologically,
and socially."[55] Such intense preoccupation, though, can quickly narrow
to anxiety and fear concerning sexuality and authority. Bleich seizes upon
this kind of anxious and fearful self-preoccupation again and again in the
responses, while passing over the complexities involved in more attentive
and sensitive student responses. (See "Q" and "U" on pages 82–84 of
Reading and Feelings for less "adolescent" and sharper, more succinct and
probing responses.) Bleich's own initial and unnegotiated response to
D. H. Lawrence's "Rocking-Horse Winner" illustrates this kind of preoccupation:

> The very outset of the story is full of excitement for me: "There was
> a woman who was beautiful, who started with all the advantages,
> yet she had no luck." For God's sake, I immediately think, if she
> is so beautiful but is just not lucky, *I'll* be only too glad to supply

---

53. Gershon Legman, *Rationale of the Dirty Joke: An Analysis of Sexual Humor; First Series*
(London: Cape, 1969), p. 9.
54. Bleich, *Readings and Feelings*, p. 93.
55. Ibid., pp. 18–19.

the missing "luck." And so I am really hooked! Before I am even introduced to the hero, I assume his burden; and with a kind of aggressive, perhaps adolescent bravado, I swallow the bait and plunge into the story.[56]

Such self-projection gives away the adolescent assumption: A beautiful woman should be available for one's fantasy. She is "bait" for "bravado," rather than a (potential) person who provokes curiosity, understanding, and the perceptive reading of character. Adolescence, a notion that occasionally seems like a synonym for subjectivity in *Readings and Feelings* and *Subjective Criticism*, cannot explain all the complexities of readings and feelings that all ages of readers can and do enact.

Bleich's theoretical ideal of the subjective authorizing of knowledge at least may provide a rationale for adolescent self-assertion, but I think it a great mistake to believe it offers an adequate epistemological justification for understanding literature. It would appear to rationalize projection and aggression and their attendant feelings rather than responsive attention to a situation that wants and warrants understanding. The anxiety over authority merely heightens the lack of real understanding. Of course, when Bleich turns to formulate specific guidelines for the "subjective recreation" of literature, the problem persists:

> . . . the essence of a symbolic work is not in its visible sensory structure or in its manifest semantic load but in its subjective recreation by a reader and in his public presentation of that recreation.[57]

The "visible" and the "manifest," the real sources of feeling ("sensory structure") and thought ("semantic load"), are discarded in favor of a private reauthoring and reauthorizing of what is read. The re-created, reauthored, projected text resembles the detextualized text and the textualized reader already discussed in connection with the work of Norman Holland. For Bleich, the "public presentation of that re-creation" is, of course, the written response statement. In general, the response statement operates much like Holland's ongoing re-creation of an

56. Ibid., p. 58.
57. Ibid., p. 21.

individual identity theme: The reader re-creates what he or she reads in
terms of his or her own personality.[58] As Bleich puts it:

> The reading transaction is in fact conceived altogether as a
> relationship between the reader and his feelings, a relationship that
> is regulated by the author, who will either facilitate or prevent the
> reader from having a satisfactory experience.[59]

This formulation for re-creation more or less drops the work out of "the
reading transaction." The reader reacts to a *facilitator* (the author or the
teacher in the classroom) whose authority and presence can provoke
satisfactory or unsatisfactory feelings. Knowledge of a distinctively other,
and perhaps more developed, way of looking at and responding to things,
as well as the nature of the reader's relationship with it, is elided as "the
reading transaction" is reduced to looking at a limited sense of "personality" and the perpetually self-replicating feelings to which it can be
provoked. Under the subjective paradigm, the activity of reading a literary
work loses all its specificity. Reading a record of the managed solicitation
of adolescent projections and free associations scarcely offers an adequate
substitute.

In summary, neither the reification of beginnings nor controlled
experiments with readers' response would seem to allow a meaningful
placement of the activity of reading a literary work within the field of
ordinary or general experience. Both strategies displace the nature of
experience and the complexities of reading in their pursuit of authority
and a single theoretical ideal. Here the quest for authority, however
variously conceived, and the control that theoretical ideals exert leads to
such ends as an idealized apologetics for absolute beginnings (Said), an
extremely limited experimentalism or scientism of the process of reading

---

58. As another commentator puts it: "Despite their differences, Holland and Bleich can be
grouped together when compared to other reader-response critics. They define their critical
paradigm (subjective or transactive) from a psychological perspective (not a sociological one).
They emphasize the individual over the group; reading is a function of personality not shared
strategies." See Steven Mailloux, "Reader-Response Criticism?" *Genre* 10 (Fall 1977): 423. This
essay provides a good general introduction to the work of Stanley Fish, Wolfgang Iser, Jonathan
Culler, and Holland and Bleich on reader-response. In "Learning to Read: Interpretation and
Reader-Response Criticism," *Studies in the Literary Imagination* 12 (Spring 1979): 93–108,
Mailloux generalizes about the basic assumptions and "critical moves," as he terms them,
involved in the diverse spectrum of reader-response critics.

59. Bleich, *Readings and Feelings*, p. 93.

and response (Cohen and Squire), or an unnecessary experimental channeling and psychologizing of the mind and motives of readers responding to literature (Holland and Bleich).

Poor idealism and poor empiricism, poor modes of speculation and experimental manipulation, are but poor substitutes for an open and pragmatic inquiry into specific cases of literary reading. Theories of reading must be submitted to the complexities of actual readings. To fail to do so entails the severance of theoretical inquiry and ongoing activity, the severance of experiment and experience. The elaborate literary-critical experiment of Part One of this book, moreover, embodies just such an engagement of literary-pragmatic experience. It tests practically and thoroughly the range of possibilities offered by the rich complexities of numerous readings and various patterns of reading "A slumber." The experience of referential confusion in the activity of reading Wordsworth's lyric, for instance, intricately focuses an entire spectrum of critical and interpretive problems that are to be found at play throughout the history of reading and interpreting Wordsworth's poetic text. The real challenge in this radically experimental approach to the nature of reading, though, comes in keeping critical thought and analysis alive to the actual experience of literary reading.

Memorably and provokingly, experiment and experience were not always at odds with one another:

> The two words *experiment* and *experience* lay close together in the seventeenth century. The very breadth of their division now leaves us, in the twentieth century, with the currently notorious "two cultures": science and poetry.
>
> The scientific instruments that excited the seventeenth century were the telescope and the microscope. Both were instruments of revelation. One showed the spots on the sun. The other opened on the myriad atomies embraced in a drop of water. Whichever instrument was used resulted in an experiment that was also an experience. Maybe for this reason the words were felt as being almost interchangeable: both meant a finding out.[60]

60. John F. Danby, *William Wordsworth: "The Prelude" and Other Poems* (London: Arnold, 1963), p. 7. In this connection, Wordsworth, in the "advertisement" to the 1798 edition of *Lyrical Ballads*, said that "the majority of the following poems are to be considered as experiments." In the "Preface" to the 1800 edition as well as in subsequent revisions of this

The attempt to recover experiments as experiences, as ways of finding out things and our relations to them, can and should become once again the well-practiced activity, and not merely a "theoretical ideal," of scientists and humanists alike.

"Preface," Wordsworth calls the whole volume "an experiment." See *PWWW*, I, pp. 116, 118–19.

9

Empirical Naturalism, Culture, and Practical Inquiry: Toward a Deweyan Sense of Experience and Knowledge

One of the chief values of a Deweyan approach to the activity of reading and responding to literary works would be the emphasis placed upon the embeddedness of literary experience in the texture of general or ordinary experience. Textual experience or textual meaning would not be privileged or discontinuous vis-à-vis other areas of our experience, nor would controlled or managed experiments with literary respondents be necessary to determine the supposed laws or mechanisms governing individual literary responses. Literary experience and the complexities of literary response would be recognized as integral elements of our general capacities for perceptual experience and conceptual understanding. Moreover, general and shareable patterns for literary experience and for the operations of critical inquiry would be ascertainable. Edward Said's discursively privileged beginnings and Norman Holland's and David Bleich's individualized and highly contingent psychologies of the authorizing personality do not adequately confront the problem of how the intentional and experiential authority of an individual person (or author of experience) can claim to speak for the experience of others. The commonality or communal patterns of experience and inquiry must be examined and must be taken seriously if experience and the perception of individualized intentions are to hold any measure of cognitive authority in literary experience and critical thought about literary reading. I propose to probe into and to elaborate a Deweyan sense of literary experience—especially focused upon the activity of literary reading. However, such probing must begin with a general account of John Dewey's central concepts of experience and knowledge. Only such an account can begin to disclose warrantable and shareable patterns for literary experience and critical inquiry.

John Dewey's writings are broad in scope and ambition, and the work that marks out more ground than any other is his *Experience and Nature*. Here Dewey develops most fully his metaphysics of experience by showing the ways in which human experience puts pressure upon and helps to disclose nature as well as give rise to social interactions, individuation, scientific inquiry, art, and criticism. In his retrospective "Preface to the Second Edition" Dewey calls this approach "the method of empirical naturalism" and claims that it is "the way by which we can be genuinely naturalistic and yet maintain cherished values, provided they are critically clarified and reinforced."[1] This formulation promotes experience as the quite *natural* medium in which human beings both engage nature and engage in various levels of valuation and criticism.

Perhaps the latter half of this formulation is easier to accept. Many thinkers will often limit human experience to the realm of social constructions or conventions—culture, that is to say. Indeed, this constriction can be found most recently in the highly influential work of Richard Rorty and Stanley Fish. Both men generally resort to a pragmatist sense of operative cultural constructions or conventions in order to dispel a variety of epistemological problems in literary and critical theory. The sense that human experience engages nature in some interesting or significant manner becomes precluded by the trying epistemological dilemmas of verifiable mental representations (Rorty) and demonstrable objective meanings (Fish).[2] Rorty's and Fish's critical work greatly empowers the constructive capacities of various ideal communities of critical thinkers. However, it does so at the grievous cost that the sense of

1. Dewey, *Experience and Nature*, 2d ed. (LaSalle, Ill.: Open Court, 1929), p. xiv.

2. Richard Rorty, *Philosophy and the Mirror of Nature* (Princeton, N.J.: Princeton University Press, 1979) and *Consequences of Pragmatism* (Minneapolis: University of Minnesota Press, 1982), especially pp. xiii–xlvii, 3–89, 139–210. For Stanley Fish, see his *Is There a Text in This Class?* (Cambridge, Mass.: Harvard University Press, 1980), pp. 301–71, and *Doing What Comes Naturally: Change, Rhetoric, and the Practice of Theory in Literary and Legal Studies* (Durham, N.C.: Duke University Press, 1989).

one's experience and critical knowledge concerning it merely instruct one about general enabling conventions, never about true features or epistemologically irremediable qualities of particular experiences. Dewey insists as well, however, on the other, the more epistemologically complicated half of his formulation of empirical naturalism. His method also

> . . . points to faith in experience when intelligently used as a means of disclosing the realities of nature. It finds that nature and experience are not enemies or alien. Experience is not a veil that shuts men off from nature; it is a means of penetrating continually further into the heart of nature. There is in the character of human experience no index-hand pointing to agnostic conclusions, but rather a growing progressive self-disclosure of nature itself. The failures of philosophy have come from lack of confidence in the directive powers that inhere in experience, if men have but the wit and courage to follow them.[3]

Such an epistemological project follows "the directive powers that inhere in experience" even "into the heart of nature," and it manifestly counters the more strictly convention-bound "neopragmatism" of such critical thinkers as Rorty and Fish.

Dewey's more capacious and more confident strain of pragmatism may also seem merely nostalgic or naive in the wake of the writings of Claude Lévi-Strauss and many of his structuralist adherents in the social sciences. Lévi-Strauss and many structuralist theorists assume a duality of nature

---

3. Dewey, *Experience and Nature*, p. xv. See also pp. 1–36. For a more recent philosophical defense of the continuity of nature and experience that is based on William James and John Dewey, see Stephen D. Ross, "The Inexhaustibility of Nature," *Journal of Value Inquiry* 7 (Winter 1973): 241–53.

Dewey's "faith in experience" may recall the "perceptual faith" described by the phenomenologist Maurice Merleau-Ponty in "Preobjective Being: The Solipsist World," *The Visible and the Invisible*, trans. Alphonso Lingis (Evanston, Ill.: Northwestern University Press, 1968), p. 158. Merleau-Ponty can tend to personalize, idealize, and mystify "natural man" and his "originating encounter" with nature in ways that would embarrass Dewey's "empirical naturalism." Nonetheless, as Victor Kestenbaum has so ably demonstrated in *The Phenomenological Sense of John Dewey: Habit and Meaning* (Atlantic Highlands, N.J.: Humanities Press, 1977), Dewey's work is amenable to the existential phenomenology of Merleau-Ponty. Kestenbaum singles out and develops Dewey's concept of habit as a theory of pre-objective, lived meaning. Merleau-Ponty's "pre-objective intentionality of the habitual body" helps to recover a basic phenomenological sense of Dewey's notion of habit as "the pre-objective intentionality of habit" or "habitual lived meaning" (pp. 110–12).

(including mankind's own biological nature) and culture—a duality of biological influence and social environment. Lévi-Strauss states, for instance, that "culture is not merely juxtaposed to life nor superimposed upon it, but in one way serves as a substitute for life, and in the other, uses and transforms it, to bring about the synthesis of a new order."[4] The cultural order, the "new order," is distinctively marked by the presence of networks of institutional rules that supposedly are not to be found in nature, even in the "pre-cultural behavior" of various animal "societies" such as insects or apes: "In fact, a vicious circle develops in seeking for the origin of institutional rules which presuppose, or rather, are culture, and whose establishment within a group without the aid of language is difficult to imagine."[5] According to the late nineteenth-century American anthropologist Lewis H. Morgan, language does indeed constitute the crucial difference between humans and animals (or what he calls "mutes"). However, Morgan, quite unlike Lévi-Strauss, recognizes no categorical or scientific imperative to impose an absolute difference between culture and nature, between cultural or institutional rules and natural behaviors. Animals do act intelligently, and the term "instinct" fails to explain their "intelligent acts." Indeed, the notion of "instinct" for Morgan reveals highly questionable and methodologically insidious assumptions:

> This term was an invention of the metaphysicians to assert and maintain the mental principle of the human species and that of the inferior animals. With its multiform definitions, and with the repeated enlargements of its signification, it is wholly incapable of explaining the phenomena of animal intelligence. . . . [Instead,] the mental phenomena manifested by the mutes can be investigated and explained on philosophical principles.[6]

Indeed a far cry from the duality that Lévi-Strauss will help to interpose so influentially, Morgan's alignment of nature and culture tends to accentuate how much the two realms actually already share. Both humans and animals are born with similar mental capacities that enable them to

4. Lévi-Strauss, *The Elementary Structures of Kinship*, trans. J. H. Bell, J. R. Needham, and R. Needham (Boston: Beacon Press, 1969), p. 4.
5. Ibid., pp. 5–8.
6. Lewis H. Morgan, *The American Beaver and His Works* (orig. pub. 1868), quoted by J. H. Moore, "The Culture Concept as Ideology," *American Ethnologist* 1 (1974): 540.

acquire the knowledge necessary and appropriate for functional living in their different evolutionary niches. Animals, Morgan states,

> are endowed with a mental principle which performs for them the same office that the human mind does for man; that this principle is free to act in view of motives and premises; and that it is ample in measure to enable each animal, within his sphere of action, to preserve his life and govern his conduct. This conclusion seems necessarily to follow from their possession of the organs of sense, from their manifestation of the appetites and passions, and from their ability to perceive, to remember, to reason, and to will.[7]

The general view that Morgan expresses here would be compatible with "the method of empirical naturalism" that Dewey strives to develop. Lévi-Strauss's dichotomy of nature and culture is not philosophically and anthropologically unshakable. The French structuralist's anthropological godfather, early and empirico-naturalist as he is, nonetheless recognizes significant commonalities in function and conduct between creatures of experience that later structural anthropology will tend to polarize categorically and differentially.

The nature-culture duality also possesses an extensive cultural history of its own. The political philosopher George H. Sabine, for example, has pointed out that for early Greek political philosophy the problem of what was permanent and lawful in the order of nature and culture was of paramount and often troublesome interest. In Athens of the fifth century B.C., such discussion seems to have circled about the opposition between nature and convention.

> Before the close of the fifth century, then, the contrast of nature and convention had begun to develop in two main directions. The one conceived nature as a law of justice and right inherent in human beings and in the world. This view necessarily leaned to

---

7. Morgan does not claim, of course, that there is *no* difference: ". . . we are led to the conclusion that the difference is one of degree, and not of kind" (p. 540). Language makes that difference, as well as helping humans develop, and continue to develop, their abilities and modes of conduct far beyond the degree and range of their neighboring "mutes."

Dewey frequently compares human and animal experience and capacities. See, for instance, his *Art as Experience*, pp. 18–19, where he turns to the activities of the fox, dog, and thrush for examples of the unity of present experience.

the assumption that the order in the world is intelligent and beneficent; it could be critical of abuses but it was essentially moralist and in the last resort religious. The other conceived nature non-morally, and as manifested in human beings it was self-assertion or egoism, the desire for pleasure or for power.[8]

The former, or naturalistic, view soon gave rise to such works as Aristotle's *Politics*, with its empirically oriented and critically intelligent description of the development of institutions and rules from the lawfulness of nature. Plato, and later on the Epicureans, adhered to the conventional-istic side of the "contrast" and developed what Sabine calls "social contract" theories of political philosophy or "utilitarianism" or "a kind of Nietzschean doctrine of self-expression."[9] The nature-culture duality itself, then, lies embedded within basic political and philosophical choices. The duality itself would not appear to be an ontological, epistemological, or anthropological necessity but a matter of an im-mensely significant, socially open, and debatable moral and political choice.

   This choice, however, does remain rooted in a sociohistorical and philosophical context that can itself be recovered and used to appraise and critique the intelligence and wisdom exemplified in the particular choice. The classicist F. M. Cornford sets forth some basic elements toward just such a reconstruction of pre-Socratic Greek philosophical thought and, by implication, its philosophical progeny. The practical art or technique of medicine, for instance, was quite well advanced in ancient Greece. The Hippocratic writings yield adequate testimony to the thoroughness of observation and description and the careful experimental probing of nature through hypotheses. However, medicine is not the only practical art for which "the impulse to build up a theoretical science on the basis of particular observations" can be traced in classical Greece.[10] Sculptors, architects, and craftsmen, like doctors, increasingly refined their observa-tions and developed their practical abilities as their arts grew in scope and efficaciousness. All these practical thinkers had "always a particular

   8. George H. Sabine, *A History of Political Theory*, rev. ed. (New York: Holt, Rinehart & Winston, 1961), p. 32 and pp. 29–32 in passing.
   9. Ibid., p. 32.
   10. F. M. Cornford, *Principium Sapientiae: The Origins of Greek Philosophical Thought*, ed. W. K. C. Guthrie (New York: Harper & Row, 1965), p. 8 and pp. 3–10 in passing.

problem to solve in practice," and their success demonstrates "that the Greeks (like other peoples) could turn common sense and ingenuity to practical account and were capable of observing closely what interested them for practical purposes."[11] Pre-Socratic philosophers, though, discarded such "common sense and ingenuity" for nonempirical speculation on the origins of the world (causality) and the ultimate constituents of matter (substance). This speculation now appears misguided, if not utterly untenable. That is to say, "the philosophers neglected, to an extent which strikes the modern mind as astonishing, to check their statements by experiment in the scientific sense of putting to nature a question the answer to which could not be foreseen."[12] The origins of Greek philosophizing, thus, are marked by a distinct break from the method generally employed in the practical arts. Observation, careful inferences, hypothesis testing, and empirically grounded generalizations—the whole set of procedures for putting practical questions to nature in order to disclose its realities—are discarded or forgotten. It is no small wonder, then, that unguided, speculative metaphysics produced curious dogmatic statements about cosmological causality and substance. Anaximenes could generate such peculiar pronouncements on the nature of water basically because he felt no need to adjudicate them with the kind of practical investigations into the properties of water that at least one early Hippocratic writer had conducted and recorded.[13] The eventual and finest product of this pre-Socratic mode of philosophizing, the purportedly scientific atomism of Epicurus, is, according to Cornford, still dominated by conceptual procedures shared by the earlier speculators: "his actual method of reaching all his most important doctrines was totally inconsistent with his notion of how knowledge is obtained."[14] Epicurean metaphysics is irreconcilable with an empirical theory of knowledge and reaches all its deductive conclusions *a priori* on the basis of a few assumptions or hypothetico-deductive principles.

In contrast with the untenable parameters of nonempirical cosmological speculation, the sociohistorical and philosophical context of practical inquiry perhaps can begin to situate the eventual production of a nature-culture or nature-convention duality in fifth-century Athens and

11. Ibid., p. 10.
12. Ibid., p. 11.
13. Ibid., pp. 6–7.
14. Ibid., pp. 12, 44.

in post-Socratic Greek philosophizing. Quite generally speaking, the Greek conventionalists prefer and privilege the power and self-expressive utility of speculation and the egoistic free play it allows the self. In sharp distinction, such adherents of a naturalistic view as Aristotle remain closer to the procedures of intelligent and practical inquiry—that is to say, the procedures of the architect, the artist, and the doctor. This view, moreover, can explain the social and historical development of conventions and rules as the progressive development of consensual procedures and critical knowledge regarding various practical areas of human conduct and inquiry. The adherents of conventionalism, on the other hand, have philosophically undermined (or disregarded) the possibility of describing and explaining the origin of cultural conventions. Indeed their purely conventionalist and often highly speculative terms border upon the sophistic and the circular.

This abbreviated excursion into the nature-culture problem helps to unsettle the belief that nature and culture are wholly separate realms and that the operational conventions of culture have no cognitive access to the processes of nature. The matter, indeed, *cannot be settled*, demonstrated, proven beyond a doubt. It remains *problematic*, in the sense of the word soon to be developed. However, there is a choice to be made—one in which our knowledge of our own experiences, our procedures of inquiry and reality testing, and our reconstructions of past knowledge situations and problems can support and guide us. Speculation provides unnumbered pleasures as we tease our minds and flex untried conceptual capabilities, yet time and again we seem to know when and how to appropriate the satisfactions yielded only by practical inquiry into what our experience offers us. The choice, at least, is always actually and already available.

John Dewey proposes an active and operational approach to dealing with human experience and acquiring knowledge of ourselves and of our environment. He does not assume that self-generating and self-disclosing sets of enabling conventions offer the sole parameters of what can be known about and by ourselves. Ordinary experience contains a mixture of the uncertain and the unsettled as well as the already secured, stable, and uniform. Our existence, says Dewey, is a

> . . . conjunction of the precarious and the assured, the incomplete and the finished, the repetitious and the varying, the safe and sane and the hazardous. If we trust to the evidence of experienced

things, these traits, and the modes and tempos of their interaction with each other, are fundamental features of natural existence.[15]

In other words, the immense variety of our daily experiences and our ability to recognize characteristics and temporal interactions constitute basic features of what it is to be human by nature. The uncertain, the unsettled, and the precarious amid this great pool of experiential existence, moreover, form obstacles in our general experience. In so doing they summon us into deliberate and intelligent action. An impediment in the ordinary course of living brings about the phenomenon of *having an experience*. The state of being uncertain induces a self into examining the conditions of his or her present experience and into preparing tentative actions that can resolve satisfactorily what is currently uncertain.

Such a state of uncertainty manifests itself, for instance, in the referential confusion undergone by a reader in trying to construe the antecedent for the pronoun "she" in Wordsworth's poem "A slumber." Such a syntactical, conceptual, and interpretive impediment is a pivot in having an experience of Wordsworth's poem. It prompts or induces the reader to attend upon and to begin shaping the particulars of his or her perceptions toward finer definition and potential resolution. Because a self generally attends to his or her inchoate experience, probes into it, questions it, begins to shape it toward resolution, Dewey indicates that the segment of experience under examination becomes a whole and stands out as a distinct entity—*an experience*.[16]

In Chapter 1 of this book, an experience was generally characterized as possessing four definitive features: (1) a body of experiential material, (2) an experiencing agent, (3) an emergent and temporal progress, and (4) a distinct and developed character or quality. With the whole complex of these features in the foreground, Dewey also calls the occurrence of "an experience" by the name "situation." This term more adequately distinguishes what is crucial about "an experience" from the general course (and often inchoate mixture) of ordinary, ongoing experience. A situation is distinctively marked by a "pervasive quality" that "has a binding force holding together and giving unity to the perceptions, feelings, impulses, and thoughts" that constitute the temporal progress or interaction of "the

15. Dewey, *Experience and Nature*, p. 65 and pp. 37–66 in passing.

16. John Dewey, *The Quest for Certainty: A Study of the Relation of Knowledge and Action* (New York: Capricorn Books, 1960; orig. pub. 1929), p. 223, and *Art as Experience*, p. 35.

things and persons involved."[17] The four definitive features of having an experience can also be recognized as strong structural features in the characterization of a situation. A situation develops when a self probes into what is uncertain or unsettled about an obstacle or impediment in a body of experiential material. If no inquiry is needed or instituted, the situation is said to be "determinate"—the necessary knowledge is already operative, and activity remains routine. If the situation developed admits of no other pervasive quality than confusion or disorientation, then it is called "indeterminate." However, if such an indeterminate situation permits an intelligent inquiry into the problems it presents, then the situation becomes "problematic." A *problematic situation* involves a *situation of provisional indeterminacy that demands, warrants, and enables practical and critical inquiry into its vexed cognitive issues.* Ultimately, if a problematic situation can itself be resolved and confusion dissipated, then the situation becomes a newly determinate one.

> The problem, we say, has been solved. But this determinate situation is not the original one. The live creature is now in some degree a different being operating within an environment which has also to some extent been changed. A new and different sort of equilibrium has been achieved.[18]

In other words, we have acquired new knowledge about ourselves and our environment through active inquiry into experience. The *developed* experience or situation constitutes the very medium in which this knowledge can be actively constructed. Such new knowledge can also enlarge the reservoir of determinate knowledge that a self can call upon to handle future experiences or situations.

Literary-critical knowledge, of course, comprises a highly complicated network of cognitive constructions—and one that seems constantly open to new, active inquiries. However, the development of the experience of

---

17. Gail Kennedy, "Dewey's Concept of Experience: Determinate, Indeterminate, and Problematic," *Journal of Philosophy* 56 (October 8, 1959): 804.

18. Ibid., p. 806. Alfred Schutz deploys an intriguingly similar analysis of determinate, indeterminate, and problematic knowledge situations. Schutz, however, uses a Cartesian or rationalist groundwork and hence talks about "self-evidencies" and "that which is taken for granted" rather than Dewey's more pragmatic and less intuitional sense of experience. See Alfred Schutz and Thomas Luckmann, *The Structures of the Life-World*, trans. R. M. Zaner and H. T. Engelhardt, Jr. (Evanston, Ill.: Northwestern University Press, 1973), pp. 8–15.

reading such a lyric as "A slumber did my spirit seal" can exhibit precisely and pragmatically the active construction of new literary knowledge. Active inquiry into the experience of reading Wordsworth's poem can and does yield new knowledge about that work and its intertextual and sociocultural relations. It can also help construct new knowledge about oneself as a reader.

Experience, then, for Dewey and his pragmatic approach to the nature of human or cultural knowing puts a claim on knowledge. Knowledge is necessarily embedded in and linked to experience. The progressive clarification and refining of indeterminate and problematic situations yield new determinations because the practical and constructive activity of a self provides the single intelligence that can both feel and inquire, experience and know.

10

The Knowledge Situation, the Types of Evidence, and Two Modes of Attention: Characterizing Purposive Activity and Literary Experience

John Dewey's concept of experience would appear to "maintain a doctrine of intelligible continuity between experience and thought" and to "allow to experience the right to sit in judgment upon all claims to knowledge."[1] Such sweeping claims for a critical account of experience can run the grave danger of failing to address adequately the need for a successfully balanced and intelligible mediation of both the perceptual and conceptual poles of the knowledge-producing situation. As the philosopher John E. Smith has maintained:

> The development of modern empiricism has shown that in every concrete analysis of actual knowledge and of the knowledge situation it becomes necessary at some point to acknowledge a distinction between a perceptual and a conceptual pole. That is to say, without the encounter of a reality beyond the thinking activity and without categorial forms of thought by means of which to

---

1. John E. Smith, "Three Types and Two Dogmas of Empiricism," *Christian Scholar* 43 (Fall 1960): 205, 206.

grasp, explain, and interpret the encounter, there can be no knowledge of reality at all.[2]

There must be some consideration of both the *sensible* and *rational* components of knowledge and the nature of their relationship. Without the perceptual pole or sensible component of the knowledge situation, potential knowledge of reality would collapse into mere congeries of fictional projections or fantasies. The "thinking activity" would be isolated, self-enclosed, adrift, its range of action limited to its projectional resources. The conceptual pole or rational component of the knowledge situation provides the necessary intellectual categories and capacity for synthesis that the "thinking activity" relies upon in order "to grasp, explain, and interpret the encounter." What is sensed or experienced must also be organized and interpreted to be known and understood.

   This bipolarity of the knowledge situation has been for European philosophy an ongoing "problematic situation," in Dewey's sense of that phrase, and often approaches sheer paradox. Indeed, an "impasse has resulted from the radical separation of the domain of fact (frequently denoted by the terms 'experience' or 'sense perception') and the domain of thought," as Smith has noted. Moreover, "along with this radical separation has gone *a persistent rejection of any attempt at mediation.*"[3] David Hume and Gottfried Leibniz furnish two representative and classic instances:

> Each in his own way aimed at the denial of one of the poles or, more precisely, at the reduction of one to the other. Hume tried to get on with a continuum of perception or sense, taking an idea as a decaying or less vivid sense impression, while Leibniz working from the other direction tried to establish a continuum of conception or thought, making sense perception into confused conceptions. In both cases one pole was interpreted as an inferior form of the other, and in both cases there was a denial of autonomy and distinctness of kind between the poles.[4]

Immanuel Kant perhaps understood this philosophical problem better than his predecessors Leibniz and Hume. His equal theoretical emphasis

2. Ibid., pp. 209–10.
3. Ibid., p. 212.
4. Ibid., p. 210.

upon both sense and understanding in his philosophical account of reason demonstrates that he realized that neither the perceptual nor the conceptual pole of the knowledge situation should be collapsed into or conflated with the other. For Kant the logical structure of knowing was *also at the same time* the very possibility of experience. However, Kant *separated* and *isolated* sense and understanding as two distinct and heterogeneous "elements" at the very beginning of the *Critique of Pure Reason*. He distinguished and counterposed sensibility (*Sinnlichkeit*) to understanding or thought (*Vernunft* or *Verstand*). The principles of passive "receptivity" or "pure intuition" (that is, the element of sensibility) are deduced in Kant's Transcendental Aesthetic, while the principles of active or productive "spontaneity" (that is, the element of understanding) are deduced in his Transcendental Logic.[5] Indeed, the passage in which Kant asserts this monumental segregation of mental principles is worth citing at length:

> The science of all the principles of sensibility *a priori* I call *Transcendental Aesthetic*. There must be such a science, forming the first part of the Elements of Transcendentalism, as opposed to that which treats of the principles of pure thought, and which would be called *Transcendental Logic*.
>
> In Transcendental Aesthetic therefore we shall first isolate sensibility, by separating everything which the understanding adds by means of its concepts, so that nothing remains but empirical intuition (Anschauung).
>
> Secondly, we shall separate from this all that belongs to sensation (Empfindung), so that nothing remains but pure intuition (reine Anschauung) or the mere form of the phenomena, which is the only thing which sensibility *a priori* can supply.[6]

The language of this passage exhibits Kant striving to delineate and preserve a radical separation of sense and thought, percepts and concepts, as two isolated "elements" or "stems" of knowledge (i.e., "separate but equal"). Kant's transcendental critical philosophy does achieve an impressive articulation of the synthetic power of our cognitive faculties, yet his persistent imperative to impose categorical distinctions says more about

5. Immanuel Kant, *Critique of Pure Reason*, trans. F. Max Müller (Garden City, N.Y.: Anchor Books, 1966), pp. 18, 21–22, 44–46.
6. Ibid., pp. 22–23.

his own desire to map a purely rational structure of the complexities of cognition than it does about the actual vagaries and particulars of acts of cognition. Kant apparently declines to explore the unity or common connection his two distinct cognitive domains may have from the beginning prior to their critical and analytic factoring out. As he confesses in a rare moment in the first *Critique*, "there are two stems of human knowledge which perhaps may spring from a common root, unknown to us, viz., *sensibility* and *understanding*."[7] This possibility of a common root is not explored. The two poles of the knowledge situation are left thoroughly and radically isolated by Kant's analysis of their distinctly different principles.[8]

There is, however, an American philosopher who has produced a philosophical position or "world hypothesis" that seeks to reconcile the perceptual and conceptual aspects of cognition—that is to say, that seeks out and explores the "common root" of the two poles of the knowledge situation that Kant depicted so radically and so skillfully. In *Concept and Quality* Stephen C. Pepper performs an elaborate and far-ranging description and analysis of what he calls a "root metaphor" that can be recognized as the "common root" of the "two stems of human knowledge" that Kant would maintain must remain "unknown to us." For Pepper, a "root metaphor" is

> . . . an area of empirical observation which is the point of origin for a world hypothesis. When anyone has a problem before him and is at a loss how to handle it, he looks about in his available experience for some analogy that might suggest a solution. This suggestive analogy gives rise to an hypothesis which he can apply towards the solution.[9]

This search for a hypothesis-generating and empirically grounded analogy or root metaphor is not a very Kantian procedure. However, it is one that

---

7. Ibid., p. 18.

8. Kant's Transcendental Dialectic does not mediate between the Transcendental Aesthetic and the Transcendental Logic. It is one of the two divisions of the Transcendental Logic and operates as a critique of logical illusions, semblances, and sophistries that may be brought against the logic of "pure understanding" proper—the Transcendental Analytic. See Kant, pp. 48–51, 221–30.

9. Stephen C. Pepper, *Concept and Quality: A World Hypothesis* (LaSalle, Ill.: Open Court, 1966), p. 3.

echoes the practical techniques and strategies of Hippocrates and other classical Greek observers, questioners, and problem solvers. However, Kant and so many modern philosophical and critical speculators in his wake dismiss such empiricism and hypothesis testing as useless to "the discipline of pure reason." Indeed, in the section of the *Critique of Pure Reason* that addresses hypotheses, Kant calls them "mere opinions." He claims that hypotheses can serve as grounds of explanation *only* for that which is already "really given and therefore certain"—namely, the pure concepts of reason.[10] But for Pepper, Kant's claim of self-evident certainty for his *a priori* concepts would amount to a dogmatic claim to certainty. In Pepper's systematic philosophy based on the root-metaphor approach, claims for the self-evident veracity of rational principles, propositions, or axioms are disallowed as dogmatic. Systems of self-evident principles, such as the axioms of Euclidean geometry, have failed or eventually come into conflict in the past. As a clear consequence, then, Pepper contends that

> . . . the criterion of self-evidence itself is discredited. For if in one good instance the criterion of self-evidence fails, how can it ever be trusted again? The criterion could not have been better tested than in the example of the Euclidean axioms. These for centuries were accepted as self-evident by the keenest minds. If the claim must be abandoned for these, how can it be legitimately offered for the truth of any other principles?[11]

So-called self-evident principles, therefore, do not have evidence at hand adequate to the claim for absolute cognitive certainty. Principles or axioms actually are postulates in a system whose interrelations and probability must continually be tested and refined by checking them against currently available evidence.[12] To examine philosophically the knowledge situation with full regard to evidence and legitimate (nondogmatic) claims to cognitive adequacy (relative certainty), then, necessitates attention to empirical observation and available experience. Pepper's root-metaphor method of philosophy achieves such needed attention:

10. Kant, pp. 495–502, especially p. 496.
11. Stephen C. Pepper, *World Hypotheses: A Study in Evidence* (Berkeley and Los Angeles: University of California Press, 1942), p. 22 and pp. 21–24 in passing.
12. Ibid., p. 22.

A man desiring to understand the world looks about for a clue to its comprehension. He pitches upon some areas of common-sense fact and tries if he cannot understand other areas irt terms of this one. This original area becomes then his basic analogy or root metaphor. He describes as best he can the characteristics of this area, or, if you will, discriminates its structure. A list of its structural characteristics becomes his basic concepts of explanation and description. We call them a set of categories. In terms of these categories he proceeds to study all other areas of fact whether uncriticized or previously criticized. He undertakes to interpret all facts in terms of these categories. As a result of the impact of these other facts upon his categories, he may qualify and readjust his categories, so that a set of categories commonly changes and develops. Since the basic analogy or root metaphor normally (and probably at least in part necessarily) arises out of common sense, a great deal of development and refinement of a set of categories is required if they are to prove adequate for a hypothesis of unlimited scope.[13]

This basic statement of Pepper's root-metaphor method indicates that an attempt "to understand the world" depends upon "basic concepts of explanation and description"—"a set of categories"—that are not intuited or determined self-evidently but are derived from a singularly significant region of experience and observation. These concepts or categories can then be used to study and interpret other areas of "common-sense fact" while at the same time being progressively developed and refined through such practical contact. In *Concept and Quality* Pepper offers the root metaphor of the "purposive act"—and two sets of categories, the qualitative and the conceptual—as a world hypothesis that can describe and help analyze the basic unity and interactive cooperation of the perceptual and conceptual aspects of cognition and actual knowledge situations. Purportedly, this hypothesis, diverging as it does from the cognitively problematic Kantian way of proceeding, can probe the unknown and unexplored "common root" of Kant's sundered "stems of human knowledge."

Pepper chooses typical goal-seeking or appetitive behavior, behavior that humans seem to share with many other creatures—or what Lewis H.

13. Ibid., p. 91.

Morgan calls "mutes"—as the "area of common-sense fact" from which the root metaphor of the purposive act is derivable. Pepper describes in ample and insightful detail the factors involved in the goal-seeking purposive act of wanting and going in search of a drink of water. This activity is characteristic and representative of many other such purposive acts.[14] Three basic reasons inform the choice of the purposive act as Pepper's root metaphor. The first one is that it

> . . . is the most highly organized type of simple purpose—
> possibly the most highly organized activity in the world of which
> we have any considerable evidence. It is the act associated with
> intelligence. And so it entails the features of the organism which
> performs the act.[15]

This reason foregrounds the intelligent and organized nature of any purposive act. By this fact, it implicates an agent who is capable of organization, intelligence, and performative action. In other words, there are no acts without active agents. The second reason for the choice of the purposive act as root metaphor has to do with such an act's feelingful impact on consciousness.

> We can feel its whole qualitative course from initial impulse to
> terminal satisfaction. We can have the immediate feel of the
> perceptual demands of an environment in all its qualitative variety
> and graded intensity upon the search for the means of satisfaction.
> And we can feel the shock of a blocked anticipation when a wrong
> choice is made.[16]

This reason foregrounds the felt quality of a satisfying interaction with the environment on the part of the active agent. The "perceptual demands" made by the environment upon the active agent are themselves integral features of the agent's purposive act and its felt quality. Finally, Pepper's third reason involves the "qualitative structure" of a purposive act. Such

---

14. Pepper, *Concept and Quality*, pp. 19–23. Pepper describes and analyzes purposive behavior, drives, objects, and values in A *Digest of Purposive Values* (Berkeley: University of California Press, 1947), pp. 1–100.
15. Pepper, *Concept and Quality*, p. 17.
16. Ibid.

an act can be "submitted to a detailed conceptual analysis in behavioristic terms"—that is to say, a purposive act provides "an ideal opportunity to see how a set of effective and well elaborated concepts come to apply to a qualitative structure lived through in a man's [or a woman's] immediate experience."[17] This third and final reason argues the accessibility of a purposive act to systematic interpretation and conceptualization. In summary, then, the choice of the purposive act as a basic analogy or root metaphor is itself a hypothesis that the typical perceptual and purposive interactions of an active agent and his or her environment are accessible to conceptual understanding through a detailed analysis of the act itself.

Pepper's description of his purposive search for a glass of water yields two results: "a detailed conceptual description, and an immediate qualitative act to which the description applies."[18] The "immediate qualitative act," however, does not remain mysterious, private, or unpresentable:

> Perhaps at this point, someone is asking just what the description is describing. Is it describing my inner feelings or someone's observations of my outer behavior? It is basically describing my qualitative activity between the awakening in the night and the quenching of my thirst. Fortunately in this instance (and I chose it partly for that reason) I have access to the qualitative activity. I performed it and I can remember it and verbally describe it. And I am thinking that my readers have had similar experiences and can follow my description in their own qualitative terms. I suppose we have all read novels about qualitative acts much more intricate than this one and were not utterly mystified by the symbols.[19]

From our own extensive experience and observation, we have felt, performed, followed, recognized, read, and described our own and other people's qualitative activity. Through introspection, retrospection, and empathy, we have normal access to ordinary knowledge of qualitative acts. Yet at the same time, or perhaps later in retrospect, we can institute a conceptual analysis of the same purposive act. For literary critics and theorists, of course, that Pepper mentions readers' comprehension of the kind of conceptual reports on qualitative acts that novelistic discourse

17. Ibid., pp. 17–18.
18. Ibid., p. 23.
19. Ibid., p. 24.

typically articulates might be especially intriguing. Literary uses of language afford some of a culture's most probing, even provocative conceptual reportage on qualitative activity. So also does the conceptual analysis of acts of literary reading. Indeed, I have provided descriptions of qualitative acts of reading specific lyric poems in the first part of this book. Such descriptions have enabled conceptual analyses of specific, qualitative acts of reading—my own as well as those of other professional readers and critics. I will return near the end of this chapter to discuss literary reading as purposive activity, yet it may be useful to note at this point that my conceptual reports on the activity of reading a poem by Wordsworth follow out features and implications of qualitative acts of reading the poem.

Conceptual analyses, though, may not square with qualitative descriptions at all points and, indeed, will very likely go well beyond them in terms of their rigorous probing of conditions and operations. However, regardless of their exact relation, the two kinds of "reports" on purposive activity—the qualitative and the conceptual—"are wedded to each other" because they both describe the same "segment of fact." As Pepper phrases this situation,

> . . . we have a highly articulated qualitative description and a highly articulated conceptual description which refer to exactly the same actual process. The bifurcation of nature into conceptual system and qualitative experience meet here at this point.[20]

The purposive act, then, can be recognized as the "common root" of the "two stems of human knowledge" that Kant analyzed in separation. It is the one and same basic activity that both qualitative and conceptual descriptions come to bear upon and from which they bifurcate in their articulations of its two cognitively distinct aspects or poles. Kant's radical separation of sensibility and understanding can be radically altered through Pepper's situating of the problem of knowledge or cognition in the domain of commonsense fact, observation, and hypothesis. Purposive activity constitutes the meeting point of felt qualities (or percepts) and concepts. For Pepper, the "gap" between qualities and concepts is philosophically and pragmatically manageable.[21]

20. Ibid., pp. 26–27.
21. Pepper says of *Concept and Quality*: "This book regards the gap as nothing other than the

Pepper's root metaphor of the purposive act and its set of qualitative and conceptual categories can lend cognitive underpinnings to John Dewey's concept of experience and his embedding of knowledge in experience. Dewey's notion of a cognitive situation could be thought through more expressly as goal-seeking, purposive activity—a project not at all incompatible with Deweyan "empirical naturalism." The main point for this discussion, though, is the way in which Pepper clarifies the claim that experience has on knowledge. His root-metaphor method successfully balances and renders intelligible the meeting or mediation of both the perceptual and conceptual poles of the knowledge situation.

Pepper also clarifies the nature of fact, or of evidence, and its dynamic relation within the knowledge situation. Claims to self-evident or absolutely certain evidence must be dismissed as cognitively weak, inadequate, and dogmatic. Instead, Pepper asks:

> . . . why should knowledge begin with certainties? Why should it not dawn like day out of a half-light of semiknowledge and gradually grow to clarity and illumination?[22]

Like Dewey, knowledge for Pepper emerges through and from the progressive clarification and refining of indeterminate and problematic situations. Pepper says:

> There appear to be two broad types of evidence: uncriticized, and criticized or refined evidence. Socially and individually knowledge begins with the former and gradually passes into the latter.[23]

Pepper also calls uncriticized evidence "common sense," "common-sense fact," and "uncriticized fact": what Plato in *The Republic* and elsewhere termed "opinion."

Basically, uncriticized evidence (or common sense) consists of two broad areas of human experience. The first includes a great array of

---

failure to notice the distinction between the immediate felt quality of a cognitive process and its referential functioning in a problematic situation—or, more generally, between immediate intuitive cognition of felt quality, and the referential cognition of concepts" (p. 68).

22. Pepper, *World Hypotheses*, p. 39.

23. Ibid. Throughout the rest of this paragraph and the next three, I will draw freely upon pages 39–51 of Pepper's book. These pages are perhaps the best and most concise statement of his theory of knowledge.

common and shared sensations and perceptions—a kind of sociocultural sensorium or sensibility. The second holds common and shared opinions, beliefs, and ordinary or everyday facts and habits of our human form of life. The qualitative aspect of our purposive activity generally would appear to draw from and refer to these two areas of uncriticized evidence or commonsense fact. The evidential or factual descriptions of our qualitative acts are characteristically phrased in terms of our common, shared sensations and perceptions and our opinions and beliefs concerning their immediate import.

Such uncriticized facts or evidences of our purposive behavior, moreover, generally possess three distinctive traits that bear upon their uncriticized yet cognitively central role. First, uncriticized facts are indefinitely or imprecisely cognized. Second, though unstable, they are secure because they are never lacking; they are always there, insisting on cognition, but never allowing perfect or absolute cognition. Third, they are cognitively limitless, vague, unorganized, and contradictory. Such unreliability seems endlessly irritable and problematic. Uncriticized evidence or fact is bountiful, supportive, and seemingly always on the verge of exceeding our control.

Such evidence, though, naturally and often quite continually sets up a tension with a second broad type of evidence—namely, criticized or refined evidence or fact. This second type of evidence emerges from the process of critically clarifying and refining the cognitive material of common sense. Through focusing attention on the further cognitive possibilities of the indefinitely, vaguely, yet insistently cognized facts of common sense, we seek more reliable, responsible, and consistent knowledge. However, such refined knowledge must maintain a tensile relation with its secure, always bountiful cognitive source. As Pepper explains:

> This tension between common sense and expert knowledge, between cognitive security without responsibility and cognitive responsibility without full security, is the interior dynamics of the knowledge situation. The definiteness of much detail in common sense, its contradictions, its lack of established grounds, drive thought to seek definiteness, consistency, and reasons. Thought finds these in the criticized and refined knowledge of mathematics, science, and philosophy, only to discover that these tend to thin out into arbitrary definitions, pointer readings, and tentative

hypotheses. Astounded at the thinness and hollowness of these culminating achievements of conscientiously responsible cognition, thought seeks matter for its definitions, significance for its pointer readings, and support for its wobbling hypotheses. Responsible cognition finds itself insecure as a result of the very earnestness of its virtues. But where shall it turn? It does, in fact, turn back to common sense, that indefinite and irresponsible source which it so lately scorned. . . . And critical knowledge hangs over a vacuum unless it acknowledges openly the actual, though strange, source of its significance and security in the uncriticized material of common sense.[24]

The "interior dynamics of the knowledge situation," thus, exhibit a varying tension between uncriticized commonsense fact and the critical knowledge that can gradually be refined and made determinate from it. Responsible critical knowledge cannot usefully or securely exist apart from its actual and material source in common sense. This is not to say, however, that criticized evidence or critical knowledge fails to have a reconstructive or redirective impact on common sense. Socially regarded, such reconstruction would tend to be extremely gradual. Individually regarded, it can have far more redirective and overt impact. An individual can and at times will be sharply redirected (changed, reformed, converted) on the basis of new, especially unforecast, critical knowledge. For the most part, though, the tension involved in the knowledge situation "drive[s] thought to seek definiteness, consistency, and reasons" for uncriticized evidence while drawing criticized evidence back toward its source by always posing the threat of cognitive insecurity and insignificance.

Refined or critical knowledge here would involve the detailed conceptual description and analysis of purposive activity that Pepper provides in *Concept and Quality*. Conceptual analysis of the same purposive act of which we have an uncriticized and qualitative description can provide critical or refined knowledge of the act's occurrence and processes. The qualitative act and its conceptual analysis constitute two different types of evidence of purposive activity: the first, immediate, felt, secure, insisting on clarification and refinement; the second, reflective, criticized, consis-

24. Ibid., pp. 44–45.

tent, and cognitively responsible to the qualitative act it conceptually elaborates. For instance, in the case of Wordsworth's poem "A slumber," the experience of referential confusion over the antecedent of "she" involves a qualitative act and immediate, insistent, though unrefined or uncriticized evidence of purposive activity. The conceptual analysis of "A slumber" carried out in the first five chapters of Part One, moreover, offers a refined and consistent conceptual elaboration of the qualitative description of the referential confusion. This analysis involves the production of reflective, criticized, and cognitively responsible critical knowledge—namely, literary criticism and scholarship—regarding the reading and understanding of the poem.

Pepper also indicates that criticized evidence or critical knowledge can and must be corroborated in two distinct ways. Critical knowledge is verified through "corroboration of man with man, and corroboration of fact with fact." The first type Pepper calls "multiplicative corroboration" and the second "structural corroboration."[25] The first type of corroboration charts critical agreement—that is, the ways in which cognitively adequate criticized evidence can be achieved between or among various refiners of knowledge. My efforts to sort out adherents of one line of interpretation for "A slumber" or another involve the search for evidence of multiplicative corroboration of interpretive possibilities. Indeed, my own suggestion of a third line of interpretation for Wordsworth's resilient lyric gains important plausibility and credence as I can multiply evidence of critical agreement, however partial or parenthetical. The second type of corroboration of critical knowledge stems from the degree of interrelation and self-consistency among criticized facts. The overall structure and fit of refined or criticized facts helps corroborate their cognitive legitimacy and adequacy. That my rather unusual, third line of interpretation regarding Wordsworth's "A slumber" enables the mediation and structural interrelation of two other divergent lines of interpretation lends it structural corroboration and explanatory elegance and consistency. Moreover, the detection of pronominal play in "Strange fits" and "She dwelt" structurally corroborates my claim about the pivotal role of such linguistic play in "A slumber." Critical agreement (consensus) and self-consistency (coherence) constitute two distinct ways that critical knowledge can be evaluated and judged. These two ways of evaluation and judgment of

25. Ibid., pp. 47–48.

critical knowledge comprise two basic criteria for the acceptance of criticized evidence as cognitively adequate and conceptually descriptive.

Pepper's two general types of evidence and the corresponding qualitative and conceptual descriptions of purposive activity postulated by his root metaphor of the purposive act imply two modes of attention, two general ways of cognitively attending to the world and the actions performed in it. The word "attention," moreover, carries both a general sense of cognitive experience and a more specific sense of a consciously directed or intentional act of cognition. Because of this additional specific sense, the word "attention," sufficiently qualified, may be used to demarcate a particular area of purposive activity that is especially aware and directed. Not all purposive acts exhibit active agents who show particular awareness of and focused interest in the actual proceeding of such acts. The arts, however, do appear to demand and cultivate an aptitude precisely for such self-conscious and directed purposive acts. Pepper, for one, recognizes the fine state of conscious development that aesthetic qualities have attained in the arts in the final, capstone chapter of *Concept and Quality*. Such qualities, he shows, achieve in the arts a maximum of aesthetic intensity and virtually unparalleled depth and spread of significance.[26] For the purposes of this exposition, two modes of attention will have to be distinguished.

The first mode marks out the more or less usual performance of purposive acts. Qualitatively felt acts and conceptual descriptions serve to move us along in everyday life, instrumentally, pragmatically, and frequently satisfyingly. We attend to the performance of such acts in no undue or extraordinary manner. We are not really interested in the actual movements and precise course of these purposive acts. Our interest is limited for the most part to a relatively determinate and familiar purpose or objective. We can even institute inquiries, in the full Deweyan sense developed above, into these acts and their performances in order to gain clarification or further information or a satisfactory interpretation of their occurrence. However, these purposive acts, or what Dewey would call "experiences" or "situations," remain primarily, if not completely, instrumental. This first mode of attention I choose to call the "instrumental mode of attention."

We may also attend to purposive activity in a second mode, distinct

---

26. Pepper, "Aesthetic Quality," *Concept and Quality*, pp. 561–619.

from the instrumental mode of attention. Human beings can attend to past, present, and imaginary purposive acts in a way that brings into the foreground the actual movements and workings of the acts themselves. Instrumentality is here self-reflectively aware of itself. Such attention usually inhabits the arts but by no means is or should be restricted to them alone. For instance, working out in detail the covert cognitive assumptions implied in the barbarous use of diction, syntax, and argumentative organization in an article on chemical engineering or circumspectly exhibiting the subliminal use of sadomasochistic sexuality in American media advertising would both yield nonartistic examples of this second mode of attention. What these two examples do have in common with the arts, however, is the performance of careful and exacting reading and interpreting of words, images, textures, sounds, and other tools or instruments of thought. Such acts of reading and interpreting characterize this mode of attention. Indeed, they are the representative and exemplary instances of experiences that are also at the same time full inquiries into their own occurrences and particulars. Questions about the appropriateness, meaning, and depth of perceptions, feelings, and responses (felt qualities) as well as questions about the appropriateness, significance, and fit of thoughts, ideas, and contexts (conceptions) insist on being recognized and confronted in all their fullness and complexity. Performers of purposive acts double up—like William Wordsworth in his letter to Lady Beaumont about reading a poem—in order to function as attentive readers of their own acts as well as those of others. This second mode of attention I choose to call the "aesthetic mode of attention."

It is now possible to offer a provisional description or characterization of literary experience and inquiry based on the foregoing assessment of the work of John Dewey and Stephen Pepper. This characterization, moreover, will be augmented and refined progressively in the remaining chapters of this book. First and foremost, literary experience cannot be disencumbered of literary inquiry, neither vice versa. The activity of literary reading is an experience that insists on instituting an inquiry into the evidences of its own occurrence. Literary inquiry constitutes the way and means readers, and readers as critics, have for gradually clarifying and refining the indeterminate and problematic situations that most reading involves into literary or critical knowledge. Knowledge is inextricably implicated in the activity of reading because reading is an act of cognition that is best described as purposive. As such, reading is accessible to both qualitative description and conceptual analysis. Such is the case, for the structural characteristics of the purposive act disclose that it is both immediately qualitatively felt and open to conceptual probing, description, refinement, and explanation. The qualitative and the conceptual "reports" on the activity of reading may not square at every juncture. However, they both do arise from, or actually already meet at, the one and the same actual process of literary reading. Uncriticized evidence or facts, indefinitely cognized in the qualitative act of reading, are secured and available for clarification and refinement into criticized evidence. Again, the confusion in reference undergone in the activity of reading Wordsworth's "A slumber" constitutes a perfect example of uncriticized evidence or fact in need of clarification and critical refinement. Through corroboration by critical agreement or consensus ("multiplicative corroboration") and by conceptual self-consistency ("structural corroboration"), this criticized evidence can be evaluated, judged, and accepted as persuasive and adequate critical knowledge. Criticized evidence, the product of literary inquiry, however, maintains a tensile relation with its cognitive source in the qualitative act of literary reading. To fail to do so would eventually render critical knowledge arbitrary, brittle, unreliable, and cognitively irresponsible.

The activity of literary reading, moreover, demarcates a particular area of our purposive behavior that can strike us as especially aware and directed. As such, we do not attend to the world and our own activity in it merely in the usual or ordinary way. We do not suspend attention, alertness, or cognition but instead attend closely and with circumspection to the actual movements and workings of our literary reading and inquiry. Literary purposive activity is able to achieve heightened and exacting awareness as well as extended self-reflection. In other words, we are able to direct what I have called the aesthetic mode of attention upon our instrumental mode of attention. Literary experience involves a compounded act of awareness: Instrumentality has become self-reflectively aware of itself and its tools of articulation. In an exemplary manner, this compounded awareness characteristic of the activity of literary reading recovers an earlier sense of the word "attention": stretched toward some other thing in expectation, heeding, listening, tensed with taut awareness.

In her book *Literature and Knowledge* Dorothy Walsh develops a Deweyan case for the recognition of literature as eliciting "the duality of self-reflexive awareness." As Walsh articulates this situation: "*An* experience, as life experience, is self-consciously recognized by the experiencer as *his*. An experience is not just awareness; it is awareness of awareness."[27] This compounded awareness happens to any given self in and through an experience. Walsh employs Dewey's concepts of experience and knowledge and connects them to a philosophical psychology of the self that attains its most exemplary exfoliation in the encounter with a literary work.

A literary work, remarks Walsh, elicits a "revelatory or cognitively significant" relation with an attentive reader and "his perceptive insight and his funded knowledge of other works of literature." This literary encounter offers "some intimate engagement with knowledge": "knowing by living through."[28] Walsh throughout distinguishes "knowing by living through" from "knowing about," and these two types of knowledge can be likened to Pepper's one broad type of criticized and refined evidence or critical knowledge. What Walsh's distinction in critical knowledge helps to clarify is the prevailing mode of attention being elicited in an experience. When a self is aware of "knowing about" something in his or her experience, then that self can be said to attend instrumentally to his or her own awareness.[29] However, when a self is aware of knowing something 'in an intimate and revelatory way, of "knowing by living through," then he or she can be said to attend aesthetically to possibilities of experience yet unrealized or left unrealized and unknown in ordinary life experience by the instrumental mode of attention. Or as Walsh herself phrases this point, we "look to literary art for a disclosure of the possibilities of experience, for an understanding of what things might come to *as* forms or modes of human experience."[30] This understanding characteristically takes the form of a "realization." We understand our

27. Dorothy Walsh, *Literature and Knowledge* (Middletown, Conn.: Wesleyan University Press, 1969), pp. 81, 84. See pages 81–84 for her full development of the Deweyan concept of experience. Generally Walsh tends to summarize and remain rather close to the letter of Dewey, but she does disagree with his stress on the temporal pattern of experience.

28. Ibid., pp. 5, 11, 13, and pp. 3–15 in passing.

29. Walsh's designation "knowing about" would seem to be a composite of two aspects of cognitive behavior that Gilbert Ryle, in the second chapter of *The Concept of Mind* (New York: Barnes & Noble, 1964; orig. pub. 1949), distinguishes as "knowing how" and "knowing that." An ordinary cognitive act can be described and explained by the ability or capacity demonstrated and the content or information made present or evoked. The former involves descriptions of rules and procedures; the latter, qualities, attributes, or predicates. If we have in mind Walsh's naming of "knowing by living through," a consummate form of understanding that she also calls "realization," we can think of Ryle's notion of "knowing how" as "realizability" and of "knowing that" as "that which is available for realization."

30. Walsh, p. 90.

experience by realizing it, by living through it, and by "attend[ing] to the qualitative character of our mode of having or undergoing it."[31] And so, as Walsh concludes, "literary art, when functioning successfully as literary art, provides knowledge in the form of realization: the realization of what anything might come to as a form of lived experience."[32] In solid

31. Ibid., p. 87.

32. Ibid., p. 136. A different but not wholly unrelated approach to action and qualities in literature can be found in Charles Altieri, "The Qualities of Action: A Theory of Middles in Literature," *Boundary 2* 5 (Winter 1977): 323–50, and "The Qualities of Action: Part II," *Boundary 2* 5 (Spring 1977): 899–917. In the first essay Altieri proposes a theory of cultural middles in place of the metaphysical obsessions with beginnings (Edward Said) and endings (Frank Kermode) that belie "the full complexity of human behavior" (p. 326). Altieri claims that the critical and philosophical muddles that literary theorists make of literary response can be resolved by recovering "cultural middles" as the "space of response." Culture provides the realm of actions and knowledge that human beings share, and literary discourse dramatistically enacts a certain range of actions that foreground qualities of human response to experience. Literary texts are taken as imaginary worlds or cultural images of human experience that readers and critics focus upon in order to recognize, assess, and judge "the qualities performed by [them]" (p. 345). Such recognition, assessment, and judgment of quality "depend on one's cultural education and can only be justified by leading others to see the images of human value one is relying on" (p. 326). In the second essay Altieri fully develops his concept of action and analyzes the basic properties of actions and the consequences of his theory for practical criticism. "Literature expands the space of response," he concludes; "it does not provide more secure beginnings and ends. And in so doing it is continuous with our normal processes for learning to live in and to appreciate the facets of cultural life" (p. 915).

For the most part, this theory of cultural middles as the space of literary response is commensurate or coextensive with the Deweyan approach to the activity of literary reading developed here. The key difference is that the notion of "cultural middles" could easily displace the actual space of response that individual readers establish through their particular activity of reading. The issue here is not the choice of one "space of response" over the other, because the two are really not exclusive of one another. However, very generally considered, culture and cultural education do not always freely or graciously provide the actions, knowledge, and "images of human value" that readers need in order to read responsively or attentively. Reading, most especially literary reading, constitutes one major way to attain critical distance and insight into culture and cultural education. The space of this culturally critical response cannot merely inhabit cultural middles, though it is almost always related to and frequently dependent upon them at many points. This space of response, critical of prevailing cultural middles, would appear to seek or propose or forge new or additional "middles." These middles and their evocative power and value, of necessity, are still too well rooted or embedded in the particular actions, qualities, and concepts of the activity of reading that has performed, developed, refined, or constructed them.

Besides this general consideration, the actual space of response developed in the course of reading seems to be unduly displaced by cultural middles through the use of such phrases as "the qualities performed by literary texts." This phrase reveals the apparent displacement of the reader and his or her activity onto just the text itself. Perhaps another way of formulating this situation would be to say that within the particular space of a literary response, namely, the purposive activity of attending to a specific literary work, a reader evokes the qualities of actions that the

Deweyan fashion, Walsh is able to relate the broad terms "literature" and "knowledge" and make a case for "the recognition of the distinctive kind of cognitive significance literary art can have."[33]

Walsh also argues that this "distinctive kind of cognitive significance" is grounded in what amounts to a philosophical psychology of the self. Literary experience depends upon the understanding and realization that "the duality of self-reflexive awareness" can seek out and achieve. As already indicated, an experience is awareness of awareness. However, this dual or doubled character of self-reflexive awareness can be qualified a little more precisely:

> An awareness of awareness is *both* an awareness of something given in experience, *and also* an awareness of a mode or manner of experiencing it, in short, it is a "me-experiencing-this." How much emphasis there may be on "me" and how much on "this" will vary from occasion to occasion.[34]

Having an experience, then, literary or otherwise, characteristically involves a self aware of something given in his or her own experience and aware of the mode in which the experience occurs. Summarily, we can phrase this doubled awareness as an awareness of "me" and "this," "self" and "other," both involved in a particular way in the one experience. This kind of doubled, self-reflexive awareness constitutes precisely the sort of awareness, by the way, found defective in the solipsistic purview of the speaker of "A slumber." Wordsworth, moreover, limns in a lyrical mode the fatal consequences of an "I" who fails to be doubly aware of himself and the lovely "other." But the poet, with great acuity and patience, abundantly shows the ramifications of such self-reflexive awareness when he attends to his movements as observer, author, and reader of his sonnet "With ships the sea was sprinkled far and nigh." His act of literary

---

work is disposed to enact because both it and its readers generally share in a space of cultural response characteristically marked by actions and their qualities.

In *Act and Quality: A Theory of Literary Meaning and Humanistic Understanding* (Amherst: University of Massachusetts Press, 1981), Altieri presents a wide-ranging philosophical defense and humanistic application of his literary and cultural theory of actions and qualities. For an appraisal of this important work in literary theory, see my review-essay "A Grammar of Actions and Attitudes: Unfolding a Humanist Theory of Literary Studies," *Pre/Text* 6 (Spring/Summer 1985): 31–49.

33. Walsh, p. 15.

34. Ibid., p. 85.

awareness in this instance reveals a self doubly aware of himself and his relations to others.

Chapters 11 and 12 will investigate the type of relation between "me" and "this," "self" and "other," that usually obtains in an experience or a knowledge situation. They will also assess the Deweyan sense of self and social milieu. These two sections can be understood as deploying a Deweyan philosophical psychology of the self suited to placing philosophically the role of literary readers and their activity of reading within a framework of cognitive social psychology.

11

Self, Environment, Interaction: The Interactive Paradigm

In developing the common patterns that are to be found in various experiences, Dewey states that the "outline" of the most basic and shared pattern

> . . . is set by the fact that every experience is the result of interaction between a live creature and some aspect of the world in which he lives. A man does something; he lifts, let us say, a stone. In consequence he undergoes, suffers, something: the weight, strain, texture of the surface of the thing lifted. The properties thus undergone determine further doing. The stone is too heavy or too angular, not solid enough; or else the properties undergone show it is fit for the use for which it is intended. The process continues until a mutual adaptation of the self and the object emerges and that particular experience comes to a close. What is true of this simple instance is true, as to form, of every experience. The creature operating may be a thinker in his study and the environment with which he interacts may consist of ideas instead of a stone. But the interaction of the two constitutes the total experience that is had. . . . [1]

The interaction of a "live creature" and "some aspect of the world," whether stone or idea, sketches the basic shared pattern of an experience. This interaction, furthermore, involves a temporal process that "continues

---

1. Dewey, *Art as Experience*, pp. 43–44.

until a mutual adaptation of the self and the object emerges." Once the self and the object have adapted themselves to one another over a particular course of time and in a particular way, the experience can come to closure. This sense of determinateness or determination at the end of an interaction constitutes an essential feature of the interactive paradigm of experience. Dewey generalizes this interactive paradigm for all types and complexities of having an experience. It provides the basic paradigm for his metaphysics of experience, namely *Experience and Nature,* for his inquiry into epistemology, *The Quest for Certainty,* for his aesthetics, *Art as Experience,* and even for his social psychology, *Human Nature and Conduct.* For Dewey a careful understanding of the social-psychological nature and conduct of human beings is fully enabled by an interactive paradigm: "We can recognize that all conduct is *interaction* between elements of human nature and the environment, natural and social."[2] Moreover, when two or more human beings engage in mutual interaction, each one helps to provide a complex natural and social environment for any one or more of the others.

More recent work on the Deweyan theory of knowledge helps to confirm the centrality of the interactive paradigm for Dewey's concepts of experience, knowledge, and inquiry. Anthony Quinton, for instance, locates Dewey's epistemology within the tradition of American "anti-Cartesianism," most notably exemplified by C. S. Peirce and William James.[3] "Absolute certainties," "secure and certified knowledge" of things in the world, are not to be had. Neither is "the subject or possessor of knowledge . . . a pure mind or consciousness, a Cartesian *res cogitans.*" Only "rational and warranted belief" is possible; and "the knower or inquirer, the pursuer of rational and warranted belief," must be seen "as an active being, an experimenter, not as a contemplative theorist." Indeed, Quinton maintains that the knower is "an intelligent organism, an embodied thing, animated by primarily bodily purposes" who constructs his or her beliefs concerning the world by means of practical, "bodily" interaction:

2. Dewey, *Human Nature and Conduct: An Introduction to Social Psychology* (New York: Modern Library, 1930; orig. pub. 1922), p. 10. The general context involves the question of how to examine the relation of morals (social psychology) and human nature without falling into the alternative of either a mysterious "inner freedom" or a cynical naturalism.

3. Anthony Quinton, "Inquiry, Thought and Action: John Dewey's Theory of Knowledge," in *John Dewey Reconsidered,* ed. R. S. Peters (London: Routledge & Kegan Paul, 1977), pp. 1–8.

> Our rational beliefs about the world in which we live and act are
> not the result of a kind of Augustinian illumination, passively
> received, and then privately worked up and systematized in the
> recesses of our own minds. They are, rather, the outcome of
> deliberate, experimental interaction with our environment.

The knower must and does actively and fully engage the world that resists,
prods, irritates, puzzles, and satisfies him or her. Neither one nor the
other can be elided from the cognitive situation, even though the knower's
"intellectual apparatus" or "conceptual equipment" is his own and "the
pervading structure of the world outside" eludes absolute ascertainability.[4]
It is their relative and instrumental interdependency within our experience and our pursuit of rational and warranted beliefs that constitute and
manifest the knower and the world, the self and the environment, as
interactive coparticipants in any given experience. As Quinton phrases it,

> . . . our conceptual apparatus is not a direct reflection of the
> nature and structure of the world but the result of an interaction,
> worked out in an evolutionary way, between the world and two
> things located in us: our perceptual equipment, on the one hand,
> and our needs on the other. . . . The mind or knower, then,
> can be admitted to be conceptually creative without denying that
> the conceptual outfit it creates is some kind of reflection of the
> world; for surely, if it did not in some way reflect the similarities
> and differences to be found in the world it would be descriptively
> useless.[5]

Cognitive experience, then, is perhaps best explained by the interactive
paradigm, by the interaction of a self and his or her "bodily purposes" and
"conceptual apparatus" with the environment whose resistant and often
challenging otherness helps orient, guide, and direct the "conceptual fit"
of the self to the world.

The persistent skeptic's question, though, will remain: If the nature and
structure of the world, or even some small segment of an environment,
cannot be known with absolute certainty, how can we say that a *real*

4. Ibid., pp. 3–5.
5. Ibid., p. 11.

interaction occurs? Does not a self merely project his or her own needs, powers, and fictions upon what is otherwise believed to be reality? However, in order to put this very question, the skeptic must suspend, interrupt, and even disregard his instrumental mode of attention and what it can teach him qualitatively and conceptually about his usual purposive activity in the world. What is more, this skeptic must either disregard or grievously transvalue his aesthetic mode of attention and what it can make known to him about the movements and manner of his instrumental relation to the world. Both modes of attention offer bountiful, qualitatively felt and conceptually accessible evidences of a self's interactive contact with objects and entities that are distinctively and insistently different. Neither utter skepticism nor solipsism with regard to our cognitive dealings with the world can suffice as responsible or defensible positions. The utter or dogmatic skeptic chooses not to attend to the complexities of interaction but to believe dogmatically in illusion and in the activity and power of doubting utterly or absolutely. As Stephen Pepper limns the troublesome situation of the dogmatic skeptic:

> To doubt utterly the products of knowledge, one must believe implicitly the deceptive structure of knowledge. And apparently one must dogmatically believe this, for otherwise some products of knowledge may be more credible than others. . . . [Such dogmatic belief] sets demands upon the nature of fact and judgment and indeed of the whole universe which must be believed to guarantee the possibility of utter unbelief. An utter skeptic thus turns into a dogmatist.
>
> The position of the utter skeptic is, we find on careful scrutiny, impossible. It amounts to the self-contradictory dogma that the world is certainly doubtful.[6]

6. Pepper, *World Hypotheses*, pp. 8–9 and 3–10 in passing. In general, the critical and philosophical work of Jacques Derrida and Paul de Man expound the dogmatism of utter unbelief. Their deconstructions of figural language supposedly demonstrate the impossibility of holding relatively coherent and adequate senses of the self and of otherness, or of act and reference (to reduce the parameters to linguistic terms). The deconstructive power that riddles absolute belief in tropes and figures spreads out and utterly undermines the possibility of all speech, communication, belief, action, reading, and philosophical thinking. See, especially, Jacques Derrida, *Writing and Difference*, trans. Alan Bass (Chicago: University of Chicago Press, 1978), and Paul de Man, *Allegories of Reading* (New Haven, Conn.: Yale University Press, 1979).

For two excellent essays that fault Derrida's excessive positions on the self, action, language,

The solipsist as well chooses not to attend to the complexities of interaction. In the first part of this book the dangers of solipsism were rehearsed as factors involved in developing the character of the speaker of Wordsworth's "A slumber." In general, the solipsist *"believes* in his solitude in the universe" and does so on the basis of various unquestioned and largely unexamined motives that are clung to against insistent evidence to the contrary.[7] The solipsist is a dogmatist because his *belief* in his own solitude and lack of responsive and responsible interaction will always exceed the cognitive grounds for such belief.[8] Any refined and critical consideration of the evidences of cognition will eventually lead to the undermining and disavowal of the utter skeptic's as well as the solipsist's dogmatic positions on activity and knowledge of the world.

Dorothy Walsh's notion of "the duality of self-reflexive awareness" already discussed can also be of assistance here. An experience, "an awareness of awareness," shows any given self the dual or doubled awareness of which he or she is capable. In any given experience, a self has, as Walsh has phrased it, "an awareness of something given in experience." In other words, an experience characteristically makes a self aware of some thing that is and can only be given in and through experience. A self, moreover, can and does make present in that conscious act of awareness something that is markedly other or different. At the same time and through the same act, then, a self can have an awareness of some aspect of the world and an awareness of the act of attention to that aspect in a particular manner. This dual awareness is a consequence of the capacity and power of self-reflexivity, but it is a self-reflexivity that still must engage and act upon the world. Such purposive activity cannot be utterly the monopoly of any given self because our experience shows us being aware of other things and entities *in order to be aware of ourselves acting, feeling, and thinking.* In other words, *we are interactive in order to be active.* After the fact or in retrospect, the clarification and refinement

---

and meaning, see John Searle, "Reiterating the Differences: A Reply to Derrida," *Glyph* 1 (1977): 198–208, and Charles Altieri, "Wittgenstein on Consciousness and Language: A Challenge to Derridean Literary Theory," *MLN* 91 (1976): 1397–1423. For an extensive examination of Paul de Man's mature work, see my essays *"Allegories of Reading*: Positing a Rhetoric of Romanticism; or, Paul de Man's Critique of Pure Figural Anteriority," *Pre/Text* 4 (Spring 1983): 9–51, and "Recovering the Figure of J. L. Austin in Paul de Man's *Allegories of Reading*," in *The Textual Sublime: Deconstruction and Its Differences,* ed. Hugh Silverman and Gary Aylesworth (Albany: State University of New York Press, 1990), pp. 139–46, 240–43.

7. Pepper, *World Hypotheses,* p. 10.
8. Ibid., p. 11 and pp. 11–19 in passing.

of the evidence of an experience, of a purposive act, will progressively help
clarify and define the interactive participants in a particular "awareness of
awareness." This situation of interaction and retrospective clarification
involves precisely the relation between speaker and other in my analysis of
Wordsworth's "A slumber." The rather strange verbal and mental action of
the speaker eventually can disclose a refined critical conception of his
interaction with the lovely other. Moreover, this situation of interaction
and retrospective refinement of experience implicitly structures my
conception of a critical reader's handling of the actual evidence of the
problematic of reading Wordsworth's poem. The awareness of a referential
confusion regarding the identity of the "she" of the poem can lead into a
self-reflective awareness regarding Wordsworth's verbal craft and the
alluringly puzzling identities of speaker and other in the lyric.

This conception of the interactive paradigm and its general implications
for experience, knowledge, and the self-reflexive quality of experiential
awareness are not without problems. After his various major works on
logic and epistemology had been in circulation for some years, John
Dewey, in collaboration with Arthur F. Bentley, published a revised view
of the notion of interaction. In *Knowing and the Known* Dewey and
Bentley undertook a search "to find a few firm names for use in
connection with the theory of knowledge."[9] Among other things, they
distinguish "interaction" from "self-action" and "transaction" within a
trilevel scheme of inquiry. These "three levels of the organization and
presentation of inquiry in the order of their historical appearance" are:

> *Self-action*: where things are viewed as acting under their own
> powers. *Inter-action*: where thing is balanced against thing in
> causal interconnection. *Trans-action*: where systems of description
> and naming are employed to deal with aspects and phases of
> action, without final attribution to "elements" or other presump-
> tively detachable or independent "entities," "essences," or "reali-
> ties," and without isolation of presumptively detachable "relations"
> from such detachable "elements."[10]

9. Dewey and Bentley, *Knowing and the Known* (Boston: Beacon Press, 1949), p. 287. See
also their introduction, "A Search for Firm Names" (pp. xi–xiii), and the first two chapters,
"Vagueness in Logic" (pp. 3–46) and "The Terminological Problem" (pp. 47–78), for "a startling
diagnosis of linguistic disease" in logic and epistemology (p. xii).
10. Ibid., pp. 107–8.

Purportedly this scheme depicts the evolutionary development of these three levels of intellectual activity both for society and for individuals, whose abilities at inquiry grow progressively as they develop into adults in society. Individuals and societies as a whole advance from the earliest stage of "self-action" through the intermediary stage of "interaction" toward the ultimately progressive stage of "transaction."

Dewey and Bentley consider the first level of inquiry, self-action, to be a "pre-scientific" or "primitive" form of thought. Two additional definitions of "self-action" make this general sense of the term clear:

> [1] Pre-scientific presentation in terms of presumptively independent "actors," "souls," "minds," "selves," "powers" or "forces," taken as activating events.

> [2] Used to indicate various primitive treatments of the known, prior in historical development to interactional and transactional treatments. Rarely found today except in philosophical, logical, epistemological, and a few limited psychological regions of inquiry. [11]

The self-actional model of inquiry remains "pre-scientific" or "primitive" because it involves a cognitively unsound acceptance of or belief in an excessive, or even mythic, authority and power of the self's own activity. The attribution of godlike powers to *genii loci* on the part of primitive peoples, the deification of royalty or charismatic persons, the personification of inanimate objects, and the crises over the possession of authority on the part of children and adolescents are examples of self-action being used as a paradigm for explanation. The need that Edward Said describes to postulate "a strong seminal figure" with power to authorize beginnings, as well as Norman Holland's and David Bleich's theories of the continual re-creation of identity or personality in all the self's activities, are examples of self-action that still persist "in philosophical, logical, epistemological, and a few limited psychological regions of inquiry." More than likely, though, self-action would be found upon investigation to be no more than one mode or aspect of inquiry actually used in primitive societies. Its evolutionary or historical appearance should not be so easily and securely typed. The concept of self-action and its theoretical disjunction from

11. Ibid., pp. 72, 301.

better developed and more circumspect levels of inquiry, however, usefully schematizes the cognitively weak presumption of the priority and authority of personality or subjectivity. Theories of experience, knowledge, and literary meaning rooted in conceptions of the prior authority of personal or subjective identity generally construct cognitively inadequate myths of childish or adolescent self-action. Such theories usually neglect or disregard the enabling matrices of interaction that undergird the often alluring yet illusory beliefs and powers in unrestrained personal authority and self-authorization. By doing so such theories also neglect the shared and shareable grounds for experience and inquiry that the enabling matrices of cognitive interaction generally offer the knowing self.

Interaction stands at a more complex level of inquiry than self-action. Until the appearance of *Knowing and the Known*, "interaction" had sufficed for Dewey to name what he and Bentley mutually felt the need to separate into two distinct levels of inquiry, "interaction" and "transaction." Accordingly, as schematized above, Dewey and Bentley limit "interaction" to describing the "causal interconnection" between two counterbalanced things, while "transaction" becomes the term for designating the description of "aspects and phases of action" in which the participating things or "elements" cannot be categorically isolated or detached. The term "interaction," then, takes on a mechanical sense; it no longer seems to be a way of inquiry into *actions* but instead charts offsetting parts and their causal linkage. Another phrasing of the term by Dewey and Bentley definitely carries this sense: "Presentation of particles or other objects organized as operating upon one another."[12] The term "interaction" in *Knowing and the Known* has lost the sense of a way to describe and explain actions; it is a little too mechanical and causally oriented for that sense to carry now. However, this later redefinition and restriction of "interaction" involves a terminological choice that appears seriously counterproductive to the enormous epistemological advance that an interactive paradigm offers.

This terminological problem has arisen because of an ambiguity in the use and meaning of the prefix "inter":

> This prefix has two sets of applications (see Oxford Dictionary). One is for "between," "in-between," or "between the parts of." The

---

12. Ibid., p. 73.

other is for "mutually," "reciprocally." The result of this shifting use as it enters philosophy, logic, and psychology, no matter how inadvertent, is ambiguity and undependability. The habit easily establishes itself of mingling without clarification the two sets of implications. It is here proposed to eliminate ambiguity by confining the prefix *inter* to cases in which "in between" is dominant, and to employ the prefix *trans* where the mutual and reciprocal are intended.[13]

This elimination of ambiguity, however, means that "cases in which 'in between' is dominant" would inadvertently be dropped out of the study of human actions. "Transaction" is glossed, in the meantime, as "the knowing-known taken as one process in which in older discussions the

13. Ibid., pp. 295–96. Dewey did not easily give up the term "interaction." Dewey's and Bentley's impressive correspondence from 1932 to 1951 shows the younger Bentley slowly and insistently introducing an elaborate, new terminology and the need for careful clarification of terms. The correspondence eventually issues in the collaborative work *Knowing and the Known*. The term "interaction" receives a massive amount of attention and debate, from July 1942 onward. Though Dewey has reservations concerning the term, and does eventually concur with Bentley about the more restricted sense of "interaction" and the epistemologically more advanced sense of "transaction," it is clear that Dewey had striven to use "interaction" in its doubled sense. See especially pp. 115, 125, 126, 138, 139, 157, 169, 188, 193, 207–8, 235, 236, 244, 280, 298–302, 305–7, 309–10, 320, 348, 384, 460, 471, 527–29, 531–33, 614, and 657 of *John Dewey and Arthur F. Bentley: A Philosophical Correspondence, 1932–1951*, ed. Sidney Ratner and Jules Altman (New Brunswick, N.J.: Rutgers University Press, 1964).

In his introduction to the volume, Sidney Ratner recognizes that Dewey's and Bentley's choice of "transaction" over "interaction" can cause serious difficulty in exploring deeds that involve active human agents:

> Valuable as the transactional approach is, when the need arises to stress the moral value or historic significance of individual choice and action, a non-transactional phrasing is justifiable. Too rigid an adherence to the "transaction" formulation could liquidate the special qualities of individuality. Although some readers have inferred that the transactional approach must be mechanistically applied, or interpreted, this was not the intention of Dewey and Bentley, as I understand their writings.
>
> In some respects retention of the "interaction" form guards against this type of misinterpretation and conduces to the development of a theory of the self that Dewey and Bentley never worked out adequately. (p. 45)

My reintroduction and theoretical defense of the term "interaction" picks up on this serious problem of terminological choice and underscores the epistemological value of an interactive paradigm for understanding the social, historical, and psychological implications of complex human actions.

knowings and knowns are separated and viewed as in interaction."[14] The one action, the single process of "the knowing-known," upon any further inquiry, however, will begin to yield not "the knowings and knowns [as] separated" but will characteristically yield at least one actively cognizing and inquiring agent who has some form of history or memory and a distinctive, spatiotemporal, bodily, or organic existence. Other such agents may be implicated in the same action or process; or the process may yield particular goals, objects, purposes, or ideas that themselves will be marked by a history and some form of spatiotemporal duration. These interacting "elements" sooner or later emerge from any inquiry into purposive activity or the knowledge situation. Activity occurs "in between" things, at least one of which assuredly will be a complex organism. The term "interaction" thus needs to have and use both senses of the prefix "inter": (1) mutual and reciprocal action, and (2) action that occurs "in between."[15] The first sense indicates the unity and reciprocal nature of an action. The second sense *unambiguously* indicates that this reciprocity, upon further inquiry, happens as it does in the interaction between things. If this interactive quality of actions were not the case, processes could not actually be (or even be recognized as being) purposive actions; we could not locate, even provisionally, processes as the distinctive behavior of active agents.

As Dewey and Bentley use the term "transaction" in *Knowing and the Known*, it implies an eventual appeal to systems analysis. Indeed, in at least one place, they gloss "transaction" in such a way: "functional observation of full system."[16] The transactional model proposed in

14. Dewey and Bentley, p. 304.

15. Dewey and Bentley are aware that they must force the prefix *"trans"* to carry this reciprocal sense of *"inter"*; *"trans"* has the sense of "beyond," "across," and "side to side," but they choose to redefine as they see fit. See Dewey and Bentley, pp. 296, 304.

16. Dewey and Bentley, p. 73. See also page 303 for the gloss on "system." In "Viewpoints: Transaction versus Interaction—a Terminological Rescue Operation," *Research in the Teaching of English* 19 (1985): 96–107, Louise Rosenblatt attempts to rescue the term "transaction" from its associations with business and information processing and to underwrite Dewey's and Bentley's characterization of "interaction" as mechanistic. However, when she turns to characterize the activity of reading as transactional, the very terms of her analysis echo the interactive paradigm:

   . . . we need to see the reading act as *an event* involving *a particular individual* and *a particular text*, happening at a *particular time*, under particular circumstances, in a *particular social and cultural setting*, and as *part of the ongoing life of the individual and the group*. (p. 100; italics mine)

Knowing and the Known moves in the direction of a systemic analysis of a complex of agent-free processes. In many respects Dewey and Bentley relish the clear emphasis placed on the knowledge situation, now regarded as an ongoing process or flow of systemic activity. However, complex, purposive activity of human beings involves not only mutual and reciprocal action but also an awareness of purposive agents who decide to engage in mutual and reciprocal activity. The interactional model developed in Dewey's earlier and primary work is comparatively less systemic than the later transactional theory. However, it is more schematic, organismically oriented, and attentive to the reality of purposive agents who can decide to interact with one another or with aspects of their environments. The scheme, in outline, is the interaction of organism and environment. For the purposes of this discussion, I choose to adhere to the earlier, better developed, and, I think, far more cognitively adequate and defensible interactional model.

Some experimental and theoretical work in cognitive social psychology that provides broad-based evidence in support of this Deweyan interactional model can be cited. Such supportive evidence involves work carried out in diverse yet overlapping fields of perceptual cognition, neurological behavior, and cognitive and developmental psychology. For instance, in a book directed against "sense data" theories of perception, the distinguished psychologist James J. Gibson proposes a holistic interactive model of the senses. Under varying and plentiful stimulation from a complexly conceived environment, a particular self's unified system of senses and repertory of learned responses can perceive and discern "new properties of the world" and develop the capacity for further responses.[17] Gibson limits his explorations to perceptual learning and so does not directly examine highly performative behavior or performatory learning. Nevertheless, his model for perception is decidedly interactive. Roger Gurney, in a study that concentrates on neurological processes, develops a model of those

---

I will discuss Rosenblatt's work in Chapter 14. Her study of the nature of literary reading is eminently suitable to the interactive paradigm, even though she prefers to subscribe to Bentley's and Dewey's later usage of the term "transaction."

17. James J. Gibson, *The Senses Considered as Perceptual Systems* (Boston: Houghton Mifflin, 1966), pp. 5–6, and 7–30 in passing. According to Gibson, there are four interconnected levels of the environment: the terrestrial environment, the organismic habitat, the animate or social environment, and the cultural environment (pp. 14–26). See Edward S. Reed, *James J. Gibson and the Psychology of Perception* (New Haven, Conn.: Yale University Press, 1988) for a critical biography of Gibson and his lifelong development of a model of perception based on purposive acts of attention by organisms seeking ways to interact with the complexities of environments.

processes that collectively provide the basis for the human capacity to learn language. He integrates biological, neurological, psychological, and linguistic evidence in order to elicit the complex set of interactive processes that carry throughout these domains of activity that linguistic behavior depends upon. In words that resonate with Dewey's, Gurney can claim: ". . . the different interactive processes are logically connected as different aspects of biological activity. They stem from the basic ability of all biological material to interact with the environment."[18] The extensive work of Jean Piaget, however, provides perhaps the finest and most widespread corroboration of Dewey's interactive paradigm. Working in cognitive and developmental psychology, Piaget, like Dewey, investigates the connections between biology and epistemology in an attempt to chart the human organism's environmentally nurtured and self-regulated development of cognitive structures and functions. Piaget's "guiding hypothesis" postulates the interaction of complex organisms with the environment in a distinctively Deweyan fashion:

> *Cognitive processes seem, then, to be at one and the same time the outcome of organic autoregulation, reflecting its essential mechanisms, and the most highly differentiated organs of this regulation at the core of interactions with the environment,* so much so that, in the case of man, these processes are being extended to the universe itself.[19] (Piaget's italics)

The evidential support supplied by such researchers and theorists as Gibson, Gurney, and Piaget will not be enlarged upon here. However, their work does in general provide a large body of experimental data and theoretical integrations and hypotheses in support of interaction as the most cogent and compelling model for cognition and purposive activity.

18. R. Gurney, *Language, Brain and Interactive Processes* (London: Arnold, 1973), p. 92.
19. J. Piaget, *Biology and Knowledge: An Essay on the Relations between Organic Regulations and Cognitive Processes,* trans. Beatrix Walsh (Chicago: University of Chicago Press, 1971; orig. pub. 1967), p. 26.

12

Habit, Integration, Character, and Reasons for Action: A Deweyan Sense of the Self

In *Art as Experience* John Dewey calls the self a "live creature," a complex organism who, in being fully animate and present in the world and to itself, is capable of having experiences, both ordinary and aesthetic.[1] Dewey's sense of the self or individual creature does not really get beyond this organismic model in this particular work on aesthetic philosophy. Other books and articles by Dewey, though, do help to elaborate a fuller and more distinctively psychological sense of the self. The key notion for Dewey is "habit," a term traceable to David Hume and to various eighteenth-century discussions of the nature of human physiological and mental behavior. Dewey recognizes and reintegrates a wide range of possibilities for the notion in the wake of Freud's work on psychic impulses, drives, complexes, and repetition compulsions. Dewey's notion of habit, however, is far less deterministic and far more socially and environmentally oriented than Freudian conceptions. Dewey dwells upon the individual and the collective workings and integrations of habits in human behavior and the ways in which habits prepare us for and dispose us toward certain kinds of action. Human habits, moreover, are mediated by a uniquely human set of capacities and procedures—namely, the uses of language. Even though Dewey may frequently seem to limit the uses of

---

1. Dewey, *Art as Experience*, pp. 18–19, but also the first two chapters, "The Live Creature" (pp. 3–19) and "The Live Creature and 'Etherial Things'" (pp. 20–34), in passing. Chapter 11, "The Human Contribution" (pp. 245–71), discusses the psychological aspect of aesthetics but remains very general and does not concretely refine the organismic conception of self.

language to purely instrumental functions, as reflected in his recurrent metaphor of it as a "tool," the acquisition of language appears critical to human experience, to human self-regulation and interaction with others, and to the development of human habits and their integrations. Recognition of the fundamental, formative, and informative way in which language shapes and directs development of human experience will start us on the path toward a rich, Deweyan sense of the self.

In a collaborative article, three linguists coordinate current research into the acquisition of language with Dewey's understanding of language and experience. What interests them most is Dewey's "view about language comprehension as an active, constructional process."[2] Quite contrary to Noam Chomsky and transformational or deep-structural grammars, but quite in line with the active, constructional approach to experience and learning espoused by Dewey, these linguists—on the basis of a theoretical elaboration of experimental evidence—make the following claims:

> Language acquisition does depend upon mastery of non-linguistic concepts (although it is not explained by them); the mastery of syntax *is* dependent upon meaning and it may well be better to think of initial syntax as itself serving a semantic function; and finally, the corpus of speech that is the input upon which acquisition is based is not a sample, not overheard, not indifferent. In fact, the corpus of speech to which the child is exposed is governed by rules of interdependent interaction between child and adult and the uses to which language is put are powerfully important in how the child gets into the language.[3]

This view of language acquisition emphasizes the embeddedness of the development of linguistic abilities in the general development and ability to use other sorts of concepts. Language, like knowledge in general, is embedded in experience, in our general purposive activity. Language develops along with, mediates, and is mediated by our whole range of pragmatic and performative acts. Such activity has been constructed over time in rule-governed interactions with other speakers, in the case of

---

2. Jerome Bruner, Eileen Caudill, and Anat Ninio, "Language and Experience," in *John Dewey Reconsidered*, ed. R. S. Peters (London: Routledge & Kegan Paul, 1977), p. 20.

3. Ibid., p. 22.

language, or with other things, in the case of our general purposive activity. Linguistic activity thus continues to be a constructional process as learning itself continues. In the case of language acquisition or linguistic construction, the child starts off slowly with "an extraordinarily limited and repetitive range of learning" until an initial set of linguistic habits are acquired.[4] Language learning continues with the construction, reconstruction, and integration of additional linguistic habits—such as the need to presuppose or ascribe antecedents for pronouns. This learning happens only through interaction with other speakers and already acquired and usable habits, but it provides the active basis for recognition and response for later complex behavior. We generally take the activity of presupposing or wanting to ascribe an antecedent for the pronoun "she" or "he" or "it" as a fairly fundamental linguistic habit for speakers of the English language, for instance. That fundamental linguistic habit cannot or should not be overlooked or trivialized in the complex purposive activity of reading and interpreting Wordsworth's poem "A slumber did my spirit seal." Like all competent speakers of a language, a poet relies upon and employs a wide range of fundamental linguistic habits that have been actively learned or constructed over time by his or her presumed, projected, or potential readers.

Such an active, constructional view of language acquisition as well as the interactional scenes in which our linguistic habits get constructed would seem to discourage a "private" or "inner" or highly "mentalized" conception of any given self and his or her habits and uses of language. Indeed, Dewey can wax vehement on this very point:

> . . . the idea of perfecting an "inner" personality is a sure sign of social divisions. What is called inner is simply that which does not connect others, which is not capable of full and free communication. What is termed spiritual culture has usually been futile, with something rotten about it, just because it has been conceived as a thing which a man might have internally—and therefore exclusively. What one is as a person is what one is as associated with others, in a free give and take of intercourse.[5]

4. Ibid.
5. Dewey, *Democracy and Education: An Introduction to the Philosophy of Education* (New York: Macmillan, 1916), p. 122.

Indeed Dewey would appear to be correct in making this rather expansive connection between "the idea of perfecting" a "private" or "inner" personality and the attenuation of what he calls a "full and free communication" and association with others. An "inner" or highly "mentalized" conception of the self produces or coins a "valorization"[6] of the self that has serious, if not grievous, social ramifications. As Stephen Toulmin has insightfully written, the highly inward and mentalized conditions of thinkers (and ordinary people as well) constitute a "*postso*-cial" state of society—one that is antipathetic to communal life and surfaces in the symptomology of fixated "fantasy" life, "personal isolation," and "civic decay." Toulmin claims that this "*post*social" condition is the outcome of our inheritance from Locke, Hartley, and Hobbes of privatistic theories of mind and the quality of the isolated self's relation to others.[7]

A full philosophical appraisal of the idea of the "inner" personality, of course, has been carried out most notably by Gilbert Ryle. Ryle combats what he calls "Descartes' Myth" or "the dogma of the Ghost in the Machine": namely, the bifurcation of the self into two "lives"—its external, physical, bodily life and the "inner life" of its own mental workings.[8] Ryle shows that this bifurcation of physical and mental processes is a mistake in logical reasoning that also has historical and theological promptings and influences.[9] He contends that the exercise of qualities of mind and the acts or utterances in which these qualities can be recognized by others are one and the same. Such qualities and acts cannot be separated into mental processes, on the one hand, and physical processes, on the other. Through the exercise of intelligence and by practice guided by example, we learn from the acts and utterances of

6. "Valorization" and "valorize" are much abused terms in certain quarters of literary discourse. Many critics and theorists seem to take them mistakenly, as synonyms for "to place a value on," "to assign a value to," or simply "to value." The primary use of "valorization," though, is to mean: the policy and action of supporting commodity prices by any of various forms of government subsidy. A definition of the verb "valorize," following its nounal use, is: to inflate commodity values (prices) arbitrarily and systematically through deliberate manipulation on the part of elites, usually through legal or administrative means. I use "valorization" here to carry the sense of *an arbitrary and inflated valuation of a commodity within a particular group or society.* Such valuation also implies the (socioeconomic and sociopolitical) risk of *misvaluation.*

7. Stephen Toulmin, "The Inwardness of Mental Life," *Critical Inquiry* 6 (Autumn 1979): 15, and pp. 1–16 in passing.

8. Ryle, pp. 11–16.

9. Ibid., pp. 18–22, 23–24.

others what concepts fit and do not fit a particular situation within which we are just beginning to habituate ourselves. In such manner we learn to act, think, speak, and gain competency and skill in the use of "mental-conduct concepts."[10] Our own abilities and sense of our own minds develop from our extensive interactions with others. As we learn to characterize conceptually our own mental conduct, we also learn to attend to and follow the workings—the acts and utterances—of other minds. As Ryle sums up this point:

> I discover that there are other minds in understanding what other people say and do. In making sense of what you say, in appreciating your jokes, in unmasking your chess-stratagems, in following your arguments and in hearing you pick holes in my arguments, I am not inferring to the workings of your mind, I am following them. Of course, I am not merely hearing the noises that you make, or merely seeing the movements that you perform. I am understanding what I hear and see. But this understanding is not inferring to occult causes. It is appreciating how the operations are conducted. To find that most people have minds (though idiots and infants in arms do not) is simply to find that they are able and prone to do certain sorts of things, and this we do by witnessing the sorts of things they do. Indeed we do not merely discover that there are other minds; we discover what specific qualities of intellect and character particular people have.[11]

The performances of particular acts or utterances, then, are not the private property of "inner" or "private" selves or personalities.[12] As a conse-

---

10. Ibid., pp. 25–26, 40–51.
11. Ibid., pp. 60–61.
12. Of course, Ryle admits and considers the exceptions of "silent soliloquies and other imaginings," as well as pain and dreams. These "covert" doings are "private" or "inner." However, notice that soliloquizing and unvoiced imaginings are internalizations of utterances and acts learned in social settings and interactions. Also, once we express our pain or our dreams, they become intelligibly accessible to others. See Ryle, p. 61, and the chapter "Imagination" (pp. 245–79) in passing. Ludwig Wittgenstein, moreover, confronts this problem in the "private language" section of *Philosophical Investigations*, 3d ed., trans. G. E. M. Anscombe (New York: Macmillan, 1968), pp. 88e–104e (Part I, #243–316). Wittgenstein is generally concerned to show that private sensations, or the private use of feelings, do not count as criteria for understanding linguistic operations. The criteria we use are behavioral, shared, public—or, as Wittgenstein prefers, "grammatical."

quence, the discussion of a fuller, richer sense of self that begins to emerge with the trial-and-error acquisition of linguistic habits does not move toward an *inward* sense of self but toward a *habitual* sense of self, one that opens directly onto the social and cultural interactions that shape human activity.

Victor Kestenbaum has conducted a full-scale inquiry into Dewey's notion of "habit." Kestenbaum seeks to recover the "phenomenological sense," as he calls it, of Dewey's notion. However, a major benefit of the inquiry is its recovery of the concept from inattention and disuse. As he has correlated the terms, Kestenbaum shows that for Dewey "habit" is that large area of human experience of "had" or "lived" meanings, meanings that are not yet refined or "known." Habits are also called "accepted meanings," "funded meanings," and "acquired meanings."[13] Habits, as such, are much like Stephen Pepper's common sense and commonsense facts in that they exist and are operative—"had" or "lived"—prior to being more fully recognized and refined into critical knowledge. Characteristically, habits require "the cooperation of organism and environment" because "they are things done by the environment by means of organic structures or acquired dispositions" possessed by the organism. Or, a little more precisely: "habits are ways of using and incorporating the environment in which the latter has its say as surely as the former."[14] Just as with the acquisition of linguistic habits, habits in general are acquired through interaction. Any given self tends to be disposed toward accepting and developing what the environment brings to bear. The habits acquired by a particular self also remain social, shared, and never purely subjective. Habits, as Dewey himself phrases it,

> . . . are not private possessions of a person. They are working adaptations of personal capacities with environing forces. All virtues and vices are habits which incorporate objective forces. They are interactions of elements contributed by the make-up of an individual with elements supplied by the out-door world.[15]

Essentially, habits cannot be private because individuals all must adapt their "personal capacities" to the same, or predominantly the same, set of

---

13. Kestenbaum, pp. 2–4. See also footnote 3, p. 163.
14. Dewey, *Human Nature and Conduct*, pp. 14–15.
15. Ibid., p. 16.

"environing forces." The individual members of a particular society, to return to the example of linguistic habits, all tend to grow into and develop a working use of the same language because they all must adapt their own capacities to predominantly the same set of "environing forces"—namely, competent speakers of the language. Honesty, garrulity, gaiety, forgetfulness, alacrity, and procrastination are all habits to which particular individuals may have adapted themselves to differing degrees. However, these habits are social and shared because they are supported by the environing forces and conditions of a particular society or aggregate of human beings.[16]

Nevertheless, because an individual has acquired a particular set of "working adaptations" or habits, they are quite significantly *his* or *her* habits. These habits, that is to say, constitute the particular individual's character. Dewey notes that a particular habit, especially such a "bad habit" as procrastination, has a powerful and intimate hold over a self:

> A bad habit suggests an inherent tendency to action and also a hold, command over us. It makes us do things we are ashamed of, things which we tell ourselves we prefer not to do. It overrides our formal resolutions, our conscious decisions. When we are honest with ourselves we acknowledge that a habit has this power because it is so intimately a part of ourselves. It has a hold upon us because we are the habit.[17]

16. A general set of such habits for a society would be comparable to what Raymond Williams, in *Marxism and Literature* (Oxford: Oxford University Press, 1977), pp. 128–35, calls a "structure of feeling." A "structure of feeling," as a "cultural hypothesis," designates "meanings and values as they are actively lived and felt" (p. 132). The "elements" within such a "structure of feeling" are marked for their "specificity" and for their "sociality" (p. 133).

The sociologist and cultural anthropologist Pierre Bourdieu, in *Outline of a Theory of Practice*, trans. Richard Nice (Cambridge: Cambridge University Press, 1977), pp. 72–95, develops the notion of "the habitus" in order to name and analyze social systems of structured and structuring dispositions that generate possible perceptions and recognitions within given sociocultural environments. Bourdieu's elaboration of "the habitus" yields a quite current sociological and anthropological analogue to Dewey's predominantly philosophical and psychological investigation of the constructional and generative powers of habits. Indeed, Dewey's notion of cultural habitude—a notion to be addressed in Chapter 13—appears to have strong affinities with, if not to anticipate by some fifty years, Bourdieu's theoretical outline of the explanatory force of "the habitus" in practice.

17. Dewey, *Human Nature and Conduct*, p. 24. Considered etymologically, the word "habit" derives from the Latin noun "habitus"—meaning "condition," "appearance," "attire," "character," or "disposition." The noun is related to the Latin verb "habere"—meaning "to have" or "to hold." Psychologically considered, "habit" carries a far more active and integrated and far less

"We are the habit" because it is a basic and formative "predisposition" of the self toward activity and thought. Habits are our "energetic and dominating ways of acting":

> All habits are demands for activity; and they constitute the self. . . . They form our effective desires and they furnish us with our working capacities. They rule our thoughts, determining which shall appear and be strong and which shall pass from light into obscurity.[18]

Habits, then, are the particular capacities selves have acquired and that, as a consequence, constitute and have an intimate and powerful hold over us. They predispose us toward, even demand, activity in the world. They form the desires, skills, and thoughts basic to initiating purposive activity.

A particular self, furthermore, progressively becomes individuated through the increasing degree of integration and character of his or her own habits. Habits do not remain separated or isolated. A self is not "a bundle, an untied bundle at that, of isolated acts."[19] Any given self achieves some degree of integration of his or her habits. Though the integration can never actually be total, it does yield a relatively determinate and working integration that we call "character." Character, thus, emerges from a relative yet specific integration of habits. Dewey also limns "character" as "the working interaction of habits" and "the mutual modification of habits,"[20] the latter phrase an allusion to Wordsworth and his pronounced concern for the interactive powers and consequences of human habits. Both of Dewey's synonymous phrases for character emphasize the continual and ongoing work involved in shaping and performing the character of the self. "Character," says Dewey,

> is the interpenetration of habits. If each habit existed in an insulated compartment and operated without affecting or being affected by others, character would not exist. That is, conduct would lack unity being only a juxtaposition of disconnected

---

mechanical and determined sense of psychological processes than do such terms as "instinct," "drive," "unconscious behavior," "compulsion," or "repetition."

18. Ibid., p. 25.
19. Ibid., p. 38.
20. Ibid., pp. 40, 39.

reactions to separated situations. But since environments overlap, since situations are continuous and those remote from one another contain like elements, a continuous modification of habits by one another is constantly going on. A man may give himself away in a look or gesture. Character can be read through the medium of individual acts.[21]

A particular self works to integrate and enact his or her character in assorted looks, gestures, acts, and utterances. This self's abundant, overlapping, and remembered interactions with numerous specific environments support the activity of this integration. Other selves too have learned how to read individual acts and know how to recover the sense of another self from them. The evidence of habits is recognized in the particular acts of any given self, and other selves can and do adequately integrate such habitual evidence into a character they can come to know and with which they can pursue further interactions.

Since habit is a basic and formative predisposition toward activity and thought—or, as Dewey says elsewhere in his discussion, "an acquired predisposition to *ways* or modes of response"[22]—habit supplies our basic reasons for and disposals toward action. A self generally does not act randomly or at mere whim and with utter caprice. Neither does a self act with unrestricted choice or unhindered preference. A particular self's direction and freedom are not left to chance but are based in the habits of that self. Habits carry us into new actions and thoughts, variations and repetitions of past or present activity, and thus substantially *direct* us forward, if only but poorly:

> Concrete habits do all the perceiving, recognizing, imagining, recalling, judging, conceiving and reasoning that is done. "Consciousness," whether as a stream or as special sensations and images, expresses functions of habits, phenomena of their formation, operation, their interruption and reorganization.[23]

However, the choices that the self can make do not leave it at the mercy of already acquired habits. The power of making choices—freedom—

21. Ibid., p. 38.
22. Ibid., p. 42.
23. Ibid., p. 177.

instigates a conscience and consciousness about the self's direction and disposals toward further and future actions. "Freedom," as one Deweyan writer has phrased it, "is the intelligent harmonizing of habits for the open-ended purpose of becoming an intelligent human being."[24] This "intelligent harmonizing of habits" is part and parcel of the character-forming "mutual modification of habits." Yet there is also the additional sense here of a self assuming decisive and effective control of the changes being wrought upon and among his or her habits. The developing exercise of intelligence and conscious choice reveals that a self is actually already and always under some degree of active construction.

A particular self fully capable of direction and freedom, moreover, has decisively moved this process of construction of the self into one of continual and continuous *self-construction*. Such a self

> . . . is always in a state of becoming and the conscious search is a search for himself. The search is not a treasure hunt, however, since there is no pre-existent self to find. The search creates the self by bringing habits into harmony . . . and constructing a man who is free and human.[25]

The idea of a "pre-existent self," or what Dewey also types as "the doctrine of a single, simple and indissoluble soul," is a "psychological monster." Human beings create such a monstrous "soul" by "transforming the (truistic) fact of acting *as* a self into the fiction of acting always *for* self." This fiction deceives us into believing that a self must preexist all his or her habits and acts. However, it is a fallacy, a "material error," to believe in "the fixity and simplicity of the self." This fallacious belief has been "fostered by . . . the theologians with their dogma of the unity and ready-made completeness of the soul." Instead, we arrive at a more adequate conception of the self by recognizing that "selfhood (except as it has encased itself in a shell of routine) is in process of making, and that any self is capable of including within itself a number of inconsistent selves, of unharmonized dispositions."[26] Since any given self is not prior,

---

24. Martin Hollis, "The Self in Action," in *John Dewey Reconsidered*, p. 63. This essay offers an excellent integration and overview of the implications of Dewey's concept of person or self-identity.
25. Ibid., p. 67.
26. Dewey, *Human Nature and Conduct*, pp. 176, 136–37. See also Karen Hanson, *The Self*

unitary, or fixed, the project of continual making, constructing, and reorganizing can in fact *and in deed* include inconsistent "selves." They may well be various contradictory or unharmonized modes of response and general dispositions toward activity in the character of a self. The disposals toward action that concrete habits provide do not demand absolute self-unity in order to instigate conscious choices. Intelligent levels of integration and organization are not absolute, but they are adequate and actualizable. The ongoing and intelligent activity of self-construction, then, is the most substantial measure and cognizable evidence of "selfhood." A self is neither mysteriously secreted nor only elusively glimpsed. A particular self presents himself or herself before us, or within us, in habits and their harmonizings.

This conscious search of the self perhaps makes itself most apparent in those situations that are new or unusually demanding. Such situations occasion activity that may not be easily reconciled with a self's current harmonizing or integration of habits:

> . . . a novel factor in the surroundings releases some impulse which tends to initiate a different and incompatible activity, to bring about a redistribution of the elements of organized activity. . . . Now at these moments of a shifting in activity conscious feeling and thought arise and are accentuated. The disturbed adjustment of organism and environment is reflected in a temporary strife which concludes in a coming to terms of the old habit and the new impulse.[27]

With novelty new impulses toward activity, which differ from that toward which old habits dispose a particular self, disturb and perhaps distress that self. The self is more acutely aware in such moments and can feel and think more consciously and attentively than in more settled and habitual situations. In the novel and unsettling situation, furthermore, habit must yield direction to impulse until the habitual self can probe the situation

---

Imagined: Philosophical Reflections on the Social Character of Psyche (New York: Routledge & Kegan Paul, 1986), especially pp. 66–133.

27. Dewey, *Human Nature and Conduct*, p. 179. Or, as Dewey says elsewhere: "With conflict of habits and release of impulse there is conscious search" (p. 180). Victor Kestenbaum calls these demanding and conflictual situations "imaginative experiences," with "imagination" itself being a function of habit as it responds to impulses and promptings. See Kestenbaum, pp. 107–9, 24.

and reorganize old habits, perhaps with more awareness and better integration:

> In this period of redistribution impulse determines the direction of movement. It furnishes the focus about which reorganization swirls. Our attention in short is always directed forward to bring to notice something which is imminent but which as yet escapes us. Impulse defines the peering, the search, the inquiry. . . . During this search, old habit supplies content, filling, definite, recognizable, subject-matter. It begins as vague presentiment of what we are going towards. As organized habits are definitely deployed and focused, the confused situation takes on form, it is "cleared up"—the essential function of intelligence.[28]

Inquiry into the novel and the unsettling demarcates the path of a particular self's conscious search for self-definition, for the exercise of intelligence and choice, for the acquisition or clarification of new knowledge, and for the reorganization of habits. An impulse that conflicts with or confuses habits gives movement and direction to a self disposed toward inquiry. Such an impulse directs us forward, tentatively, toward "something which is imminent but which as yet escapes us"—for instance, my sudden recognition of a syntactical inversion in the first line of "A slumber did my spirit seal" and its chilling implications for the referent of "she." Habit, conflicted or confused as it may be, masses to support the effort toward new understanding. It fills in where needed, deploying its concretions and established working procedures and adaptations when they are intelligently of use. Through inquiry a particular self most actively probes into, constructs, and reconstructs habits of comprehension and response and most actively pursues the insistent direction and movement of an impulse into the novel, the unclarified, and the unrecognized.

The shared and shareable modes of acquiring and reorganizing habits, moreover, provide the social psychological medium for understanding the nature, need, and results of this inquiry engaged upon by a particular habitual self. It will be the burden of the next chapter to demonstrate the viability of a Deweyan sense of the self and inquiry into human habit for understanding the structure of inquiry, especially with regard to social and communal patterns of literary inquiry and judgment.

---

28. Ibid., p. 180.

13

The Structure of Inquiry:
The Construction of Judgments; or,
Grounding Judgments in the
Intelligent Purposive Activity
of the Self

John Dewey's own inquiry into the nature and structure of inquiry spans approximately forty years and includes at least four major works and numerous essays. The principal work is his voluminous book of 1938, *Logic*. This consummate effort builds upon three previous volumes: *How We Think: A Restatement of the Relation of Reflective Thinking to the Educative Process* (1933), *Essays in Experimental Logic* (1916), and *Studies in Logical Theory* (1903). The central problem in all of these works can be put generally: How does thought or intelligence logically relate to its subject matter? Dewey states early on in *Studies in Logical Theory*:

> Thinking is a kind of activity which we perform at specific need. . . . The measure of its success, the standard of its validity, is precisely the degree in which the thinking actually disposes of the difficulty and allows us to proceed with more direct modes of experiencing, that are forthwith possessed of more assured and deepened value. . . . Our attention is taken up with particular questions and specific answers. What we have to reckon with is not the problem of, How can I think *überhaupt*? [transcendentally]

but, How shall I think right *here and now?* Not what is the test of
thought at large, but what validates and confirms *this* thought?[1]

The practical emphasis is abundantly clear: Thought or thinking is taken
as an activity, a *purposive* act furthermore. It is summoned to perform in
specific instances when the habitual self is not fully adequate to the
difficulty at hand. The success and validity of thinking, then, is its
adequacy and appropriateness to a difficult or even novel situation.
Thought logically relates to its subject matter by being able to clarify or
resolve a difficulty that impedes or puzzles habit. Moreover, this relation
is active and practical, not transcendental and universal.

The term "inquiry" is Dewey's more formal way of denoting this use of
thinking. In *Logic* he expressly identifies "reflective thought" with what he
calls "objective inquiry" or the "determination of an indeterminate
situation." A difficulty arises in a knowledge situation, and as such the
situation appears indeterminate. By thinking, by instituting an inquiry,
the situation can be resolved, made determinate. The *consequences* of the
thinking, of the inquiry, are themselves the "necessary tests of the validity
of propositions, *provided* these consequences are operationally instituted
and are such as to resolve the specific problem evoking the operations."[2]
This pragmatic focus connects the purposive operations of thought with
problems arising from, as well as the consequences for, subject matter.
Reflective thought should not remain abstract, unfocused, or disjunct
from a situation that necessitates its operations. By conceiving of thinking
as inquiry, this pragmatic focus establishes an unusual relationship
between thought and logic. Logic as the formal theory of inquiry, or as the
inquiry into inquiry, no longer demands a rigid separation of logical forms
and subject matter as is so often the case in axiomatic, deductive, and
transcendental systems of thought and logical relations. As Dewey casts
the "thesis" of his *Logic*, it is clear that logical forms and operations are
pragmatically inseparable from subject matter, situations, and the insti-

1. Dewey, *Studies in Logical Theory* (Chicago: University of Chicago Press, 1903), pp. 2–3.
This book is a collaborative effort by Dewey and other members and fellows of the University of
Chicago Department of Philosophy from that school's first ten years of existence. Dewey authored
the first four of the eleven essays included. All of his essays take the collective title "Thought and
Its Subject Matter" (pp. 1–85) and serve as the working core of his three subsequent books on logic
and inquiry.

2. Dewey, *Logic: The Theory of Inquiry* (New York: Holt, Rinehart & Winston, 1938), pp.
iii–iv.

tution of inquiry: "Logical forms accrue to subject-matter when the latter is subjected to controlled inquiry."[3]

The generation of logical forms occurs in the operations of inquiry and not in some intellectual process or intellection set apart from subject matter and actual knowledge situations. There is no need to "suddenly evoke a new power or faculty like Reason or Pure Intuition" as Kant felt compelled to do in the *Critique of Pure Reason*.[4] The theory of inquiry, as Dewey summarizes it, shows that

> . . . all logical forms (with their characteristic properties) arise within the operations of inquiry and are concerned with control of inquiry so that it may yield warranted assertions. This conception implies much more than that logical forms are disclosed or come to light when we reflect upon processes of inquiry that are in use. Of course, it means that; but it also means that the forms *originate* in operations of inquiry. To employ a convenient expression, it means that while inquiry into inquiry is the causa cognoscendi of logical forms, primary inquiry is itself causa essendi of the forms which inquiry into inquiry discloses.[5]

Logical forms, then, are neither intuited nor rationally deduced from a set of basic principles or axioms. They are generated in the operations of "primary inquiry." Such inquiry is none other than the cause of their being and coming into being. Logical forms *control* inquiry so that "warranted assertions," or "knowledge" as Dewey calls them cumulatively, may be the issue of the inquiry. In a way, logical forms can be regarded as the *regulative guidelines* for the operations of inquiry. The operations themselves and the nature and quality of the indeterminate situation being inquired into *constitute* the inquiry. In other words, they provide the *constitutive guides* for inquiry or the *constitutive sense of being guided* in inquiry rather than the regulative guidelines of inquiry. Logic or the theory of inquiry, meanwhile, is the result of reflection upon logical forms and the operations from which they arise. Logic is our way of knowing about and cognitively refining (causa cognoscendi) logical forms and processes of inquiry.

3. Ibid., p. 101
4. Ibid., p. 24.
5. Ibid., pp. 3–4.

Dewey calls his theory of inquiry "the naturalistic conception of logic." Since logic constitutes thoroughgoing inquiry into our ways of pragmatically instituting thought or inquiry into problems and difficulties and indeterminate cognitive situations, logic cannot escape the experiential and cultural matrix that occasions primary inquiries. Consequently, logic is both "*a naturalistic theory*" and "*a social discipline*":

> . . . every inquiry grows out of a background of culture and takes effect in greater or less modification of the conditions out of which it arises. Merely physical contacts with physical surroundings occur. But in every interaction that involves intelligent direction, the physical environment is part of a more inclusive social or cultural environment.

> All inquiry proceeds within a cultural matrix which is ultimately determined by the nature of social relations.[6]

This naturalistic conception of logic as a social discipline firmly and securely locates inquiries and the theory of inquiry within experience and the sociocultural environment.

Furthermore, inquiry, and correspondingly logic, can probe into and reflect upon experience and the sociocultural environment in two general ways—through commonsense inquiry or through scientific inquiry. Scientific inquiry is experimentally and quantitatively oriented, whereas commonsense inquiry is more directly, individually, and behaviorally oriented. In distinguishing common sense from scientific inquiry, Dewey states:

> I shall designate the environment in which human beings are *directly* involved the common sense environment or "world," and

---

6. Ibid., pp. 18–20, 487. Dewey also designates this conception of logic and inquiry "*cultural naturalism*" (p. 20, Dewey's italics). As discussed in Chapter 9, "empirical naturalism" is Dewey's term for his philosophy of experience, where human experience is closely connected with nature. With the phrase "cultural naturalism," the close link between the contexts of human experience and the operations of thought becomes foregrounded. Dewey's whole philosophy of experience might usefully be called "empirical and cultural naturalism," a phrase that exhibits the continuity of nature and culture and the adequacy of practical inquiry for gathering evidence and acquiring an understanding of this continuity.

inquires that take place in making the required adjustments in behavior common sense inquiries.[7]

I intend to elaborate the structure of commonsense inquiry because, of the two forms of inquiry that Dewey describes and analyzes, it is the one closer to literary and critical inquiry. Scientific inquiry does not suit the subject matter involved in literary studies, even though experimental and quantitative research, such as that of Gillian Cohen and James Squire discussed in Chapter 8, does indeed occur. Literary and critical inquiry involves a direct and individually conducted investigation of a segment of our commonsense environment that characteristically intensifies perceptions, conceptions, and reflective questionings of that environment at large. Such inquiries issue in at least five types of pragmatic "adjustments in behavior" on the part of the inquirer and his or her audience. First, there are augmented, reintegrated, or reconstructed linguistic and stylistic habits. Second, insights into the integration of modes of presence of character are possible and are frequently realized. Third, new knowledge concerning the evidences and complexities of the interactions of habit, character, and environment is discovered and critically refined. Fourth, finer, more perceptive, and better conceptualized integrations of one's reading and interpretive habits are possible for both critic and critical readers. Fifth and final, perhaps the most difficult behavioral adjustment with regard to literary studies potentially occurs: the progressive development of the range and acuity of the aesthetic mode of attention. All five of these types of pragmatic adjustments in behavior remain potential in and for any particular commonsense inquiry in the literary and critical field, but the point is that commonsense inquiry in literary studies does manifestly involve a form of reflective thinking that purposively shapes and reshapes our habits of recognition and response and our knowledge of ourselves and others.

Commonsense inquiries, furthermore, probe into the interactions of habitual selves and their environments through the use of symbols that are "determined in the habitual culture of the group."[8] Such inquiries, though reflective and open to generalizations, usually remain concrete and enmeshed in particulars. They must remain concrete and particular-

7. Ibid., p. 60. For the full development of the distinction between common sense and scientific inquiry, see pp. 60–80 and 105–19.
8. Ibid., p. 115.

izing because they cannot be freed of direct and practical reference to the habits, concerns, and interests of the limited (nonuniversal) group for whom a commonsense inquiry bears greatest import. Not everyone and for all time, for instance, should be assumed as having an abiding interest in the reading and interpretation of Wordsworth's lyric "A slumber did my spirit seal." However, for Anglo-American scholars and critics of Words-worth's lyric art and the qualities of his lyrical balladry, this poem constitutes a central and very problematic text. Moreover, the text and the contingencies of its interpretation have become a major and intriguingly problematic prooftext for the development and the critique of Anglo-American theories of Romanticism, tropological figures, interpretation, evidence, and reading theory. For these specific, well-demarcated, yet nonuniversal groups a commonsense inquiry into the concrete particulars of reading and interpreting Wordsworth's poem can and does bear great import. This same kind of recognition and targeting of audiences for commonsense inquiries usually occurs implicitly and sometimes explic-itly, but always with the sense that such inquiries cannot be globalized transcendentally or universally without serious qualification.

Dewey lays down his most succinct definition of "inquiry" in the following sentence:

> *Inquiry is the controlled or directed transformation of an indeter-minate situation into one that is so determinate in its constituent distinctions and relations as to convert the elements of the original situation into a unified whole.*[9] (Dewey's italics)

The antecedent condition for the initiation of an inquiry, then, is an indeterminate situation. I discussed an indeterminate situation above as being *an* experience that occurs as uncertain or unsettled; it is marked generally by a pervasive quality of confusion or disorientation. For instance, in reading such a poem as "A slumber did my spirit seal," a reader, such as myself, may be confused or disoriented in presupposing the antecedent of the pronoun "she." This experience yields an indeter-minate situation—the antecedent condition, in this case, for literary inquiry. The indeterminate situation may then occasion or release an impulse toward activity, or a sequence of acts, that subjects the situation

---

9. Ibid., pp. 104–5. My discussion of the structure of inquiry will often draw freely from Dewey's *Logic*, pp. 99–280.

to a process of inquiry. The impulse to look about for who "*she*" is in the case of "A slumber" initiates a quest for an adequate ascription of identity (or more exactly, pronomial reference). When an impulse toward such purposive activity arises, then the inquiry proper has been instituted. Another way of putting this initiation of inquiry is to say that a problem has been instituted. The problem (one of at least four altogether) initially instituted in the case of "A slumber" is the question of the referent of "she." With the institution of a problem, or a series of interconnected problems in complex cases, we can then say that the situation is no longer "indeterminate" but is now "problematic." Indeed, as Dewey himself observes, "the indeterminate situation becomes problematic in the very process of being subjected to inquiry."[10]

As the inquiry proceeds, the problematic situation progressively moves toward determination or resolution. The thinker or thinkers engaged in an inquiry generate ideas and possibilities, and those so engaged work to develop and relate the implications of useful ideas to one another. At this point an inquiry fully engages a complex of symbolic operations that can be ordered and presented in reasoned discourse. This complex of symbolic operations constitutes the "constituent distinctions and relations" of the situation that an inquirer moves toward determination: Their full development and interrelation yields a "conversion" of the initial indeterminate situation into a determinate "unified whole." In the case of "A slumber," two lines of interpretation open up as possibilities; and both can be advanced. Further problems and ideas are encountered, and a new impulse abruptly opens up a third interpretive possibility. By clarifying the relations that obtain among these possibilities and the major problems in reading and thinking about the poem, the literary inquiry can move toward a determinate "unified whole." In addition, the "operative force of facts," a force that derives from the capacity of facts for being organized to support possibilities and ideas and their development and interrelation, critically secures the adequacy and appropriateness of the determinate situation. Facts are evidential and are the means to test the adequacy of an idea or to direct the thinker or inquirer to a new idea.[11]

However, in speaking about facts and evidence and the "operative force of facts," by no means is a naive realism or a correspondence theory of truth being advocated. Indeed, Dewey's sense of the "operative force of facts" might best be compared to Michel Foucault's notion of "certain

10. Ibid., p. 107.
11. Ibid., p. 113.

historical facts that serve as guidelines for research." In pursuit of knowledge about the development and history of a social and cultural institution such as the prison (*Discipline and Punish*) or of a social science of sexuality (*The History of Sexuality*), Foucault uses documented facts as a wealth of evidential "instances" of regularities that require patient elucidation and articulation. He contends that "the singularity of events" must be recorded and must guide "meticulous" historical or "genealogical" inquiry.[12] The experienced and documented singularity of events is available to responsible inquiry and serves as a host of potential tests for the cognitive adequacy of hypotheses and conceptual patterns that aspire to high levels of coherence and consistency.

Now "the settled outcome of inquiry," what is *made determinate* in the course of inquiry, Dewey calls a "judgment." A judgment is an affirmation of some content or meaning as evidentially adequate to the knowledge situation in which it is produced. This judgment, "as finally made, has *direct* existential import."[13] In the case of "A slumber did my spirit seal," for example, one such judgment articulates and affirms the *effect* of the initial confusion in the reference of "she": A reader's experience of referential confusion can initiate him or her on one or both of two lines of inquiry into who "she" is. This judgment possesses "*direct* existential import" for the activity of reading and interpreting the poem as well as similar import for understanding a powerful instance of the Romantic death fantasy.

Judgments constitute reflective, reasoned, critical knowledge of situations and are built up, constructed, made cognate with the structure and operations of inquiry. However, as knowledge and affirmation, judgments attain a level of articulation that permits them to issue forth from the precise acts and movements of an inquiry. In inquiry, a particular self constructs judgments in terms of grammatical subjects and predicates. As Dewey is quick to indicate, these subjects and predicates are logical and not ontological determinations. The grammatical subjects of judgments are not "substances" or "essences" but the logically warranted "objects" or even "agents" that characteristically can be found in knowledge situations. The grammatical predicates are properties or qualifications of subjects that

12. Michel Foucault, *The History of Sexuality*, Vol. I, trans. R. Hurley (New York: Random House, 1978), pp. 12–13, and "Nietzsche, Genealogy, History," *Language, Counter-Memory, Practice*, ed. D. F. Bouchard (Ithaca, N.Y.: Cornell University Press, 1977), pp. 139–40.

13. Dewey, *Logic*, p. 120.

bear a hypothetical, contingent, or accidental relation to the latter. Dewey adopts a very Aristotelian stance here and even adds that "there is no *reason* why accidents occur as they do"; they simply do occur and can be judged as doing so.[14]

The embedding of the construction of judgments in the structure and operations of inquiry means that judgments will be warranted: They will have a firm, testable, or verifiable basis in evidential fact. Judgments can always be examined and validated on the basis of the evidence that justified their construction during the course of the inquiry. Affirmations or judgments, then, are "warranted assertions," or what can also be called "grounded assertions." They are *grounded* in inquiry and are *warranted* by the evidence or facts discovered, accumulated, and organized. In other words, through the use of symbolic operations—not exclusively yet primarily linguistic—judgments are inferred from the facts and constructed logically and grammatically as sentences (propositions, assertions) capable of affirmation when the "operative force of facts" warrants it.

In addition, Dewey maintains that judgments or all forms of grounded and warranted assertion regularly and unavoidably involve the conceptual activity of mediation. A representative passage runs as follows:

> . . . all knowledge as grounded assertion involves mediation. Mediation, in this context, means that an inferential function is involved in all warranted assertion. The position here defended runs counter to the belief that there is such a thing as immediate knowledge, and that such knowledge is an indispensable precondition of all mediated knowledge.[15]

Critical knowledge or judgments derive from the function of inference. Intuitional knowledge and so-called *a priori* knowledge, forms of immediate knowledge, attempt to bypass or even elide mediation altogether. Such forms of knowledge have been the pride and the bane of Platonic idealism, Cartesian rationalism, and Kantian transcendentalism in the past. The idealist and absolutist quest for immediate, or unmediated, knowledge, however, implies a neglect, a truncation, or even an abuse of our nonindubitable and nonabsolute powers of cognition, inference, and

14. Ibid., p. 138. The discussion of the grammatical construction of judgments can be found on pp. 124–38.
15. Ibid., p. 139.

judgment. The nature of the knowledge situation, the operations of inquiry, the use and function of evidence and inference, and the construction of judgments or warranted assertions indeed warrant and pragmatically affirm the Deweyan judgment that "all knowledge as grounded assertion involves mediation."

This cognitive mediation appears in another aspect of judgments as well. The "existential subject-matter" of judgments—meaning content that has direct import—possesses temporal and spatial phases. These phases are *expressed linguistically*, and this linguistic expression consti- tutes a mediation of the existential subject matter involved. In its "temporal phase," existential subject matter is "expressed in narration." In its "spatial phase," it is "expressed in description." Moreover, Dewey qualifies this bold distinction further:

> For purposes of analysis and exposition the two phases must be distinguished. But there is no separation of the subject-matter which is analyzed. Whatever exists in and for judgment is temporal-spatial. In a given proposition, either the temporal or the spatial aspect may be uppermost. But every narration has a background, which, if it were made explicit instead of being taken for granted, would be described; correspondingly, what is described exists within some temporal process to which "narration" applies.[16]

Subject matter appears in, is mediated by, is expressed through narration and description. Experientially, logically, and linguistically, these two phases of expression mediate knowledge of the temporal-spatial aspects of what we can and do experience.

Dewey indicates and discusses three types of temporal or narrative mediation and one type of spatial or descriptive mediation. These four types of temporal-spatial mediation all ultimately work to support one another in a given inquiry, but it is useful to be analytically precise in charting the differences. For instance, three types of temporal mediation can be distinguished—judgments of personal recollection, judgments of events outside of personal recollections, and historical judgments. The narration of my own activity of reading "A slumber" yields an example of

16. Ibid., p. 220.

temporal mediation as personal recollection, and my narration of Wordsworth's reading of his poem "With ships the sea was sprinkled far and nigh" constitutes an instance of the second type. My attempt to show that Coleridge's reading and interpretation of "A slumber" and two other so-called "Lucy" poems may very well have helped him to structure his grief and sense of loss at the news of his son Berkeley's death, moreover, constitutes a plausible historical narration, the third type of temporal mediation. The sole type of spatial mediation indicates and describes in varying detail the *location* or *site* in which temporal mediations happen: "But things which happen take *place* in the literal sense of the word."[17] The narration of my activity of reading "A slumber" occurs in the space of my response to the poem. This *site* of interaction allows a fair measure of description, though it continually recedes into the background of the ongoing temporal activity. Likewise, Wordsworth's letter to Lady Beaumont of May 21, 1807, and Coleridge's letters to Thomas Poole and Sara Coleridge in the spring of 1799 are *sites* that offer access via inference and warranted assertion to larger biographical and psychological "sites" or situations. Again, these specific locations, even capaciously described, often serve as background for the establishment of some type of temporal mediation. The combination of temporal and spatial phases—the conjunction of narration and description—in the construction of judgments that mediate "existential subject matter" exhibits the logical structure of what is quite often called "context" in literary studies. Any one, particular judgment still carries within its very expression a clear bearing upon the specific spatiotemporal *con-text* that it mediates, by means of language, into knowledge.

Besides judgments that constitute the field of knowledge, a second class of judgments also exists: "judgments of practice," or what may alternatively be called "evaluations." Judgments of practice issue from inquiries into situations that involve procedural questions, intentions, and values. Such judgments or evaluations are warranted assertions concerning "doing" and "making," as Dewey phrases it, rather than "knowing."[18] Some examples of evaluations or judgments of practice can be easily gathered from Part One of this book. My judgment of the poet's art in composing "A slumber did my spirit seal" as "a compact moment in Wordsworth's cultural critique of the inhumanity of modern man" yields

17. Ibid., pp. 223–29.
18. Ibid., pp. 159–80.

a judgment of practice—and so do my connections of "A slumber" to fairly contemporaneous, culturally critical moments in Wordsworth's writing. All of these critical judgments form evaluations regarding Wordsworth's practice as a writer, a thinker, and a critic of his times and of himself. Another judgment of practice involves my articulation and affirmation of the *rationale* for and greater significance of the referential confusion experienced in reading "A slumber." The referential confusion unwittingly introduces a reader to a complex piece of evidence that proves indicative and symptomatic of the speaker's own confusion of identities.[19]

My comparative assessments of the readings and interpretations of "A slumber" by M. H. Abrams, Richard Matlack, E. D. Hirsch, Jr., Norman Holland, Paul de Man, J. Hillis Miller, and Geoffrey Hartman, moreover, *evaluate* their reading and interpretive practices. I am able to phrase such judgments of critical practice by inquiring into the ways in which the assumptions (often, their critical desires or intentions) and the rhetoric of their interpretations (their own judgments of knowledge and of practice) suppress, distort, transmute, or ignore the evidential facts and operations of a fuller inquiry into the problematic of reading "A slumber."

In the previous two paragraphs on judgments of practice, I have used the first-person pronoun far more than during the entire discussion of judgments involving knowledge situations. In commonsense inquiries, evaluations rather than knowledge will perhaps more readily show that *both* forms of judgment are the result of the intelligent purposive activity of habitual selves who have the capacity to inquire into habits and problems. For both cognitive and evaluative judgments, the initiation and successive operations of inquiry generally involve purposive acts on the part of a particular self. At least two things make this particular self's inquiries of potential, and sometimes even of compelling, interest to others. First of all, both self and others employ *shared* symbolic operations from the "habitual culture," or what Pierre Bourdieu calls "the habitus," of their community or social group. Selves are significantly individual and individualized, but they possess an enormous range of intellectual operations in common and share the responsibility for keeping them active and adaptable. Second, all selves can use these shared operations to

---

19. See pages 56–62 of Chapter 4, where the seven paragraphs of evaluative judgments upon which I am now drawing can be found. These seven paragraphs are generally composed of judgments of practice that are based upon evidence and judgments of knowledge constructed in nearly four chapters of discussion.

probe into the interactions, environing forces, and conditions that they *all have in common* to a prevalent if not predominant degree.[20] The intelligent purposive activity of any given self, then, holds significance and insight for others.

Indeed, this mutuality can be exceptional and even regularly reinforced in the cases of selves whose judgments are characteristically regarded or even revered as informative, instructive, and insightful. The notion of a leader, an innovator, a cultural or intellectual hero or heroine can be much abused in the midst of harsh political, bureaucratic, and techno-cratic realities. Human nature and conduct, however, still rely formatively and collectively upon the extraordinary insights and innovations that often fall to the provenance of exceptional habitual selves. The notions of "genius" and "hero" have had their days and should clearly be set aside; they smack of the illusions incumbent upon the self-active view of human nature and conduct. The phrases "habitual self" and "exceptional habitual selves" will quite likely never be in vogue, but they do articulate accurately the interactive dimensions and realities of human self-construction and inquiry. To echo my epigraph taken from Keats's *Endymion*, the episte-mologically warranted "journey homeward to habitual self" may seem "crude and sore" relative to the illusory "wonders" of self-action. However, the literary and cultural work of such exceptional habitual selves as William Wordsworth, Mary Wollstonecraft Shelley, Jane Austen, Joseph Conrad, James Joyce, Virginia Woolf, James Baldwin, Kenneth Burke, John Dewey, Raymond Williams, Studs Terkel, and Maya Angelou—to name an even and exemplary dozen—certainly lends a sense of wonder to those who recognize the habitual character of the human self and sociocultural activity.

---

20. This point intersects with and can be corroborated by the dominant orientation of a number of works in social science and epistemology. For instance, Pierre Bourdieu, especially pp. 72–158, sketches the "structuring structures," the shared social practices by which a culture in Algeria (as well as culture more generally) interactively constructs and governs the linguisti-cally mediated schemes of social lives and cultural limits. In *The Basis and Structure of Knowledge* (New York: Harper & Brothers, 1948), W. H. Werkmeister shows how linguistic operations are basic to the "knowledge-situation" and the shared communication of knowledge. In *Knowledge of Man: A Philosophy of the Interhuman*, trans. M. Friedman and R. G. Smith (New York: Harper & Row, 1965), Martin Buber emphasizes the critical and central role of speech in shaping communities and a "world-shape" that through speech can be recognized as common to humankind. And Jürgen Habermas, in *Knowledge and Human Interests*, trans. J. J. Shapiro (Boston: Beacon Press, 1971), by examining work and interaction reveals the common interests that constitute knowledge and ground human orientations.

The intelligent purposive activity of a particular self, exceptional or otherwise, guarantees that the sequence of acts involved in an inquiry and the judgment (or sequence of judgments) constructed therein can achieve and preserve a coherent temporal continuity. Temporal continuity is not only crucial for a particular inquiry but it is also necessary for the formation and progressive reformations of a history of acts, symbolic operations, and judgments. The integration of a habitual self, who shares a habitual culture with other such selves and who is capable of initiating inquiries, supplies the characteristic and exemplary continuum where experience and purposive activity meet.

> Experience has temporal continuity. There is an experiential continuum of content or subject-matter and of operations. The experiential continuum has definite biological basis. Organic structures, which are the physical conditions of experience, are enduring. Without, as well as within, conscious intent, they hold the different pulses of experience together so that the latter form a history in which every pulse looks to the past and affects the future. The structures, while enduring, are also subject to modification. Continuity is not bare repetition of identities.[21]

A particular self with his or her biological basis, organic structures, and history of experiences, then, provides the necessary temporal continuum of and for inquiry.

Of course, all these claims concerning the temporal continuity of habitual selves situated in particular, habitual cultures seem quite abstract. However, Wordsworth again can provide an apt embodiment of these claims. *The Prelude*, for instance, can be read as a text whose unfolding not only records but also exemplifies the slow growth of the poet's self within a complex history of his own acts of inquiry into the social and transpersonal structures that shape him. The temporal continuity of the poetic self that Wordsworth projects in his long poem embodies the image of a self who responds to moments of experience, yet does so by retrospectively placing such moments in an alternately retrograde and projective history of personal response and practical contingency. The rather unusual and often critically slighted moment

21. Dewey, *Logic*, p. 245.

near the end of the final book of *The Prelude* in which the poet thanks a youthful friend, Raisley Calvert (who, dying young, left Wordsworth nine hundred pounds sterling in 1795), curiously enables him to pursue his career as poet. In a very pragmatic way, this gift can be said to help focus and center the poet's youthful wanderings. Calvert's legacy can be regarded as the contingent, historical occasion for the sudden and enthusiastic escape of the poet from London joyously articulated at the start of the preamble in the first book of *The Prelude*. Raisley Calvert's posthumous generosity opens up the possibility for pursuing the personal and social wanderings that issue in the poetic divagations of *The Prelude*. Yet it can only be retrospectively that the poetic self offers thanks for the enabling, posthumous gift of another. The temporal continuity of the poet's growth and sustained inquiry into the formative moments of his own projection through personal and historical time constitutes the only real, practical, contingent medium in which such thanking attains depth, authenticity, and sincerity. Wordsworth's remembering of his friend's grand gift yields a frank, indeed rich moment that pragmatically centers Wordsworth's sustained evocation of the restorative powers of time and memory in the historical unfolding of a poet's habitual self.

Indeed, without the potential coherence of temporal moments of experience, any habitual self would fail to materialize a capacity and ability to generalize. Without the temporal continuity of a self, it would be impossible to recognize recurrences and variations, similarities and differences and thus make inferences on the basis of them to various levels of generality. Paul Smith has offered a compact survey of the ways in which various fields of social and humanistic speculation in Western Europe and the United States have recently been conceptualizing "the subject" of discursive practices. Smith faults such theories for viewing "the subject" too abstractly and without regard to the practical, contestatory, historically contingent, gendered, and socially responsible nature that indeed marks real human agents.[22] Smith could have appealed to Dewey's articulation of the social and personal pragmatics of habitual selves in habitual cultures for a successful social-psychological theory of the human subject. Dewey offers a way to theorize responsibly the social construction of the subject as a habitual self fully capable of concerned, practical inquiry and constitutionally disposed toward alert, supple, variegated

---

22. Paul Smith, *Discerning the Subject* (Minneapolis: University of Minnesota Press, 1988), especially pp. xxvii–xxxv, 150–60.

recognition of the ways in which particular "subjects" construct themselves through an unfolding history of experiences. Moreover, Dewey
emphasizes that experience develops *temporally*. It falls to inquiry fully
instituted by actual human agents to play the intermediate role, to be the
only mediating activity in the development of human experience into
what counts for us as actual knowledge and specific judgments. Inquiry
into experience and various sustained attempts to integrate the products of
such inquiry happen in the real time, the enacted and the projected
temporality, of actual selves. The purposive activity of a self, then, clearly
opens out to embrace the field of a wider, philosophically principled
pragmatics of personal and social construction of human selfhood.[23]

Richard Rorty, though, has appropriated Dewey's pragmatism for his
own project of rethinking the tasks of philosophy and criticism along
so-called antifoundationalist lines and has criticized what he regards as a
tendency toward foundationalism or "metaphysics" in Dewey's writings.
Rorty contends that Dewey "wavered between a therapeutic stance toward
philosophy and another, quite different, stance—one in which philosophy
was to become 'scientific' and 'empirical' and to do something serious,
systematic, important, and constructive." The former or "therapeutic
stance" would purportedly open philosophy to a nontranscendental and
nonabsolutist "criticism of culture." The latter stance, however, Rorty
types as "metaphysical" because it strives to describe basic structural
features of human experience and institutions—that is to say, it attempts
to provide "a permanent neutral matrix for future inquiry."[24] I think that
the problem, though, lies *not* with the fact that Dewey attempts to offer us

---

23. Jean Piaget as well is concerned with the genesis and construction of logical and
psychological structures. Through its developing cognitive probing of the world, the human
organism engages in a process of self-construction and self-regulation that at the same time
includes construction of the structures by which the organism can act in and know about the
world. The *activity* of the organism itself is the focus and location of the process of building
cognitive structures. Piaget calls the organism "the epistemic subject," the necessary "center of
functional activity," who through its performances mediates and integrates the structures within
which we live, move, and know. See Piaget, *Structuralism*, trans. and ed. Chaninah Maschler
(New York: Harper & Row, 1968), pp. 68–70, but also pp. 52–73 in passing. See also Piaget,
Genetic Epistemology, trans. E. Duckworth (New York: Norton, 1971), in which the author
offers experimental data and epistemological coordinations of the data in order to show that
knowledge is the result of continuous and active construction. In his "Review Article: Piaget's
Structuralism," *American Anthropology* 75 (1973): 351–73, Terence Turner presents an excellent
integration of and commentary upon Piaget's concepts of "structure," "subject," "object," and
"construction."

24. Rorty, *Consequences of Pragmatism*, pp. 73, 80.

a "matrix for further inquiry" and in so doing give us "something serious, systematic, important, and constructive." The problem of typing what Dewey constructs as "metaphysical" resides in Rorty's use of the adjectives "permanent" and "neutral." Dewey does not make absolutist ("permanent") or transcendental ("neutral") claims for his *empirical* inquiries into the nature of human conduct and into the structure of inquiry itself. These investigations have a decidedly historicist, developmentalist, and socioculturally based orientation. Dewey rather clearly communicates the sense that his epistemological and logical determinations are always open to careful reconstruction. They are not set once and for all but are responsive, moreover, to specific social needs. Perhaps more important, a philosopher or critic demands a constructive and working vocabulary, one that is situated well within an understanding of the nature of human experience and social and cultural practices, in order to conceive the problems and issues worthy of cultural criticism. As Rorty himself says, Dewey "wanted to sketch a culture that would not continually give rise to new versions of the old problems."[25] Such a critical task seems thoroughly dependent upon and contiguous with a careful construction of our ways of experiencing and knowing and our ways of proceeding to inquire into the specificities of such experience.

In the final chapter of *Human Nature and Conduct*, Dewey notes a fundamentally important feature of his view of human habit and inquiry:

> . . . the formation of habits of belief, desire and judgment is going on at every instant under the influence of the conditions set by men's contact, intercourse and associations with one another. This is the fundamental fact in social life and in personal character.[26]

Human social interactions help constitute social and personal formations of what Dewey elsewhere calls "cultural habitude."[27] However, such crucial formations are often overlooked. As a consequence, "the whole matter of the formation of the predispositions which effectively control human relationships is left to accident, to custom and immediate personal

25. Ibid., p. 86.
26. Dewey, *Human Nature and Conduct*, p. 323.
27. Ibid., p. viii.

likings, resentments and ambitions."[28] In other words, social and cultural criticism will be haphazard and directionless unless and until philosophy and criticism attend to the ways in which habits and predispositions get built up within societies. *Critical inquiry into cultural habitude,* into the social and personal formations developed in the history of a society and the histories of selves, might be said to be the appropriate domain of a Deweyan criticism of culture.

Such a project, though, surfaces in a very general fashion in some research and writings by the late French social historian and poststructural theorist Michel Foucault. In a manner that might help to temporize Dewey's abiding image as an unabashedly naive, liberal optimist, it may be informative to liken Dewey's notion of inquiry into social and personal "formations of belief, desire and judgment" to Foucault's more recent genealogies of knowledge. Richard Rorty has already discussed at some length the differences between Dewey and Foucault with regard to "social hope." "We should see Dewey and Foucault," Rorty contends, "as differing not over a theoretical issue, but over what we may hope."[29] Dewey musters optimism concerning "the human sciences" and their social impact, whereas Foucault recognizes their all-too-frequent complicity in disciplining and dominating the various constituents of a society. Rorty also notes generally the historicist method of both writers. Dewey and Foucault, moreover, view discourse as a network of social and cultural forces; the former writer in terms of "structures of culture," the latter in terms of "structures of power."[30] Basically Rorty contends that

> . . . we should see Dewey as having already gone the route Foucault is traveling, and as having arrived at the point Foucault is still trying to reach—the point at which we can make philosophical and historical ("genealogical") reflection useful to those, in Foucault's phrase, "whose fight is located in the fine meshes of the webs of power."[31]

Foucault's genealogies of knowledge share a lot with Dewey's common-sense inquiries into the nature of human conduct. The factor of their local

---

28. Ibid., p. 323.
29. Rorty, *Consequences of Pragmatism,* p. 204.
30. Ibid., p. 208.
31. Ibid., p. 207.

and practical usefulness to those enmeshed in the structures of culture and power is a far from naive one. Such genealogical work constitutes empowering reflection. Foucault strikes just this note in a brief definition of his pivotal word "genealogy"; it is also a definition that resonates with Dewey's conception of critical inquiry into cultural habitude:

> Let us give the term *genealogy* to the union of erudite knowledge and local memories which allow us to establish a historical knowledge of struggles and to make use of this knowledge tactically today.[32]

Genealogical work, like critical inquiry into cultural habitude, yields an active and useful knowledge from the interplay of the "erudite" and the "local." Such knowledge is the cognitive product of inquiry and the lived memories within which the will to knowledge is secured or else founders. Dewey's own project of research and of criticism, however productive of hope, preeminently involves a serious and careful examination of cultural habitude. It also offers the possibility of greater conceptual integration and knowledge. Cultural habitude, as Foucault's researches so amply document, can also frustrate or impede new directions for social action and cultural practice. Critical activity, quite significantly then, must involve the active, contestatory struggle of inquiry within and against the resistant and supportive meshes of cultural habitude.

There is, however, a significant epistemological point of difference between a Deweyan conception of critical inquiry and a Foucauldian genealogy of knowledge. Though Dewey and Foucault would seem in agreement about historicizing and relativizing the notion of "the subject" or transcendental subjectivity and reflection, Foucault disperses the function of a historicized and temporalized self—a habitual self, for Dewey—into the meshes of discourse. In the conclusion to *The Archaeology of Knowledge*, Foucault remarks that he "wanted not to exclude the problem of the subject, but to define the positions and functions that the subject could occupy in the diversity of discourse."[33] However, the *dispersion* of some sense of the subject or the self as an active agency at

---

32. Michel Foucault, "Two Lectures," in *Power/Knowledge: Selected Interviews and Other Writings*, ed. Colin Gordon (Brighton: Harvester Press, 1980), p. 83.
33. Michel Foucault, *The Archaeology of Knowledge*, trans. A. M. Sheridan-Smith (New York: Pantheon Books, 1972), p. 200.

work within a particular and relatively integrated set of "positions and functions" in discourse prevails against Foucault's belated word of apology. Indeed, Foucault admits that his "discourse, far from determining the locus in which it speaks, is avoiding the ground on which it could find support."[34] I would like to contend that Dewey's conception of the habitual self—and the self's ongoing interactions with others and insistent impulses toward inquiry into human conduct—provides the "locus" and the supportive "ground" that Foucault self-consciously avoids in his epistemologically questionable commitment to self-dispersion.

A Deweyan criticism of culture, above all, would appear embedded within the ongoing cultivation of a habitual self who probes into and constructs judgments about his or her shared and habitual culture, however troubling and alienating, that has shaped and continues to shape that self. This social context of a habitual self and shared and shareable practices of inquiry provides the necessary and sufficient network to support the practices of literary and cultural study. The point is that the cultivation of any given self, which inquiry in general seems to involve, demands the situating of a revised concept of "the self" or "the subject" within that nexus of concepts borrowed from philosophy and the human or social sciences: "interaction," "habit," "construction," "integration," "inquiry," "judgment," "culture," and so on. A habitual self capable of and competent in instituting inquiries and constructing judgments concerning his or her interactions is indeed a precise, active, and invaluable locus of culture, criticism, and the criticism of culture. Such selves are the unavoidable and particular sites of the literary activities of writing, reading, and interpreting—activities that cannot elide the culture that permeates them. Cultures inscribe habitual selves within their structured fabrics. Yet they also, fortunately and insistently, enable such selves to explore and reintegrate—restructure and rewrite—their troublesome yet provocative textures.

---

34. Ibid., p. 205.

14

The Four Definitive Features
of a Literary Experience

Following Dewey's general conceptions of experience, knowledge, self, habit, and inquiry, a more finely tuned understanding of critical inquiry into the nature of literary experience can be developed. Literary inquiry basically comprises the intelligent purposive activity of a particular habitual self (a "character") probing into his or her own instances of literary experience. The experience may be called "reading" and the inquiry "interpretation," but I think that this distinction occasions more trouble than it offers help. The act of having a literary experience actually already institutes the activity of literary inquiry into the experience. If the particular literary experience is indeed not an easily determinate or habitual one, one that our already acquired habits are quite sufficient to comprehend, then the possibilities and ideas provoked by it can initiate us on an inquiry into what we are experiencing. Literary inquiry can clarify and refine the uncriticized evidences of an experience and can progressively transform an indeterminate cognitive situation into a problematic one, and perhaps even into a relatively determinate one. It is perhaps impossible to locate the precise moment in literary experience when literary inquiry can be said to arise. It may only occur after a first or second reading or scanning of a text—especially in the cases of brief lyrics, short stories, and the like. However, the best indication that literary inquiry into literary experience is under way would be the moment when a problem, or the first in a sequence of interconnected problems, is recognized and posed as a textual crux or question demanding more attention, clarification, and eventual resolution through the construction of judgments. What remains of the greatest critical consequence here, though, is the realignment of critical activity in relation to the activity of reading a literary work. Literary inquiry is grounded in literary experience. The operations of literary inquiry, and the judgments it can produce, arise from and are warranted by a *particular* literary experience and its unfolding evidences and problems, ideas and possibilities.

However, the nature of literary inquiry into literary experience seems by no means exhausted by the qualities and contingencies of particular literary experiences. An inquiry into the nature of literary inquiry—that is, a theory of literary inquiry—would strive to establish warranted or grounded assertions concerning the general and shareable patterns of various literary inquiries. Such an inquiry would seek to construct a logic of literary inquiry. Such a logic was briefly and provisionally sketched in Chapter 1 when I derived four definitive features of having a literary experience from John Dewey's general account of having an experience. I intend in this final chapter to redeploy these four definitive features in order to give a fuller presentation of what I want to argue is the general logic of literary inquiry.

Collectively the four definitive features of a literary experience, as they can be distinguished and clarified with regularity in and through specific literary inquiries, are (1) a literary work, (2) a reader, (3) the activity of reading—that is to say, the temporal interaction of work and reader, and (4) the quality or qualities developed and made distinct within and through the temporal interaction of work and reader. Generally considered, and in terms enriched and informed by John Dewey's and Stephen Pepper's work in epistemology and cognition, the activity of reading constitutes intelligent purposive activity operationally instituted and performed by a reader equipped with a history of acquired habits that are also well embedded in a habitual culture. The reader so engaged brings his or her habits to bear upon a particular aspect of the cultural environment—a literary work–and acts purposively upon the evidences, problems, and complexities of habit and response that the work can evoke. The issue of this activity reveals developed and distinctive knowledge of qualitatively felt activity and the possibilities of cognitive integration open to habitual selves ("characters"). The interactive paradigm, moreover, characteristically describes such purposive activity. An intelligent organism (a reader with literary and linguistic habits and impulses) interacts with environing forces and conditions (a literary work and possible contexts and habitual cultures of understanding) in order to effect a purpose, achieve a satisfactory goal, or follow and attend to the full course of a problematic situation as it develops toward qualitative and conceptual clarity and resolution (literary experience and knowledge). The activity of literary reading and inquiry, then, yields an exemplary and cognitively powerful instance of perceptual and conceptual interaction and, accordingly, demands a careful exfoliation of the interactive features and processes that constitute its general theory or logic.[1]

To orient the logic of literary inquiry along the lines and general direction demarcated by the interactive paradigm implies that the kind of "Mercator's projection" so characteristic of systematic and systems-analytic approaches to literature is seriously flawed. In "The Way We Think Now," a review-article in a special issue of *New Literary History* on "Thinking in the Arts, Sciences and Literature," Werner Berthoff points out the poverty implicit in the issue's contributors' and literary theory's general trend toward system monitoring. The central flaw seems to be the inability of critical theorists to deal, or to want to deal, with literary texts as indeed works that are read by actual readers.[2]

Literary theories that seek to collapse the "world" into the "text" or into "textuality," for instance, thereby also collapse readers and any sense of an author into the "text." Interaction, needless to say, vanishes, dispersed with the absented reader. However, the rhetoric involved in studies or "disseminations" of "textuality" cannot utterly circumvent the logically unavoidable features and functions of the reader and the work. The locution "a text reading itself," for example, still harbors three definitive features: work, activity of reading, and reader—even though the third term is collapsed into the first. More generally, however, this locution seems merely shorthand for curious and paradoxical legerdemain. Supposedly critical "strategies" can be "posited" in order to "recuperate" an allegorical "text" or a thematics of figural language from within a "text" or "textuality." In other words, a set of rhetorical tropes or markers or

1. A recent essay offers a glimpse of a conceptually related model of the process of literary understanding. In "Information Processing and the Reading of Literary Texts," *New Literary History* 20 (Winter 1989): 465–81, W. John Harker makes a case for the literary-theoretical relevance of "the information processing paradigm, a paradigm which dominates the current study of human cognition" (p. 465). In broad strokes, Harker demonstrates the interactive features of information-processing theory and contends that "meaning is generated within a framework established by the interactive participation of the reader with the text" (p. 475). Harker's model of the literary process pivots upon the interactivity of "data-driven" features (texts) and "conceptually driven" aspects (readers). See especially pp. 469–77.

2. Werner Berthoff, "The Way We Think Now: Protocols for Deprivation," *New Literary History* 7 (Spring 1976): 599–617.

signifiers can be gathered from a "text" by some nameless agent and arranged to be "read" or "interpreted" in order to disclose "the disfiguring power of figuration."[3] The surface or naive "text," then, resembles, or indeed has displaced, every sense of the extratextual and the contextual in the designs of the critical strategist. For within this surface "text," under cover of the concepts of "textuality" and "figuration," the strategist has anonymously (or "imperceptibly," as some are wont to say) insinuated himself and his interpretive assumptions and predilections. From this projected point of vantage, he can construct, from select materials offered by the surface "text," the allegorical "text" that he desires to read. A "text" can be said to "read itself," then, because the critical reader has projected himself into a world-effacing linguistic fabrication from which he can forge and circulate a "text" of his own strategic devising.

Such a contrived strategy of critical reading results from recourse to "a system of tropological transformations" in order to explore "the problematics of reading."[4] By regarding the texture of a work as merely the (illusory or deceptive) effect of a system of rhetorical tropes a critic tends to belie other possibilities for understanding the problematics of literary reading. The critical reader who sublates himself and his interpretive activity within a system of self-generating and self-transforming rhetorical figures, though, may conceal the full "problematic situation" of his interaction with a work in this way. He sacrifices a fuller engagement and testing of his reading and interpretive habits by declining to risk his sense of himself in an interactive probing of the evidences and the problems of reading a work that may yet elude him or that may insist on its own ever-articulate otherness.

In *The Critical Act,* Evan Watkins suggests "shifting attention away from second-order interpretation—whether systematic, as in Frye, or deconstructive—with its necessary dependence on an accumulation of scholarship about past literature, and toward the difficulties inherent in reading and understanding new literature."[5] This shift in attention would stress our actual strategies in reading and understanding works because readers and critics would be free of accumulated scholarship and system-

3. Paul de Man, "The Epistemology of Metaphor," *Critical Inquiry* 5 (Autumn 1978): 29. See also de Man, *Allegories of Reading,* especially pp. 3–19, 103–30, 160–220.

4. De Man, *Allegories of Reading,* p. ix.

5. Evan Watkins, *The Critical Act: Criticism and Community* (New Haven, Conn.: Yale University Press, 1978), pp. x–xi.

atic models for interpretation. Watkins argues, moreover, that the sophistication in terminology and methodology in contemporary criticism has been accompanied by an increasing distance from actual poems and works of fiction.[6] Reclaiming and redirecting practical criticism, though, can perhaps salvage what is of real use in theory:

> The effort of practical criticism then emerges as something far more important than material which theory can clarify and systemize, or even a "test case" to prove the efficacy of theory. I think it is perhaps the only way of allowing into theory the presence of another and distinctively different voice than one's own. Practical criticism prevents critical theory from lapsing into a massive and forbidding solipsism.[7]

This comment resonates well with what I have attempted to carry out during the course of this book. Critical theory needs to be realigned in terms of its relation to practical criticism and the sort of examples or test cases that practical criticism is assumed to afford theory. The consequence, then, for critical theory is that it will be most responsive and responsible to the "distinctively different voice[s]" of literary works if and when it proceeds inductively and interactively. This is the general way of proceeding in practical criticism, or what I am here calling "literary inquiry," as well as the general procedure unfolding in this book. I have, however, afforded myself the burden of reading and coming to understand the motives and purposes activating the accumulated scholarship surrounding one of Wordsworth's not-so-new lyrics in order to understand the actual strategies used by critical readers in their acts of reading and theory construction. In what follows I will try to avoid "lapsing into a massive and forbidding solipsism," as Watkins phrases it, by striving to keep my theorizing about the logic of literary inquiry fully attuned to the voices and contingencies of practical acts of criticism.

It is difficult, however, to sort out any one of the four definitive features of a literary experience for a separate and fuller characterization since they all are so intimately implicated in one another's capacity for occurrence. Nevertheless, by following roughly the course that a literary inquiry into a particular instance of reading might take, the four features may be

6. Ibid., pp. 3–23, 56–94.
7. Ibid., p. x.

unraveled and spread out sequentially for critical elaboration. The ongoing activity of literary reading seems the place to commence.

On the basis of Dewey's and Pepper's work in epistemology and cognition, I have asserted that the activity of reading is an act of cognition that is best described as a purposive one. The main purpose involved in literary reading would appear to be the achievement of a heightened and exacting awareness of some particular area of our general purposive behavior and the possibilities of action and thought to which it can give rise. For example, in a study of Alfred Noyes's popular ballad "The Highwayman," Stephen Pepper shows that the activity of reading the poem induces us to suppose and undergo a sequence of "anticipatory and apprehensive emotions" based on our past experience and familiarity with such emotions and their sources in behavior. These readerly or aesthetic emotions are "genuine emotions," but they instate a "psychical distance" between themselves and their source emotions. This distance permits voluntary control over our emotional responses.[8] From this vantage point, as it were, we can become more aware of the particular sequence of emotions undergone and their implications for our emotional response and activity in general. In the terms that I have already developed, what Pepper describes comprises the activity of reading in which the aesthetic mode of attention is directed upon both the instrumental mode of attention and itself in an act of compounded awareness. In the activity of reading, we attend to the ways in which poets and characters and, indirectly, ourselves attend to the world and a particular range of purposive acts in it. The sequence of acts that we undergo in reading leads us into supposals of purposive acts in the world. In reading, moreover, we can attend aesthetically to this compound awareness.

Louise Rosenblatt considers very generally the way in which a poem is evoked and attended to aesthetically. Her approach offers some useful general concepts for discussing the activity of reading. The term "poem" for Rosenblatt "stands for the whole category, 'literary work of art,' and for terms such as 'novel,' 'play,' or 'short story.' " The term also and more importantly "presupposes a reader actively involved with a text and refers to what he makes of his responses to the particular set of verbal symbols."[9]

8. Stephen Pepper, "Emotional Distance in Art," *Journal of Aesthetics and Art Criticism* 4 (June 1946): 235–39, especially pp. 237–38.
9. Louise M. Rosenblatt, *The Reader, the Text, the Poem: The Transactional Theory of the Literary Work* (Carbondale: Southern Illinois University Press, 1978), p. 12.

This active involvement is "an event in time," an "evocation" that develops only as "a process in time":

> The relation between reader and text is not linear. It is a situation, an event at a particular time and place in which each element conditions the other. . . . [T]he reader looks to the text, and the text is activated by the reader.[10]

Rosenblatt's sense of the activity of reading, then, seems to be interactional. The evocation of a poem, this temporal event or process that comprises literary reading, constitutes the basic and ongoing activity. This activity, of course, is occasioned by and through interaction: the reader acting upon the text, and the text being brought into action by the reader.

The activity of reading itself, then, forms the crux of Rosenblatt's concept of the "poem." Her book aims primarily at realizing "the concept of the poem as the experience shaped by the reader under the guidance of the text."[11] Even though she prefers to call her general theory of this experience a "transactional theory of the literary work," picking up on the use of "transaction" in Dewey and Bentley's *Knowing and the Known*, I think Rosenblatt's realization of her concept of the poem can be seen to subsume the interactive paradigm.[12] That is to say, the evocation of the poem, forming the basic event or process in need of critical attention, nevertheless admits an eventual analysis into two interactive roles: the enacting agent or reader and the relatively "stable" text that is open to being acted upon while imposing its constraints or limits and its guidance upon the reader.[13] For Rosenblatt the definitive features of the reader and the work are actually already implicated in the activity of reading and cannot logically be curtailed.

Rosenblatt also examines the event of literary reading, or what she prefers to call the "poem," through the concept of "aesthetic reading." She contrasts two forms of reading or "reading-events": "efferent" (from the Latin verb "effere," meaning "to carry away") and "aesthetic." In efferent reading, "the reader's attention is focused primarily on what will remain as the residue *after* the reading—the information to be acquired, the logical

---

10. Ibid., pp. 12, 69, 16–18.
11. Ibid., p. 12.
12. Ibid., pp. ix–xv. See also the subtitle of Rosenblatt's book.
13. Ibid., pp. 99, 129–30, and pp. 1–5 and 71–100 in passing.

solution to a problem, the actions to be carried out." In contrast, in the case of aesthetic reading, "the reader's primary concern is what happens *during* the actual reading event." "*In aesthetic reading,*" Rosenblatt emphasizes, "*the reader's attention is centered directly on what he is living through during his relationship with that particular text.*"[14] These two forms of reading are quite similar to the two modes of attention that I developed in chapter 10. In presenting those two modes of attention, instrumental and aesthetic, I was concerned not to limit them to the experience of literary reading alone. Rosenblatt's two forms of reading, though, offer specific formulations of the instrumental and aesthetic modes of attention as they would apply to particular reading events. In efferent reading, we attend to a text and search out information or results to be carried away and applied elsewhere. We read instrumentally, looking for that which can pragmatically advance our activity in some ordinary region of our general purposive activity. In aesthetic reading, in contra-distinction, we focus on or attend to "the qualitative living-through" of the specific activity of reading. Here the reader "turn[s] his attention toward the full lived-through fusion with the text."[15] The additional concept of "selective attention," moreover, "makes possible the adoption of an aesthetic or efferent stance, and the modulation of interest in specific details."[16] In other words, we can choose to read efferently or aesthetically and can modulate our interest in the specifics to which we may and do attend. Following Rosenblatt, then, we can derive or carry away several practical yet general concepts that can help begin to separate out and characterize the activity of literary reading: the poem (and its logical presupposition of a reader who involves himself or herself actively with a text), efferent and aesthetic reading, and selective attention. My only reservation concerning these general concepts has to do with the fact that aesthetic reading does not entail, as it seems to for Rosenblatt, that the instrumental mode of attention is in abeyance. As I have maintained above, in my own conception of literary reading, the aesthetic mode of

---

14. Ibid., pp. 23–25.
15. Ibid., pp. 25, 47.
16. Ibid., p. 46. For a favorable review, which also summarizes all the main points of Rosenblatt's book, see Alan Holinsworth in the "Books" section of *College English* 41 (October 1979): 223–27. Rosenblatt's most recent formulation of her theory takes into account aspects of the writing process. All the major features present in the book of 1978 are still very much in evidence. See Louise Rosenblatt, "Writing and Reading: The Transactional Theory," *Reader* 20 (Fall 1988): 7–31.

attention is involved in a *compounded* act of awareness. In aesthetic reading, that is to say, instrumentality has become self-reflectively aware of itself.

The concepts of "selective attention" and "aesthetic reading" eventually beg the kind of cognitive and linguistic specificity and precision that Rosenblatt's general level of argument does not address. Nevertheless, there already exists a fair amount of research into the cognitive processing of literature, or literary language, that can lend greater precision and specificity to Rosenblatt's concepts. Teun A. Van Dijk, the editor of *Text*, has published the results of "a cognitive analysis of literary communication processes." His analysis concentrates on the processes of literary reception, especially their semantic aspects. In general he "advocat[es] an *empirical* approach ('what do readers *actually do* when reading literature')."[17] Real readers receive, evoke, process, and make sense of literary texts. It is toward their manifest activity that serious research into the cognitive processes of literary reading must turn.

The cognitive processes of literary reception, according to Van Dijk, are of a piece with general cognitive processes—a claim thoroughly amenable to the work of Rosenblatt as well as of Dewey and Pepper. What begins to distinguish the cognitive processes of literary reception from general cognitive processes, though, is the invocation of a different "pragmatic and socio-cultural context." As Van Dijk explains this crucial distinction,

> . . . the poem is produced, read and understood as a speech act which need not have the usual "practical" pragmatic functions, such as a (real) assertion, question, threat, or promise in our everyday conversation, but may have only or primarily a *ritual* function. In that respect the poem, just like the novel, . . . functions in a *context* in which the speaker-writer primarily intended to change the *evaluation* set of the reader with respect to the text (or its various properties) itself.[18] (Van Dijk's italics)

In literary reception, then, a different context generally becomes operative. The poem is a "speech act" that need not have the usual or practical "pragmatic functions" that we expect and cognitively process in "everyday conversation" or normal discourse. The reader receives the poem in and

17. Teun A. Van Dijk, "Cognitive Processing of Literary Discourse," *Poetics Today* 1 (Autumn 1979): 144. (Van Dijk's italics.)
18. Ibid., p. 151.

through an altered rhetorical and social context: It has a *"ritual* function" that carries with it a generalized authorial intention "to change the *evaluation* set of the reader with respect to the text (or its various properties) itself." This merger of cognitive, aesthetic, social, and linguistic aspects in a single *empirical* approach to the understanding of literary discourse greatly amplifies the conceptual precision of Rosenblatt's notions. The unifying focus for these merging aspects, moreover, remains literary reception—the activity of reading—and the altered "pragmatic and socio-cultural context" it can characteristically invoke. This particular context, Van Dijk adds, can be further specified by means of the interlocking roles and functions of writers and readers in general, as well as teachers, reviewers, literary historiographers, publishers, booksellers, and the like: "It is this socio-cultural background which establishes for each culture which discourses *count as*, or are accepted as, ritual or, more in particular, as 'literary.' "[19] In other words, a Deweyan sense of cultural habitude provides the rich, pragmatic, and actual milieu in which particular readers can actualize their cognitive understanding of particular literary texts.

Rosenblatt's concept of "selective attention" can also be usefully grounded in the cognitive processes of literary reception. It is neither an arbitrary nor an ungrounded notion; but, following Van Dijk, the choice involved has a highly specified and warranted cognitive, social, and linguistic basis:

> . . . a reader *knows* what the typical frames, conventions and actions are which characterize literary communication. Thus, besides an interpretation of the text, the reader will be obliged to interpret the social situation, thereby constructing the specific (pragmatic) context required for adequate literary (ritual) interaction. The cues used in this pragmatic interpretation process come from various sources: (sub-)titles of the book/discourse being selected for reading, knowledge about "literary" writers and pub-

19. Ibid., p. 152. Richard Ohmann has explored this area of speech acts and discursive style and the social conventions that support them. Two representative articles are "Speech, Action, and Style," in *Literary Style: A Symposium*, ed. S. Chatman (London: Oxford University Press, 1971), pp. 241–54, where Ohmann formulates his theoretical approach, and "The Social Definition of Literature," in *What Is Literature?*, ed. P. Hernadi (Bloomington: Indiana University Press, 1978), pp. 89–101, where he examines the hegemony exerted by certain "literary" power blocs in defining and evaluating literary works for American society at large.

lishers, the specific social context frame (home, school, etc.) involved, etc. On the basis of this information, the reader knows that possibly the kind of speech act to be performed is ritual. He will therefore *expect* a number of specific properties of the discourse and the writer: he expects that the writer's primary purpose will not be to inform him about "the world" as it is, nor will he have specific intentions regarding the wishes, opinions or actions of the hearer connected to this specific knowledge of the world. In other words, the contextual constraints of ritual communication induce a specific *cognitive set* in the reader. This cognitive set will determine the ways in which the text is analyzed and interpreted.[20]

The reader's knowledge of literary conventions and the social contexts of reading aid him or her in selectively attending to a work and expecting certain aesthetic functions that he assumes the writer will have performed. Again, "A slumber" by Wordsworth provides a rich case in point. The use of a first-person speaker invites a reader to attend to the lyric with a particular cognitive set regarding the features and qualities of the speaker's speech act. The confusion over whether the "she" of the poem is the speaker's "spirit" or some other entity initiates a problematic realignment of our contextual expectations and consequently of our cognitive set toward the poem. Such selective attention, then, is built into our progressively acquired literary habits and interpretive facility. When a literary (or what Van Dijk calls "ritual") interaction does not obtain, then we attend efferently, instrumentally, ordinarily, to someone's discourse.

Rosenblatt's concept of "aesthetic reading," accordingly, can be grounded in the "specific *cognitive set* in the reader" that selective attention to literary works pragmatically and contextually induces. This "cognitive set" guides and determines the way in which a reader lives through, analyzes, and interprets his or her relationship with a work. Quite reminiscent of Rosenblatt, Van Dijk notes that, in literary reading, "the *attention*, or *focus of interpretation*, of the reader is 'on the text

<hr/>

20. Van Dijk, pp. 152–53. See also Charles Altieri, "A Procedural Definition of Literature," in *What Is Literature?*, ed. P. Hernadi (Bloomington: Indiana University Press, 1978), pp. 62–78, where, in the effort to define or generalize about "literature," Altieri emphasizes a reader's knowledge of general literary conventions and intentions and the pedagogical development of these procedures by means of examples, especially canonical texts.

itself.'" In literary reading there is an "enhanced capacity for surface structures," an emphasis on the "local" "pleasures" of a text. At the same time, the text requires the reader to process cognitively its "global" "coherences." The reader essentially must conduct "a conceptual (re-) construction of the sequences of events and actions represented." These global coherences tend to yield a "global interpretation" of the literary interaction, but one that must meld with and account for "local interpretation" that pauses over and recollects our local pleasures in reading.[21] The numerous local pleasures of reading "A slumber," "Strange fits," and "She dwelt," for example, can be constructed toward illuminating the general or global coherences of Wordsworth's pronomial playfulness and his range of creative inquiry into various aspects of Romantic death fantasy.

Two other prominent theorists of aesthetic reading have stressed the reading process and the interaction of reader and text, but their proposals, I believe, fail to be as circumspect, practical, and warranted as those of Rosenblatt and Van Dijk. Wolfgang Iser and Stanley Fish have both attempted phenomenological accounts of the process of reading.[22] Both theorists stress the temporality or the temporal nature of the activity of reading, and both try to analyze its temporal dynamics. For both, the

21. Van Dijk, pp. 152, 154, 156. Two other related and supportive studies of the cognitive processing of language and literature should be cited here. In *Language Processing and the Reading of Literature: Toward a Model of Comprehension* (Bloomington: Indiana University Press, 1978), George L. Dillon develops a theory of reading to account for the cognitive processing of literary style: ". . . we are concerned with the sources of perceptual complexity and the different types of strategies one might use to resolve them" (p. 30). In "Literary Dynamics: How the Order of a Text Creates Its Meanings," *Poetics Today* 1 (Autumn 1979): 35–64, 311–61, Menakhem Perry examines the cumulative construction of literary meanings in and through the activity of reading as well as the cognitive processes brought to bear on the specifics of the order (or "continuum") of a text.

22. The key article to consider by Wolfgang Iser is "The Reading Process: A Phenomenological Approach," *New Literary History* 3 (Winter 1972): 279–99. This essay also appears as the final chapter of Iser's *The Implied Reader: Patterns of Communication in Prose Fiction from Bunyan to Beckett* (Baltimore, Md.: Johns Hopkins University Press, 1975). Iser elaborates his notion of the implied reader and his phenomenological approach to the reading process in *The Act of Reading*. The key essay for Stanley Fish is "Literature in the Reader: Affective Stylistics," *New Literary History* 2 (Autumn 1970): 123–62. Fish later poses this essay as the opening piece of "Part One: Literature in the Reader" in *Is There a Text in This Class?: The Authority of Interpretive Communities* (Cambridge, Mass.: Harvard University Press, 1980), pp. 21–67. In the essay "Interpreting the Variorum," *Critical Inquiry* 2 (Spring 1976): 465–85, Fish revises his earlier theory and basically abandons an interactional model of the reading process for a theory of critical fictions or "interpretive strategies." See also Fish, *Is There a Text in This Class?*, pp. 147–80, 301–71.

reader actively brings the text into being while undergoing a continuous construction and alteration of his expectations and assessments as he responds to the disparities, gaps, problems, style, and ambiguities of the text. Generally viewed, such phenomenological accounts can be associated with, and even adumbrate, the pragmatic and empirical approaches of Rosenblatt and Van Dijk to literary reading as well as the Deweyan and Pepperian approach that I have been developing. The exigencies of their phenomenological orientations, however, occasion grave difficulties for their models of interaction. I will briefly address only one troublesome feature of their phenomenological models here—namely, their flawed conceptions of "the reader" who is supposed to interact with a work. Basically, Iser's and Fish's efforts to situate the reader in a dynamic interaction with a text ultimately tend to undermine the full complexity of the exchange involved and tend to treat the reader as an ideal construct.

Generally speaking, Wolfgang Iser wants to show how a self, a reading subject, enlarges his grasp of the world through structured acts of reading. Iser conceives of the text as an open "field of play" with an "inherently dynamic character" capable of being realized by the reader when he converges upon and interacts with the text.[23] Iser goes on at length to develop the specifics of this realization that occurs during the reading process. "The way in which sequent sentences act upon one another," he maintains, during the reading of a text creates the "world" of the literary text by giving rise to ongoing series of expectations and modifications of those expectations.[24] The realized text constitutes the "virtual dimension of the text" or the product of the convergence of reader and text. Indeed it is a world finally shaped by the creation and modification of expectations. The result of the reading process is that we can "absorb an unfamiliar experience into our personal world."[25] We have converged on something unfamiliar and have had our expectations with regard to it altered until it has ("virtually") come over to us. Iser claims that there is also a "dialectical structure" implicit in this particular construction of the reading process. The convergence of text and reader is actually the converging of an "alien 'me'" and a "real, virtual 'me'." Iser thus postulates a division in the reader so that the reader might be able to think

---

23. Iser, "The Reading Process," pp. 279–81.
24. Ibid., p. 281.
25. Ibid., p. 293.

"the thoughts of another" in his realization of the text.[26] The reader's "alien 'me' " is his former world. The "virtual 'me' " comprises the realized "me," the product of the interaction of text and reader. However, in this divided posture of Iser's postulated reader, the text begins to lose its reality before the absorbing consciousness of the reader. The dialectical structure of reading becomes for Iser, it would seem, a dialectical structure within the consciousness of the reader who would use a text to divide and realize himself. Consciousness, within Iser's Husserlean purview, leads itself onward by creating illusions for itself. Indeed, the fictions and expectations inherent in the sequent sentences of the text "do not correspond to any objective reality outside themselves."[27] Readerly consciousness, however implied by the "virtual dimension of the text," toys with itself. It has absorbed all (familiar and unfamiliar) into its own subjectivity. The otherness, the difference, the insistent oppositeness, of the text runs the risk of being sacrificed to a dialectic of (one) consciousness.

Stanley Fish, in a well-known essay, once set out "to demonstrate the explanatory power of a method of analysis which takes the reader, as an actively mediating presence, fully into account."[28] This method—called "affective stylistics"—is very short on active mediation, however. As one critic assesses this article, "Fish talked as if a reader was manipulated by a text—the text forced the reader to perform certain cognitive acts—and he, as critic, described that manipulative process."[29] Because the integrative and generalizing capacities and skills of readers are not taken into account by Fish in his model of the reading process, his notion of the reader is severely impaired and not really interactive. Fish's "reader" is basically at the mercy of wherever his "developing responses" to the temporal succession of the words of the text lead him.[30] And, often enough, they lead him into one baffling ambiguity or textual complexity after another. Moreover, Fish's model of reading, according to Ralph Rader, "cannot differentiate the characteristic quality of any literary work from another."[31] The "reading" is far too close and cannot assist the reader in discerning or grasping general qualities, structures, or textures of works. To some

26. Ibid., p. 298.
27. Ibid., p. 281.
28. Fish, "Literature in the Reader," p. 123.
29. Mailloux, "Reader-Response Criticism?" p. 414.
30. Fish, "Literature in the Reader," pp. 126–27.
31. Ralph Rader, "Fact, Theory, and Literary Explanation," *Critical Inquiry* 1 (December 1974): 269, and pp. 262–71 in passing.

degree, Fish has recognized this theoretical deficiency and has sought to revise his model of text-reader manipulation. Since the appearance of "Interpreting the *Variorum*" in 1976 and *Is There a Text in This Class?* in 1980, shared or communal "interpretive strategies" supposedly serve to demarcate what count as formal features of a text. However, such strategies are also announced as "fictions."[32] The rather troublesome individual reader has now been replaced by an equally troublesome "communal" or "structural" reader. Both notions yield ideal constructs that transcend the capacities and actions of real readers reading.

If an interactional model of the activity of reading purports to keep both text and reader and their temporal convergence real and practical and unidealized, then *precisely* how can a text be said to *guide* and *act* upon a particular reader who acts upon it? Louise Rosenblatt, as discussed above, claims that the text imposes constraints or limits upon the enacting reader and thereby supplies the reader "guidance." She asserts that "the text serves as a blueprint for the selecting, rejecting, and ordering of what is being called forth; the text regulates what shall be held in the forefront of the reader's attention."[33] Van Dijk's textual "cues," the "local" "surface structures" and "global" sequences of represented actions and events guide the reader in his or her cognitive processing. Such pragmatic guidance differentiates itself rather closely from the illusional or idealized exchange involved in the reading models of Iser and Fish. With the latter two theorists, the *guidance* that a text supplies is *derealized*. It becomes preempted as a "virtual 'me' " in a dialectic of consciousness (Iser) or assumed as manipulatively dominating the chain of a reader's "developing responses" (Fish). But how, precisely, can textual "guidance" of the reader be described in some sense other than the metaphorical or analogical ("blueprint," "cues")? Such a description seems necessary in order to warrant fully the temporal and interactive characterization of the activity of reading and to establish the literary work as the second definitive feature deployed in this unfolding logic of literary inquiry.

At a crucial juncture in the serial presentation of his use theory of meaning and language in the first part of *Philosophical Investigations*, Ludwig Wittgenstein inquires into reading and the phenomenon of being guided by a text or a notation.[34] Wittgenstein is at pains to show that

---

32. Fish, "Interpreting the *Variorum*," pp. 465–85.
33. Rosenblatt, *The Reader, The Text, The Poem*, p. 11.
34. Ludwig Wittgenstein, *Philosophical Investigations*, pp. 61e–72e (Part I, #156–78). A

"understanding is not a mental process," that it is not "a special experience" added to the specific circumstances of a given activity.[35] He takes "reading," especially reading a notation, as the key example or "case" for this nonidealist conception of the act of understanding. Instead of positing a special act of consciousness in order to account for the phenomenon of reading, Wittgenstein encourages a closer look at the circumstances of reading—that is, at the particular linguistic behavior involved:

> Well, what does go on when I read the page? . . . And what does the characteristic thing about the experience of reading consist in?—Here I should like to say: "The words that I utter *come* in a special way." That is, they do not come as they would if I were for example making them up. —They come of themselves.[36]

Such words are not illusions or fictions projected by the reader; they come to the reader of themselves during the activity of readerly understanding. Reading proceeds in *this* way.

> I feel that the letters are the *reason* why I read such-and-such. For if someone asks me "Why do you read such-and-such?"—I justify my reading by the letters which are there.
>   This justification, however, was something that I said, or thought: what does it mean to say that I *feel* it? I should like to say: when I read I feel a kind of *influence* of the letters working on me . . . In particular, this interpretation appeals to us especially when we make a point of reading slowly—perhaps in order to see what does happen when we read. When we, so to speak, quite intentionally let ourselves be *guided* by the letters. But this "letting myself be guided" in turn only consists in my looking carefully at the letters—and perhaps excluding certain other thoughts.[37] (Wittgenstein's italics)

Being guided by a notation or text, then, is concomitant with *attending*

---

preliminary, and occasionally more expansive, draft of this section can be found in "The Brown Book." See Wittgenstein, *The Blue and Brown Books* (New York: Harper & Row, 1965), pp. 119–25, 167–71, 177–78, 180.

35. Wittgenstein, *Philosophical Investigations*, p. 61e.

36. Ibid., p. 66e.

37. Ibid., pp. 68e–69e.

normally, or even slowly and more carefully, to a mode of transcription with which we are quite familiar. We are *influenced* and *guided* by what we *attend* to as it comes to us of itself. Free associations and random thoughts ("certain other thoughts") can occur, but we also recognize them as indeed extraneous and incidental to that which comes of itself. Through practice and progressive development, we have learned how to attend to a notation or to a text such that a special mental act or dialectic of consciousness is not necessary, after the fact, to explain how the activity and its communicative function could possibly have taken place. As Wittgenstein comments,

> . . . *while* I am being guided everything is quite simple, I notice nothing *special*; but afterwards, when I ask myself what it was that happened, it seems to have been something indescribable. *Afterwards* no description satisfies me.[38] (Wittgenstein's italics)

The temptation, then, is not to be satisfied and to posit special and superfluous illusions. The challenge, though, would be to accept the guidance and influence of that which guides *while* and *as* we attend to it, ordinarily and carefully.

The question of the ontological status of the literary work has accumulated an extensive and controversial history.[39] In terms of the logic of literary inquiry that I am developing here, the work of art comprises that entity which can be said to guide a reader in and during the activity of reading. Wittgenstein's remarks on reading and being guided by a notation logically situate the activity of reading in close connection with notations, inscriptions, and texts and the guidance they ordinarily and characteristically supply. An essay by Stephen Pepper, moreover, can serve to enlarge upon and further clarify the logical status of the literary work as a definitive feature of literary experience and inquiry.

Pepper indicates that a work of art is a perceptual object fitted with two "dispositions"; it has, in other words, "a double dispositional base."[40] First of all, the work is a physical object, a "physical control object," "with a

38. Ibid., p. 71e.

39. For a brief critical history of this question, see W. K. Wimsatt, "Battering the Object: The Ontological Approach," in *Contemporary Criticism*, ed. M. Bradbury and D. Palmer (London: Arnold, 1970), pp. 61–81.

40. Stephen Pepper, "The Work of Art Described from a Double Dispositional Base," *Journal of Aesthetics and Art Criticism* 23 (Summer 1965): 421–27.

physical configuration constituting a *passive disposition* fitted . . . for the situation of certain sensory, emotional, and meaningful responses in any person who enters its perceptual field."[41] It is fitted in order to influence and guide a perceiver who enters its field and begins to read its notation. Pepper dwells primarily upon the visual and plastic arts, but the point should be able to carry for the peculiar nature of artistic material that authors display in literary works of art. The syntactical, grammatical, and rhetorical organization of words, phrases, and utterances characteristic of a socioculturally shared language constitutes a wide field of dispositional capacities with which authors can shape their texts. Cultural attitudes, values, and habits as well as culturally mediated specifications of discursive types known as genres also figure as major factors in the articulated disposition of a literary work. However, regarded from the perspective of a reader who experiences such a work, this initial disposition appears passive, not-yet-activated, not-yet-articulated. Critics and theorists who would dwell upon intentionality or the privileged interpretive validity of authorial intention, of course, regard this passive disposition of the literary work of art as imminently dynamic. Nevertheless it is crucial to recognize that actual readers of literary works perform the task of articulating what count later on as authorial intentions, or the predisposed intentionality of texts. One could simply divorce and reify what Pepper calls the passive dispositional base of the work of art as "the author," but that preemptive move would strongly betray the actual process of literary reading. Readers do construct images of authors, even implied authors, as they read. Such active construction positions the role of author not as a definitive feature of literary experience so much as a readerly approximation of the productive faculty typically assumed to be on display in the work being read. Readerly constructions of images, roles, attitudes, and values assigned to authors, moreover, involve judgments of practice or evaluations. A reader makes judgments concerning another's practice, another's work, another's notation, as that practice itself undergoes comprehension in the act of literary reading. Authors have existed, do exist, will exist. However, in terms of the definitive features of literary experience, their historical facticity does not supplant the passive dispositional base of the literary work of art as it first appears for readers.

However, once readerly response commences, a second disposition has actually already been activated:

41. Ibid., p. 422.

> As soon as such capacities to respond to the physical control object
> are present in a person, however, they become latent *dynamic
> dispositions* for that person. . . .[42]

For instance, a literary reader's linguistic and literary competence certainly forms a quite general "dynamic disposition" toward the text; but
more specialized and more tutored responses also significantly dispose
particular readers toward the comprehension of specific genres of
literature—Romantic lyric poetry, ballads, and so on. A response to a
work in Pepper's terms, then, "is a combined result of the passive
disposition of the physical object and the dynamic disposition of a person
triggered into action by being within the perceptual field of the physical
object and receptive to such stimulations."[43] The passive disposition of the
work aptly describes its logical status as a definitive feature of having a
literary experience. In general terms, it is fitted to guide a reader who
chooses to enter its notational field. Such fitting disposes the work toward
being brought into action by the perceptual activity of a person receptive
to its guidance and influence. Pepper adds, with caution, that

> . . . the perceptual qualities are what constitute the *actual*
> qualitative content of appreciation for the work of art. The physical
> control object possesses only the dispositional capacities for evok-
> ing such actual qualitative content in a perceiver.[44]

The *interaction of work and reader*, that is, *yields actual qualities*, and not
the work itself. Pepper's "double dispositional base" description of the work
of art, then, fits in securely with an interactional model of literary
experience and inquiry and lends some measure of conceptual clarity to
Wittgenstein's remarks on reading and being guided by a notation.

Now the passive disposition of a work of art, especially in the cases of
great works of art, is virtually inexhaustible, regardless of how full and
intense a dynamic disposition it may activate. Indeed a single perception
of a literary work of art can scarcely begin to approximate the fuller
perceptual possibilities of the work that multiple encounters often intimate. A reader, however, can progressively approximate a fuller percep-

42. Ibid.
43. Ibid.
44. Ibid.

tion of a work as he or she approximates what Pepper calls "the full perceptual potentialities of the control object":

> [T]he content of one perceptual event can be revived by another through processes of memory and recall. In the gathering together of the perceptual content of a work of art towards a total perceptual grasp, the process consists of a sort of amalgamation of the content of earlier perceptions into the new.[45]

After repeated or successive interactions with a "physical control object," the perceiver or the reader

> . . . responds more and more fully to the passive dispositional structure of this object. He actualizes more and more completely the perceptual potentialities of the work of art.[46]

This increasingly more complete actualization of the potentialities of the physical control object, furthermore, carries two important qualifications. First of all, "the total perceptual experience" need not be simultaneous or present to itself all at once. "What is asked for," states Pepper, "is simply a set of perceptions centered upon the control object as their stimulating source and responsive to one another."[47] That is to say, the perceptions should arise from the perceiver's interaction with the control object and they should all be coherently related to one another. This initial qualification perhaps retrospectively can be seen governing my desire and insistence in giving a diverse range of perceptions regarding "A slumber" their due and in seeking a way to detect coherence among them. Pepper also admits as a second qualification regarding the actualization of the control object that the set of perceptions need not be completely and "internally consistent." Indeed, in Pepper's words, "alternative interpretations derivative from the control object may lie in the dispositional structure of that object."[48] Ambiguities, contradictions, or multiple lines or strands of interpretation comprise aesthetic perceptions that the physical control object can indeed dispose the perceiver or reader toward.

45. Ibid., p. 423.
46. Ibid.
47. Ibid.
48. Ibid., pp. 423–24.

The experience of referential confusion in "A slumber did my spirit seal" and the three lines of interpretation that the work gives rise to constitute a powerful instance here of the perceptual fault lines and fractures that the passive dispositional base of a literary work can harbor for its readers. The control object does not always guide us into a uniform, untroubled, and easily clarified set of perceptions or perceptual qualities.

The actualization of the perceptual potentialities of a physical control object fully depends, of course, on the aptitude and activity of a perceiving self. At this point, Pepper's description of the "double dispositional base" of the work begins to demand a third definitive feature of having a literary experience—namely, the reader, the active or enacting agent. According to Pepper, "the full discriminating capacity of a person" is "required" in order "to actualize the perceptual potentialities of a control object." If such "dispositional capacities" are not available or are impaired, then the person will not produce an adequate or appropriate "perceptual response to the dispositional structure of the control object."[49] Much depends, then, upon the capacities, competence, and purposive activity of the particular self in a dynamic disposition toward the work of art.

With the role of the reader, though, a very embattled theoretical issue comes to the fore: How real or definitive is the reader? Is he or she an actual person, or an "ideal" reader, or a "communal" or "structural" or "implied" reader? With the latter conceptions of the reader, critics construct ideals that scarcely any reader could hope to actualize. As one commentator has put it: "We seem now, however, to run some real danger of being directed by the theoreticians to read in a way that real readers, on land or sea, have never read."[50] In the logic of literary inquiry being developed here, the reader is and should be taken as a particular habitual self capable of and disposed toward at least some basic level of inquiry into his or her own instances of literary experience. The reader is actual, human, individual: a particular observer as well as agent of his or her own purposive activity of reading. As one writer has stated in his assessment of the current situation in aesthetic theory, "what matters most (at this juncture of our intellectual history) is how much the observer has been *induced to develop or reconstruct* his habitual formulations by *his experience of art* or by the perception of the human condition *which art*

49. Ibid., p. 425.
50. Robert Alter, "Mimesis and the Motive for Fiction," *Triquarterly* 42 (Spring 1978): 248–49.

has instigated in him."[51] A particular reader's own activity of reading, then, serves to develop or perhaps even to reconstruct perceptual and cognitive habits, linguistic and otherwise. The nature of this kind of experience clearly depends upon the fact that the reader is understood to be a particular habitual self and not some sort of ideal construct or theoretical fiction.

A number of literary critics and theorists variously have defended the position that "the reader," in fact and in deed, should first and foremost be recognized and admitted as oneself. Though it is possible to develop and construct generalizations about the reading habits and experiences of a communal or social "we," our reading experiences must begin with an "I." As I. A. Richards has phrased this inescapable situation:

> The main source of any view, sound or silly, which we have of how we read must be *our own observation of our own doings while we are reading.* We should supplement this by observation of others' behavior and their reports, but inevitably in interpreting such other evidence *we start from and return to that picture of a mind at work which only introspection can supply.* [52] (italics mine)

Critics as diverse as Raymond Williams, Ian Gregor, Philip Hobsbaum, Walter Slatoff, Gordon Mills, and Lowry Nelson, Jr., all share a basic consensus that theorizing about reading and criticism must begin with the individual activity of a reader, most notably oneself. Hobsbaum, Slatoff, Mills, and Nelson indicate, though in slightly differing formulations, that personal readerly response constitutes the starting point for shared and integrated responses.[53] Ian Gregor studies passages from Jane Austen, Emily Brontë, Thomas Hardy, and E. M. Forster in order to show that criticism, "an individual activity," can and "will make us more sharply

---

51. V. Tejera, "Contemporary Trends in Aesthetics: Some Underlying Issues," *Journal of Value Inquiry* 8 (Summer 1974): 141. (Tejera's italics.)

52. I. A. Richards, *How to Read a Page* (Boston: Beacon Press, 1959; orig. pub. 1942), p. 26.

53. Philip Hobsbaum, *Theory of Criticism* (Bloomington: Indiana University Press, 1970), pp. 1–14; Walter Slatoff, *With Respect to Readers* (Ithaca, N.Y.: Cornell University Press, 1970), pp. 3–26; Gordon Mills, *Hamlet's Castle: The Study of Literature as a Social Experience* (Austin: University of Texas Press, 1976), pp. 2–3, 5; and Lowry Nelson, Jr., "The Fictive Reader: Aesthetic and Social Aspects of Literary Performance," *Comparative Literature Studies* 15 (June 1978): 203–10, especially pp. 207–9.

aware of our personal responsiveness."[54] And Raymond Williams notes that there is a "necessary" and "adequate" "attention" that every individual reader must allow in practice in order to read poetry with any degree of understanding. A strict method cannot be stipulated; "but one can perhaps demonstrate by example, and then by example and repeated example, what response to a poem involves."[55]

Even though the reader and the activity of reading are necessarily individual, response and critical activity are not accordingly subjective—that is, "subjective" in the sense of arbitrary and idiosyncratic. The inadequacies of subjectively oriented criticism have already been discussed at some length in Chapter 8. An alternative position has been fully developed through the ensuing chapters. The shared and shareable grounds for complex cognitive activity provided by my analyses of the knowledge situation, the types of evidence, the purposive activity of the self within the interactive paradigm, and the construction of judgments in the procedures of inquiry also comprise shared grounds for the cognitive activity of readers. The individual reader, it can be said as a general rule of practice, also carries out his or her own purposive activity under a double ethical obligation. The reader is obliged, for one, to recognize or respect the otherness of the literary work that disposes the reader toward dynamic interaction. Walter Slatoff has even spoken of this obligation as a "moral and ethical" consideration.[56] Second, and far more subtly, the individual reader indissolubly remains obliged to that complex range of predispositions to certain feelings and thoughts as well as qualities, actions, and language—collectively, cultural habitude—that he or she shares with other individuals in a social group. Both obligations, throughout ongoing interactions, serve as transpersonal checks on the purposive activity of a self. They do not yield "objectivity," but neither do they justify or rationalize solipsism or subjectivism in matters of experience and knowledge. They also serve as pragmatic checks on any dogmatically skeptical appeal to radical forms of cognitive incommensurability in matters of epistemology and interpretation. An individual reader, oneself, myself, characteristically attempts to carry out an inquiry into an instance

54. Ian Gregor, "Criticism as an Individual Activity: The Approach through Reading," in *Contemporary Criticism*, ed. M. Bradbury and D. Palmer (London: Arnold, 1970), p. 199, and pp. 195–214 in passing.
55. Raymond Williams, *Reading and Criticism* (London: Muller, 1950), p. 58.
56. Slatoff, pp. 89–90.

of literary experience and constitute it as fully and adequately as possible as an example, in Raymond Williams's words, of "what response to a poem involves." The first part of this book, considered retrospectively, strives to mount one such example of readerly response.

The fourth and final definitive feature of the logic of literary inquiry yields the exemplary development of the experience of reading: the quality that is made distinct within and through the temporal interaction of a literary work and a reader. This quality emerges from a specific problematic knowledge situation as it moves toward resolution and relative determinacy through the activity of a self. Such a quality also provides both literary knowledge and the means to achieve, or at least to canvass, a consensus among differing interpretations. The experience of a confusion in pronomial reference and personal identities in "A slumber" yields this poem's distinctive quality: Confused perceptions, feelings, and identities plague the lyric's speaker. Such confusion of identities, emotions, and recognitions also seems to constitute our fate as readers of Wordsworth's lyric art. This distinctive quality seems to mark various problems generated during the act of reading Wordsworth's lyric: a confusion in the identity of the dead girl and a disturbing ambivalence in the character of the speaker. I named the interconnecting and intimate network that these problems, as a whole, constitute as "problematic." This designation can also be refined.

The term "problematic" best designates the *conceptual* aspect of a literary cognitive situation for which the term "quality" names the *perceptual* or *qualitatively felt* aspect. As in Pepper's analysis of purposive activity, the cognition involved has its conceptual and qualitative components. Literary inquiry into literary experience offers access to both qualitative description and conceptual analysis. The quality discovered or made distinct in the activity of reading focuses and guides qualitative description of the literary experience, while the problematic, marked out by the moments and problems of this qualitative description, centers and directs the conceptual analysis. The quality and the problematic of a given literary interaction can subsequently furnish means for discovering and establishing some measure of differentiation as well as consensus among differing interpretations. My assessment and adjudication of different lines of interpreting "A slumber" is, again, a case in point. The notion of the problematic of "A slumber" developed in Chapter 6 also helps to assess the critical practice involved in such diverse interpretations as those of Norman Holland, Paul de Man, J. Hillis Miller, and Geoffrey Hartman.

Their interpretive assumptions and rhetoric generally tend to distort, or refocus in curious ways, the quality and problems a fuller act of response and interpretive inquiry can engage.

Some overtly sociohistorical and ideological discourse has also made keen use of the term "problematic," but in a way that marks a significant difference from a Deweyan or pragmatist sense of the concept. Louis Althusser is the theorist most closely identified with the notion, but John Fekete can provide the most concise formulation of this divergent sense of the term: "A 'problematic' is a social, ideological, or theoretical framework within which complexes of problems are structured and single problems acquire density, meaning and significance."[57] Here the concept of the problematic names a kind of theoretical space in which can be located various interlinked social problems and their attendant theoretical analyses. This Althusserian notion seems intriguingly similar to the Deweyan one, yet spatial imagery tends to characterize this use of the term. That is to say, an ideological "problematic" tends to be analogized as a figure, rupture, break, or disjunctive space within some kind of architectonic structure of social discourse.[58] A Deweyan sense of the term strives to emphasize temporality and ongoing activity as characteristic of the unfolding of given problematics. A pragmatist problematic appears as conceptually dynamic and interactive rather than as spatialized, even reified figures of discursive formations.

Finally, and perhaps as a way of drawing my own discourse to a close, it is worth noticing that my chosen usage of the word "problematic" yields a slight departure from the way in which Dewey uses it in discussing a problematic knowledge situation. For Dewey, the problematic situation is a transitional one. It constitutes that intermediate stage in the course of an experience in which an indeterminate situation has been recognized by the self and an inquiry begun toward determinately resolving it. However, it seems to me that problematic situations typically encountered in the reading of literature do not always, or perhaps even characteristically, move toward a full and determinate resolution. Of course, this is not to say that determinations are not or cannot be made. It seems, though, that

57. John Fekete, *The Critical Twilight* (London: Routledge & Kegan Paul, 1978), pp. 217–18. See also Louis Althusser, *For Marx*, trans. B. Brewster (New York: Pantheon Books, 1969) and *Reading Capital*, trans. B. Brewster (London: NLB, 1970).

58. R. D. Boyne, in "Breaks and Problematics," *Philosophy and Social Criticism* 6 (Summer 1979): 205, points out that geometrical conceptions underlie Althusser's use of the term "problematic."

literary experience does not necessarily aim to *solve* the problems it generates but, instead, seems to *open* readers into the purposive activity of perceiving and reflecting on a full interplay of perceptions and problems. The aesthetic mode of attention, indeed, would be and is a willing collaborator in this demanding cognitive project. A literary "problematic" is left open. Its resolution assumes the form of a readerly understanding of its occurrence, quality, evidences, and complexities. A problematic developed in the course of a particular literary interaction, then, in a way, both shapes an instance of reading for a reader and still holds the promise of further, and perhaps inexhaustible, interaction.

Appendix

Lucy in Retrospect: A Late Wordsworth Manuscript of "She dwelt among th'untrodden ways"

While examining the second volume in a set of the 1800 edition of *Lyrical Ballads* deposited in the rare books collection of the Poetry Room at the State University of New York at Buffalo, I found a manuscript signed and apparently dated by William Wordsworth. It is a variation on the third and final stanza of "Song," better known as "She dwelt among th'untrodden ways" and later as "She dwelt among the untrodden ways." The stanza is inscribed in a careful hand on letter paper measuring 18 ×11.5 centimeters and folded in three. The letter paper itself is laid paper and bears a lightly embossed seal in the lower right-hand corner. The seal is legible from the reverse side of the manuscript and reads "Corgon Superfine," with an imperial crown set in between the two words. The paper is lightly foxed, especially at the fold that was inserted into the crease of the book. The manuscript was placed between pages 52 and 53 of the volume—that is, between the pages bearing the poems "Song" and the untitled poem "A slumber did my spirit seal." The volume itself is part of a set of the Longman and Rees impression of *Lyrical Ballads*, published in London in 1800. The set belongs to the Julian Park Collection purchased by the Poetry Room of Lockwood Library in 1966.[1] The insert had not been

1. A full bibliographic transcription of the title page runs as follows: Lyrical Ballads/ With/ Other Poems./ In Two Volumes./ By W. Wordsworth./ Quam nihil ad genium, Papiniane, tuum!/ Vol. II/ *London:*/ Printed For T. N. Longman And O. Rees, Paternoster Row,/ By Biggs And Co. Bristol./ 1800. The set itself bears the signature "Louisa Carter" on the page preceding the title page of both Volumes I and II. On the inside cover, opposite the page of Volume I just mentioned, there appears the penciled signature "Park." On the inside cover of Volume II, in the

catalogued by the Poetry Room, and no printed bibliographic recording or listing of the manuscript exists to my knowledge except for this one.

The manuscript itself reads as follows:

> She lived unknown, and few could
> know
> When Lucy ceased to be;
> But She is in her grave—and oh
> The difference to Me.!

> William Wordsworth

> Lostheth How
> 20th July
> 1848

The indentations characteristic of the printed versions of the lyric are not preserved. The second line begins further to the left than the others so as not to interfere with the last word of the first line, which had to be written below most of the line it belongs to in order to fit on the page. The four lines of the lyric and the signature are all in a very careful and easily legible hand. Though the intensity of the ink varies, with the word "grave" appearing rather faint, the expression "and oh" and the final line of the stanza stand out sharply and clearly. Individual letters and words match up well with letters and words from several facsimiles of documents written by Wordsworth in the late 1830s and 1840s.

It is also of note that the fourth line has a double punctuation at the end. Both a period and an exclamation mark are visible. The period is more heavily impressed and distinct than the faintly stroked exclamation stem and dimly legible point underneath. Also legible is a slight underlining of the first "e" of the word "difference."

---

upper right-hand corner, there appears this note in pencil: "The whole of this (2nd) /vol. was first published/here./With and stanza of/Lucy." This note, according to University of Buffalo archivist Shonnie Finnegan, is in Julian Park's handwriting. Moreover, running underneath the word "stanza" the poorly erased signature "Park" can still be read.

I thank Shonnie Finnegan and Christopher Densmore, University Archives, and Eric Carpenter, Poetry Room, of the State University of New York at Buffalo for their very helpful assistance. I also thank Professors Irving Massey and John Dings of the Department of English, SUNY at Buffalo, for their very generous assistance and advice in the writing of this essay.

The place-name and date, though apparently written in the same ink as the rest, appear less careful, less applied, and in a shaky hand. Indeed, some of the date is traced over a second time but still shows the faint first effort underneath. Perhaps the place and date were inscribed later than the rest, as an afterthought or in response to a special request. I could not completely satisfy myself that the words and numbers of the place-name and date were in Wordsworth's handwriting. They are too few, too faint, and not sufficiently well formed.[2]

Significance of the Manuscript

This brief manuscript was apparently written by Wordsworth in order to correct and update, perhaps for an acquaintance, a poem that Wordsworth may have been particularly fond of or, more likely, a poem that the assumed acquaintance and probable owner of the book had drawn to Wordsworth's attention for any number of possible reasons. In general, from 1836 to 1846, Wordsworth's collected *Poetical Works* had been going through a number of arrangements and editions. In 1846 the seven-volume revised edition appeared; this edition, moreover, would essentially be duplicated in a six-volume format when the definitive 1849–50 edition of Wordsworth's collected writings appeared. On the occasion of the 20th of July 1848, Wordsworth may have wanted to correct an early version of

2. At the Wordsworth Library at Dove Cottage, Grasmere, there is a manuscript letter written by William and Dorothy Wordsworth to Samuel Taylor Coleridge around the middle of December 1798, during the Wordsworths' four-month sojourn in Goslar, Germany. This lengthy letter contains a transcription of the original five-stanza version of "She dwelt" in Dorothy's handwriting. A transcription of this letter is provided on pages 235–43 of *The Letters of William and Dorothy Wordsworth*, Vol. I, ed. Ernest de Selincourt, 2d ed. rev. C. L. Shaver (Oxford: Clarendon Press, 1967). De Selincourt records the divergences this manuscript (which he calls MS. 1799) shows with respect to the three-stanza lyric that Wordsworth published in 1800. Also of note are the Longman MSS. originally described and edited by W. Hale White in *A Description of the Wordsworth and Coleridge Manuscripts in the Possession of Mr. T. N. Longman* (1897) and now deposited at the Beinecke Library at Yale University. Among these documents is the original manuscript for the 1800 edition; the poems for that edition were transcribed primarily by Coleridge before being sent to the printer, T. N. Longman. Besides these two early manuscripts, the only other manuscript version that I am aware of is a presentation copy dated "London—May 20th 1828" and signed "Wm Wordsworth." This document is housed at the Princeton University Library; it is a fair copy of the whole poem and shows only a handful of small variations from the text of 1805. Its existence does help to indicate Wordsworth's willingness to inscribe presentation copies or adjusted versions of "She dwelt."

one of his poems, either to please himself or the owner of the book, by making the text of its final stanza consistent with the later printing.

The corrected stanza that the manuscript presents is close to the text offered in the definitive edition of 1849–50 and differs in only two respects—the punctuation of the phrase "and oh" and the capitalization of the pronouns "She" and "Me."[3] A comparison of the 1800 and 1849–50 versions of "She dwelt" also yields little difference in the first two stanzas of the lyric. There are only some minor changes of punctuation in lines four, seven, and eight. The 1800 text of the third and final stanza does offer more significant textual variations from the later version:

> She *liv'd* unknown, and few could know
>   When Lucy ceas'd to be;
> But she is in her Grave, and Oh!
>   The difference to me.

These lines constitute the text that Wordsworth corrected. Just as for the 1805 *Lyrical Ballads* as well as his later *Works*, he removed the marks of emphasis from "*liv'd*," "Grave," and "Oh." (Thomas Hutchinson has indicated in his "Preface" to the single-volume Oxford Edition of the *Poetical Works* that Wordsworth's "use of capital letters" is "a sure index to his intentions of stress."[4]) The truncated spellings of "liv'd" and "ceas'd" had also been replaced with full spellings by the 1805 edition, and these changes were preserved in later editions. The relocation of the exclamation point, and consequently the stress it indicates, did not occur until after the 1805 edition.

These differences may not seem at first to amount to much, but apparently Wordsworth felt they did in 1848 because the final stanza, and not the whole poem, is singled out for careful correction. Since the words and grammar are substantially the same, no major alteration in meaning seems intended. Possibly, Wordsworth was concerned with how the emphases of the 1800 text would be taken. He removed them from the narrative exposition of Lucy's living and dying and from the speaker's expression of grief. Instead, Wordsworth channeled his textual emphasis

---

3. In *PW*, II, p. 30, the eleventh line of the poem reads "But she is in her grave, and, oh"—the difference appearing small yet of some significance for Wordsworth.

4. Wordsworth, *Poetical Works*, ed. T. Hutchinson, rev. Ernest de Selincourt (London: Oxford University Press, 1936), p. vii. Hutchinson's "Preface" originally dates from 1904.

into the final line, stressing the sudden difference that her irrevocable loss means for the speaker. The stress should fall, that is, on the speaker's or narrator's own apprehension of abrupt and personal loss and not on the facts of Lucy's life and death. Perhaps Wordsworth recognized that the textual emphases of the 1800 text misdirected his meaning or the affective power of his poem and that in 1848 an opportunity to exercise this recognition presented itself. This recognition can be seen developing slowly from edition to edition, but it stands out in sharpest profile in a retrospective comparison that spans forty-eight years.

This conjecture has some further support in a final observation on the significance of the manuscript. The initial letters of the pronouns "she" and "me" in the third and fourth lines of the corrected stanza are capitalized. Again the emphasis seems channeled in the direction of the difference suddenly realized as obtaining incontrovertibly between the dead "She" and the living "Me," an emphasis in agreement with the other alterations being made in the text. Of course, Wordsworth did not capitalize these pronouns in any publication of the lyric. However, this one intriguing occurrence of capitalization helps to underscore the aptness and interpretive power of my previous arguments concerning Wordsworth's highly imaginative use of pronouns and pronominal interplay in "She dwelt," "Strange fits," and "A slumber did my spirit seal." Even so late in life, correcting a stanza of "She dwelt" in the summer of 1848, Wordsworth appears to intimate that emphasis should fall on the curiously understated relation of his first-person speaker ("Me") to Lucy ("She") belatedly recognized in retrospect.

Date and Chronological Placement of the Manuscript

The manuscript dates from a period late in Wordsworth's life when he was just emerging from melancholia and reclusiveness following his daughter Dora's death the previous July. After an illness of several months, Dora died on July 9, 1847. Wordsworth withdrew into a prolonged period of sorrow that persisted until April 1848. At this time Mary Wordsworth persuaded him to visit his sons Willy and John and their families in Carlisle and Brigham, respectively, in the northern part of Cumberland. The excursion began in early April and lasted until just before May 20. Wordsworth became less melancholic and even enjoyed numerous walks with John Wordsworth in the neighborhood of his own birthplace, Cockermouth. During June and July the Wordsworths entertained family and visitors. Wordsworth received many tourists, "especially from New York," as his wife notes in a letter to Isabella Fenwick of August 2, 1848. On or about August 5, William and Mary Wordsworth made a ten-day trip to Penrith and Newbiggen by way of the Kirkstone Pass and the Vale of Ullswater in order to visit all their friends still living there.[5] Thus, after an extended period of depression and noncommunication that even provoked journalistic rumors of onsetting imbecility (Robinson, p. 671), Wordsworth began to see numerous friends and strangers and to travel about his native Cumberland and environs rather frequently. On July 20, 1848—the date of the manuscript—the Wordsworths were at home at Rydal Mount, reported in letters by Mary Wordsworth, July 22, and by the Wordsworths' son-in-law, Edward Quillinan, on July 23 (Robinson, pp. 700–702, 673–75). On August 2 Mary Wordsworth mentioned to Isabella Fenwick a ramble in the direction of Clappersgate and Fox Ghyll that Wordsworth had taken some time before to visit their longtime friend Mrs. Luff (Mary Wordsworth, p. 300). Fox Ghyll, the home of Mrs. Luff, was at one time the residence of the Thomas De Quinceys (Mary Wordsworth, p. 43, n. 5). It lay not more than two miles from the Wordsworths' and was, according to Mary Moorman, "within a quarter of an hour's walk of Rydal Mount" (p. 485).

I have not been able to locate the place-name "Lostheth How" on various maps of Cumberland and Westmorland, in standard dictionaries of English place-names, or in indexes of Wordsworth material and Wordsworthiana, though I have located a reasonable possibility. "Lostheth How" could very well be the place near Ambleside called "Lesketh How" or "Lisketh How."[6] Dr. J. Davy, Wordsworth's physician, and his wife

5. This account is a distillation of Moorman, II, pp. 599–603; *The Letters of Mary Wordsworth, 1800–1855,* ed. Mary Burton (Oxford: Clarendon Press, 1958), pp. 295–304; and *The Correspondence of Henry Crabb Robinson with the Wordsworth Circle,* Vol. II: 1844–1866, ed. Edith J. Morley (Oxford: Clarendon Press, 1927), pp. 665–77. Additional citations from these three works will be made parenthetically by using the names Moorman, Mary Wordsworth, and Robinson, respectively, as well as the relevant page numbers of these texts. Moreover, this account accords well with Stephen Gill's recent synopsis of the final years of Wordsworth's life. See Gill, *William Wordsworth: A Life* (Oxford: Clarendon Press, 1989), pp. 421–22.

6. In a personal communication in 1979, Dr. Peter Laver, Administrative Librarian of the Wordsworth Library in Grasmere, agrees that this location is the most likely one. Also, as mentioned previously, the place-name and date in the manuscript found at Buffalo are the least

Margaret resided at this spot for a great number of years. The Davys were acquainted with many of the Wordsworth circle and were instrumental in soliciting funds and materials in the 1850s and 1860s for monuments to Wordsworth's memory in Grasmere and Ambleside and for the first "Wordsworth Library" located in a room attached to Ambleside's grammar school. In a letter to Henry Crabb Robinson posted on February 8, 1851, concerning the memorial at Grasmere, Dr. Davy writes his address as "Lisketh How, Ambleside." Moreover, two letters written by Mrs. Davy to Robinson in early 1863 concerning the new Wordsworth library bear the address "Lesketh How, Ambleside" (Robinson, pp. 773–75, 840–42). The variability in the spelling of the place-name by the Davys themselves may help encourage the supposition that "Lostheth How" is another variant spelling (or, one-time misspelling).

Traveling from Rydal Mount to Mrs. Luff's at Fox Ghyll, Wordsworth would have passed by the Davys' residence at Lesketh How. He may have stopped to visit with them or with someone else in the vicinity. In her letter of August 2, Mary Wordsworth mentions only one walk that could have occurred on July 20. In addition, in an earlier letter, dated July 22 and written to H. C. Robinson from Rydal Mount, Mary Wordsworth reports that "Mrs. Davy thinks herself better" and that two of the Davys' children were on a trip with their grandmother, Mrs. Fletcher (Robinson, pp. 700–702). This news indicates some recent contact with the Davys. Wordsworth's walk to Fox Ghyll, perhaps including a visit to Lesketh How along the way, could reasonably be dated July 20, 1848. This conjecture does not in the least distort the evidence of Mary Wordsworth's letters or put unusual demands on Wordsworth's probable movements. However, it is not necessary to suppose that Wordsworth's visit to "Lostheth How" occurred on the same day as his walk to Mrs. Luff's. The proximity of Lesketh How, Ambleside, to Rydal Mount, along with Mary Wordsworth's timely hint of contact with the Davys, makes it reasonable to suppose that Wordsworth could have paid the Davys or someone else at the same locale, such as a visitor or tourist, "especially from New York," a separate visit on the day that the Buffalo MS is dated.

Even if "Lostheth How" be found to lie somewhere else, however, the general tenor of Wordsworth's life from April to August 1848 was such that any number of occasions for his interest in correcting and updating the

clearly executed of all the writing that it contains. My notes show that the "o" in "Lostheth" is not closed, and indeed it is possible to read it as a half-executed "e."

third stanza of "She dwelt" could have arisen. This late period of his life was characterized by an emergence from depression and an immersion in a grand round of touring and walking. His visits and conversations, with acquaintances and tourists alike, seem to have drawn Wordsworth out from his depression and into an unusually active period of contact and communion with others. The loss of his daughter Dora made a difference in his life in late 1847 and early 1848, but the spring and summer of 1848 reveal a renewal of energies and interests on the part of the poet.

Index

Abrams, M. H., 66, 81, 93 n. 13, 228
action, poetic, 121–22
activity, purposive, 178–88, 198–204, 212,
218, 222–23, 228–32, 238, 242, 259,
262
   action(s), 190–91 n. 32, 198–203
   critical activity, 159–60, 235–36, 238
   perceptual activity, 255–57
   "purposive act" (S. Pepper), 178–82, 242
   See also attention; inquiry; interaction; reading (activity of); self
actualization, 256–57
adolescence, 156–57
aggression, 154–57
Alfoxden (England), 68, 69 n. 7
allegory, 89–93
   allegorical model of textuality, 89–92,
   239–40
Alter, Robert, 257
Althusser, Louis, 261
Altieri, Charles, 74–75, 190–91 n. 32,
   196–97 n. 6, 247 n. 20
Ambleside (England), 268–69
analogy, 143–45, 153, 176, 178, 180, 251,
   261
Anaximenes, 167
Angelou, Maya, 229
animals ("mutes"), 164–65, 178–79
anthropology, 51–52, 163–65, 211 n. 16
anti-Cartesianism, 194
antifoundationalism, 9, 232
   See also conventions; foundationalism; neopragmatism; pragmatism
argumentation, 2–6
Aristotle, 166, 168, 225
Arnold, Matthew, 32
arts, fine, 186–87
arts, practical, 166–67
ascription, 19, 84, 207, 223

assumptions, theoretical, 12, 84–85, 228, 240
   See also ideals; methodology
Athens (Greece), 165–66, 167
atmosphere, poetic, 48, 108
attention, 79, 122, 128–29, 147–48, 157,
   186–87, 188, 242, 247–48, 252–53, 259
   aesthetic mode of, 186–87, 188, 189, 196,
   221, 242, 244–45, 262
   instrumental mode of, 186–87, 188, 189,
   196, 242, 244–45, 247
   modes of, 186–87, 189, 196, 244
   selective, 244–47
attitude(s), cultural, 4 n. 3, 72 n. 10, 73, 254
audience, 222
Austen, Jane, 229, 258
Austin, J. L., 19 n. 7
author, 77–78, 239, 247, 254
authoritarianism, 153–56
authority, 133–35, 150, 153–59, 161–62,
   199–200
autonomy, poetic or textual, 27–28, 30–33,
   41
Averill, J. H., 112 n. 21

Baldwin, James, 229
ballads, 60, 70, 103–8, 115
Bateson, F. W., 20 n. 8, 29 n. 8, 61 n. 18, 67,
   71–75
Baudelaire, Charles, 49 n. 1, 53 n. 10
Baudrillard, Jean, 10
Beaumont, Lady, 76, 78, 79, 187, 227
   and Mrs. Fermor, 76, 78
beginnings, 16, 23–24, 133–35, 158
belief(s), 4 n. 3, 12, 194–97
Benjamin, Walter, 49 n. 1, 53 n. 10
Bentley, Arthur F., 198–203, 243
Benziger, James, 143 n. 23
Berthoff, Werner, 239
Beyette, Kent, 112